FESSENDEN OF MAINE

Fessenden of Maine

CIVIL WAR SENATOR

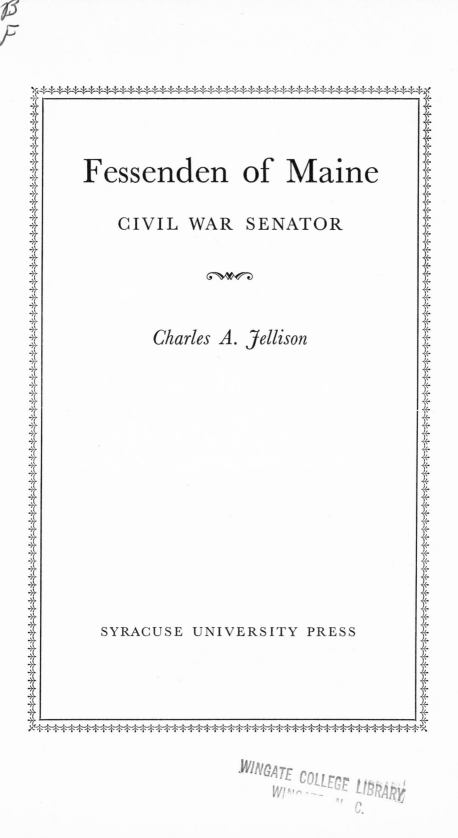

Charles A. Jellison

SYRACUSE UNIVERSITY PRESS

This book has been set in 10 point Linotype Baskerville, leaded 3 points, printed on 60 pound P. H. Glatfelter antique standard white text papers, R grade, and bound in Bancroft's Arrestox A over 80 point binder's board.

MANUFACTURED IN THE UNITED STATES OF AMERICA
BY THE VAIL-BALLOU PRESS, INC., BINGHAMTON, NEW YORK

Preface

AMONG THE national statesmen of the middle years of the past century, few played a more significant role than William Pitt Fessenden of Maine. Entering the United States Senate in February of 1854 during the convulsive Kansas-Nebraska debate, he almost at once rose to a place of leadership among that small band of anti-Nebraska Congressmen who soon after swung their support to the infant Republican party. From that time until his death in 1869 Senator Fessenden occupied a commanding position in national councils, where his powerful intellect, his mastery in debate, and his unquestioned integrity caused him to be considered by many of his colleagues as the foremost legislator of his day.

Despite the high standing he claimed among his contemporaries, however, Fessenden has been relegated by time to an undeserved obscurity. Even the most dedicated historians of the Civil War period have tended to give him only meagre attention, with the result that no satisfactory account of Fessenden's life and political activities has ever been prepared, save for a valuable but in many respects inadequate biography of the Senator written by his son some fifty years ago. It is the purpose of this book, then, to assuage this lack and to sketch within the limits of restricted space and time the outlines of the private and public life of Fessenden of Maine. To accomplish this, primary reliance has been placed upon manuscript materials, most especially upon the Senator's private papers, which have hitherto remained largely inaccessible to historians.

The story of Fessenden is the story of integrity and ability in politics. Reared and educated in a strongly Federalist and puritanical environment, he entered at an early age the arena of state politics where he experienced a rapid rise to a position of prominence among the Maine Whigs. For a time, 1841–1843, he sat in Congress as a devoted supporter of Henry Clay's American System, but not until 1854 did he emerge upon the national scene to take the Senate seat he was to hold for fifteen critical years.

During the turbulent times of the middle and late 1850's Fessenden figured as a leading spokesman in the Senate for the new Republican party against Southern demands for slavery extension; and throughout the long war that followed he labored tirelessly and with great effect, both as Senator and briefly as Secretary of the Treasury, for complete and final victory over the Confederacy. Once this victory had been won, Fessenden was named by his colleagues to head the all-important Joint Committee on Reconstruction, and consequently he wielded great influence in initiating the Congressional program for restoring the Southern States.

With the ascendancy of Radical Republicanism after the summer of 1866, however, Fessenden came to assume a role of greatly diminished importance. Inclined toward political conservatism, he held little sympathy for the Radical program, and by early 1867 Senator Fessenden often found himself in open opposition to the majority of his party. As a result he was frequently berated as an obstructionist by the more extreme of his colleagues. But for Fessenden there were stronger considerations than party fealty, and he consistently refused to be bullied out of his beliefs. When in the spring of 1868 he was called upon to make a momentous choice between party and personal convictions, he chose the latter and cast his vote for the acquittal of Andrew Johnson.

In the late summer of 1869, little more than a year after the impeachment trial and at a time when public sentiment was rapidly growing aware of the wisdom and courage of his acquittal vote, William Pitt Fessenden of Maine died at his home in Portland. For the Senate and the nation the loss was a severe one, for with Fessenden there passed from the national political scene a large measure of that honest conservative statesmanship and personal integrity with which the legislative halls of the period were far too scantily blessed.

Acknowledgments

IN THE preparation of this small biography of a big man I have sought and received help from a multitude of people, each of whom responded in a warm and generous manner to my needs. To all of them I am deeply grateful, but to none am I more beholden than to Professor Edward Younger of the University of Virginia and John Baxter of Brunswick, Maine. Without their kind aid and encouragement it is unlikely that this book would have been written.

A DuPont Senior Fellowship and two grants from the Central University Research Fund of the University of New Hampshire helped greatly to ease the financial strain involved in preparing this manuscript. For favors such as these Mr. Fessenden and I are, in his words, "much obliged."

CHARLES A. JELLISON

Newport, Rhode Island
January, 1962

Contents

He was a scholar, and a ripe and good one,
Exceeding wise, fair-spoken, and persuading;
Lofty and sour to them that loved him not,
But to those men that sought him sweet as summer.

Henry VIII, IV, 2, 51

I

The Bar Sinister

THE TOWN of Fryeburg, Maine, lies only a few yards east of the New Hampshire border. Some fifty miles northwest of Portland, the town is stretched out ribbon-like on a broad plain through which the Saco River meanders like some giant, unhurried serpent. To the west, a fair distance beyond the New Hampshire boundary, stand the White Mountains, immense masses of granite looming like monster sentinels over the plain and river below, and casting long afternoon shadows across the little village. On a clear day the mountains are nearly close enough to be touched from the main street, or so at least they seemed to the Reverend William Fessenden, who arrived in Fryeburg in the summer of 1774, afire with an enthusiastic desire to serve God and man on the frontier.

At that time the infant village of Fryeburg in the District of Maine was still being hacked out of the wilderness and was in obvious need of a spiritual shepherd. To young Fessenden, a recent product of Harvard College who had moved north soon after his graduation to take a preaching assignment in the small New Hampshire town of Dunbarton, Fryeburg seemed a promising place indeed. There was challenge there; there was blasphemy and back-sliding aplenty; God's work was in desperate need of attention. But to the local citizenry the matter of selecting a minister was not one for hurried decision. In fact, during those still Congregational days choosing a minister was a community rather than church affair—a matter to be pondered at town meeting. And so it was that the Reverend Mr. Fessenden was forced to retrace his steps to Dunbarton and there wait upon the de-liberations of the Fryeburg freemen. Ten months later his long patience was rewarded. He had passed the test of town approval and was invited to come with his new wife to Fryeburg to serve as first minister of the young community, in return for forty-five pounds a year, one-third payable in Indian corn. On May 24, 1775, scarcely a month after the first shots of the American Revolution had sounded in Middlesex, the young pastor delivered his first Fryeburg sermon —an exhortation to the men of the town to take up arms against British tyranny. "May God of his mercy sanctify what was delivered." [1]

The Reverend William and his wife Sarah almost at once became a part of the town, and as the years passed, the community looked more and more to the gentle minister for direction. Like Goldsmith's village preacher:

> A man he was to all the country dear,
> And passing rich with forty pounds a year.

For a time he served the town in the Massachusetts General Court, and when, during the final decade of the century, the need for an academy was felt, it was the Parson Fessenden who took the lead in fashioning his parishioners' plans into a one-storied, box-like reality. In matters of the flesh and the spirit alike he was, as Daniel Webster later remembered him, "a learned, amiable, and excellent minister of the gospel," and when death took him from his pulpit in 1805 he left behind a legend of good in the town.[2]

In the house of William and Sarah there was full measure of love and warmth. There was frequently less of food and clothing, however, owing largely to William's generous habits and to an irrepressible strain of fecundity in the Reverend's devoted wife. Ultimately the children numbered nine, and of these, the fifth son, born in the summer of 1784, was Samuel, a handsome child who was destined to play during the years to come no small role in shaping opinions and events for his state and country.

At the foot of Pine Hill, near the meeting of Main Street and East Conway Road, Fryeburg Academy was erected in 1791, and here in this sober frame building the sons of William and Sarah Fessenden prepared for college. Here also was born a strange and powerful friendship between Samuel Fessenden and his stern-eyed schoolmaster,

Daniel Webster, older than his pupil by scarcely two years. It was the beginning of a relationship that for nearly half a century was to bind the two men together in close ties of affection and esteem, only to be ended in sudden bitterness on March 7, 1850, when, amidst the resounding tones of Webster's Compromise speech, all friendship ceased.

Young Webster, "long, slender, pale, and all eyes," came to Fryeburg in January of 1802. Fresh from Dartmouth College, he had crossed over the line from Salisbury Lower Village, New Hampshire, sold his horse, and settled down to assume the position of schoolmaster at the Academy in return for the handsome sum of $350 a year. At this time Samuel was in his final session at the Academy, and it was probably the influence of his new preceptor that prompted him to enter Dartmouth in the winter of the following year.[3]

Money had never been plentiful with the Fessendens of Fryeburg, and matters were made especially critical by the death of the Reverend William before Samuel had completed his course at Dartmouth. Left largely to his own devices, the young man met the challenge by teaching school during the winter months, a practice not uncommon among college students of that day. In the early winter of 1805–06, just prior to the beginning of his final term at Dartmouth, Samuel's teaching assignment took him to Boscawen, New Hampshire, where his friend Daniel, having abandoned teaching for the bar, had opened a law office the year before and was by the time of Samuel's arrival doing "just about so-so." [4]

It became painfully apparent to Sam soon after his arrival in Boscawen that the place had little to recommend it. The town was a small and unexciting affair, and with Daniel's time being selfishly devoured by the demands of a new practice and an ailing father, the leisure hours at first passed by slowly for Samuel. And then in late December or early January he met Ruth Greene, and Boscawen suddenly took on a new charm. So, in fact, did the entire universe, for loneliness now gave way to love, or something akin to it, for the handsome young student. There were strolls together through the town, and sleigh-rides, and late evenings before the fire in the home of Ruth Greene's father. And after the winter had all but passed and Samuel had returned to Dartmouth for his final term, he composed tender nocturnal letters, liberally studded with original verse and classical allusions, to assure "my good girl" from afar of his everlasting devotion:

> Roseate her cheeks, her Skin with Snow may vie.
> Unconscious of her Charms so much divine
> Ten thousand Cupids wanton in her Eye,
> Her form ten thousand graces doth combine.
> Youth, innocence in every feature shine.
> Greatness of soul her every action moves.
> Reason directs what virtue e're approves.[5]

The *affaire* produced more than poor poetry, however, for although the fact was not then known to Samuel, at the time of his return to Dartmouth, Ruth Greene was already two months with child.

The boy that was born in Boscawen on October 16, 1806, was named for William Pitt, the great Tory statesman of Britain who had died earlier that year. Thus did the father indicate his own strongly Federalistic leanings, while simultaneously stamping in name the indelible brand of political conservatism upon his infant son. Nor, as matters turned out, could an apter name have been found, for whether by accident or design, in many aspects of thought, character, and career, William Pitt Fessenden bore striking resemblance to his English exemplar. As one historian has pointed out:

> Both were men of strictest personal integrity, austere in manner, and admired by most of their followers more than loved. Each was skilled in finance; neither was in the full sense of the word a great orator. . . . Like Pitt, Fessenden had a somewhat weak constitution. . . . In loftiness of character it is probable that the American was the superior.[6]

For reasons unknown Samuel Fessenden and Ruth Greene did not marry. Perhaps family interference succeeded in thwarting the union, or perhaps some final, senseless lovers' quarrel was responsible for keeping the young parents apart. Even more inexplicable is the fact that when Pitt was only a few days old he was separated from his mother and taken by Samuel to Fryeburg. Pitt was never to see his mother again. Once many years later when he was a young man setting out on the practice of law in Portland, he received a letter from his mother who had somehow managed to discover his whereabouts. She had married long since, and now had a family of her own, but she yearned to see her first-born. Would he come back to New Hampshire to visit her? Pitt showed the letter to his father and then made his own decision: No, he wouldn't. Nothing good could come of it.

Legend still persists that the separation of the infant from his mother was made possible by some sort of cash settlement, with Daniel Webster supposedly supplying the wherewithal. Since, however, Daniel was at the time scarcely in a money-lending posture, this part of the story at least is doubtless romance. One thing Webster did do for his friend Samuel, though. On a cold, blustering afternoon in the autumn of 1806, he rode twenty miles through sleet and snow to stand as godfather to William Pitt Fessenden, an onerous feat which Webster never forgot; nor in later years did he allow his godson to do so.[7]

The blight of bastardy was to hang heavily over Pitt Fessenden throughout his entire life. At an early age the awareness of his illegitimacy fastened itself forever upon him and proceeded to gnaw away mercilessly at his sensitivity and self-esteem. In a life filled with crosses to be borne, this would be the most relentlessly burdensome of them all. There would be no more powerful influence in shaping his character and attitudes than this awful, unspoken shame—this evil, irremovable stain of indecency and inferiority. Fessenden's bristling pride, his quickness to take affront, his intolerance of human weakness in himself as well as in others, and his frequent displays of pettiness and petulance, all of these were at least in some degree mechanisms of defense or compensation for the ego of a man who was always painfully mindful of the fact that he was not quite respectable and never could be, either in his own eyes or in the eyes of others.

In Fryeburg the infant Pitt was given over to his grandmother, in whose custody he remained for the first seven years of his life. From this remarkable woman he received all the benefits that love and common-sense care could bestow, and to her he owed perhaps his greatest cultural debt. Although of only limited learning herself, Sarah Fessenden fully recognized the advantages to be gleaned from education, and she urged upon young Pitt, as she had upon her own children, the importance of a trained mind and retentive memory. From her the boy developed "my habit of reading and remembering," which remained with him, to his great profit, until the end of his days.[8]

Meanwhile, Samuel had applied himself to the study of law, and in 1809 was admitted to the bar. Shortly thereafter he set out alone from the Fryeburg area for New Gloucester, District of Maine, a town of less than a thousand inhabitants which had been settled half-way through the preceding century by emigrants from Gloucester, Massachusetts. Here in this small community, some twenty miles north of Portland, Samuel Fessenden sought out an office and embarked upon his long practice of the law.

Within a few years Samuel had gained a prominent place in the community. The story is told that soon after his arrival he endeared himself to the local citizenry by thrashing the town bully in a fair fight at high noon in the courthouse square. Thereafter, the story goes, he was considered something of a popular hero by the people of New Gloucester, and was deferred to in matters great and small. Whether there is any truth to this tale is open to question, but the very existence of such a story indicates that Samuel was possessed of a goodly measure of that natural leadership upon which legends are wont to be constructed. A towering man of powerful face and frame, he was one of the most strikingly handsome figures ever produced by his state. But more than that, he was widely known throughout his life as a great force for justice and a citadel of warm good-nature and understanding. Although lacking in his son's brilliance, he was bountifully endowed with an ingredient which had lamentably not been passed on to his Pitt. He was early and always possessed of that kindly patience for humanity and tolerance of individual failing that was so noticeably missing in the make-up of his distinguished son. Between Pitt and his father there would always be the strongest bonds of affection and respect, and it is said that in later years the Senator never left Portland without first visiting the old house on India Street to kiss his father goodbye.[9]

Until he moved with his family to Portland in 1822, Samuel figured as a pillar of Federalism in the New Gloucester area. In 1811 he delivered one of his first political speeches, an anti-administration Fourth of July oration, considered by his colleagues as "correct, elegant, and patriotic." Said Samuel himself of his effort: "Should it be productive of any benefit to the cause of Federalism, I shall have the reward which a well-wisher to his country will be anxious only to obtain—that of promoting the good of the great whole." [10] Two years later he was sent by his fellow-townsmen to represent New Gloucester in the Massachusetts General Court where, in true Federalist fashion, he harangued against "Mr. Madison's War" and in 1814 supported the call for a convention of protest to be held at Hartford. By 1818 he had been advanced to the Massachusetts Senate, and in the same year, as an indication of his growing public importance, Samuel Fessenden, thirty-four years old, was elected major-general of the Maine militia.[11]

During this period of rapid political and professional growth, Samuel found time for marriage to Deborah Chandler in 1813. Soon after, Pitt was uprooted from his grandmother's house in Fryeburg and brought to New Gloucester where with Samuel and the gentle Deborah he found his first real home. Here the boy spent the next half-dozen years in a swiftly expanding household, for Samuel had apparently inherited from William and Sarah a great love of children, as well as a dominant male gene which in time accounted for nine boys before the birth of his only daughter.

These years in New Gloucester, spent in a "cultivated and Puritan atmosphere," were apparently for Pitt the boughbenders of his life. As the eldest son of a respected family much was expected of him— perhaps too much. Instead of play with his peers, there was too often a heavy assignment of serious reading for him to contend with. His contemporaries in New Gloucester would later remember him as a frail and serious boy who would frequently abandon his play in favor of his books. For a time young Pitt attended North Yarmouth Academy, then one of the most reputable schools in the District of Maine. Most of his work, however, was done under the personal direction of Samuel himself, whose task was made easier by the fact that the boy was a rapid and apparently eager learner. By the autumn of 1818 Pitt felt himself adequately prepared to attempt the entrance examinations for Bowdoin College, but in his blue-boy jacket and broad-ruffled collar he failed to impress the Bowdoin fathers as being sufficiently mature for college experience, and was sent back to Samuel for further ripening. Undaunted, the boy returned the following year to be examined, with other candidates for the freshman class, in:

Cicero's Select Orations—the Bucolics, Georgics, and Aeneid of
Virgil—Sallust—the Greek Testament—Dalzel's Collectanea Graeca
Minora—in the writing of Latin—in the fundamentals of Arith-
metic, and in Cummings' Geography. They must also produce
satisfactory credentials of good moral character.[12]

Later that same autumn young Pitt Fessenden was admitted to Bowdoin College. He was at the time a few weeks short of his thirteenth
birthday.*

The Bowdoin of Fessenden's day was entering its second quarter-
century of catering to the college needs of northern New England.
Founded in 1794 on the outskirts of Brunswick village, it was in
many respects still in a late period of infancy at the time of Pitt's arrival. The campus buildings were only four in number, all of red brick
with the exception of the square-towered chapel, which, offset somewhat from the other buildings, was a jaded white that gave the false
impression of great age. Opposite the chapel were Maine and Win-
throp Halls, of combination dormitory and classroom use for Bowdoin's sons, while at the northernmost end of the campus stood Massachusetts Hall, a box-like building topped by an awkward cupola,
which served as the great nerve-center of the college. Here on this
campus, flanked on one side by forests of "academic pines" and on
the opposite by a sprawling cow-pasture, congregated the young and
hopeful to receive from Bowdoin's six-man faculty the blessings of
a classical education, in return for six dollars and sixty-seven cents
per head per term.

Though of unassuming physical proportions at the time, the college was inordinately rich in the potential of its students. The first
half-decade of the 1820's might, in fact, be considered the golden age
of Bowdoin College, for then along its pine-fringed paths walked
many of the great and near-great of years to come: young Nathaniel
Hawthorne, serious, gentle, impulsive, fond of thinking long thoughts
by the banks of the little brook that twisted through Brunswick and
emptied into the Androscoggin River a mile or so below the falls

---

* Young Fessenden was not actually in official attendance until the late winter
of the following year, for in those early years of the 19th century the academic
session began usually in the late winter or early spring and ended in September
or October.

—fond too of gambling at cards and idling with his warm-hearted friend Franklin Pierce, who by the end of his sophomore year stood scholastically at the rock-bottom of his class; the Longfellows, Henry and Stephen, one a boy of "decided personal beauty and most attractive manners . . . frank, courteous, affable while morally . . . proof against the temptations that beset lads on first leaving the salutary restraints of home," [13] and the other—something of a rake; Calvin Stowe, possessed of grave and massive thoughts, intensely dedicated to his fearsome God, and happily unaware that his would be a reflected glory; Jonathan Cilley, friend of Pierce and Hawthorne, a boy of brilliance and great promise, who as a Congressman during the late 1830's would be cut down in the infamous duel with Graves of Kentucky; John B. Russwurm, first colored graduate of an American college, a recluse befriended by Hawthorne, later an editor of no mean ability, and still later Governor of Cape Palmas, Africa; and then too, Uncle Trench, a venerable old man with wheelbarrow who supplied for a modest price ginger-bread and root-beer to hungry Bowdoin sons. His fame would come in fiction from the pen of Hawthorne as the real-life prototype for Uncle Venner in *The House of the Seven Gables*. Into an arena of such future notables as these was cast young William Pitt Fessenden, destined to become before his sands were run something of a notable himself.

At the request of Samuel and in deference to Pitt's youthfulness, the boy was allowed to spend his freshman year at the home of a relative in Gorham. Since that town lay some thirty miles distant from Brunswick, regular class attendance during this period was for Pitt out of the question. But by directed study and attendance at special college exercises, the boy was able to remain abreast of his class, and it was as a sophomore that he came to the campus to live in the late winter of 1821.

After a long and troublesome period of adjustment, during which his grades were no better than "respectable," Pitt finally found his way, and by the beginning of his senior session had established himself as a reputable scholar. Student papers in the manuscript files of Bowdoin College indicate that during his final year the boy participated actively in public dialogues and discussions and that even at this early stage he had developed a marked felicity of expression. At a college exercise in 1823 the sixteen-year-old senior proclaimed with

some fluency his sympathy for those Latin-American peoples then
rebelling against Spanish rule:

We should . . . rejoice that such splendid prospects await our
Sister States. And while we praise them for the national gallantry
manifested in this bloody and trying contest, we contemplate with
satisfaction the time, when they who have so long groaned under
the tyrannous yoke of an European, shall establish permanently
their freedom and independence.[14]

Many years later he was remembered by a classmate as "a good writer,
and an excellent debater, and he took high rank as a scholar." Not
so high, however, was his popularity rating among his fellow-students,
for while at Bowdoin Pitt impressed his peers as being "ardent,
haughty, and defiant. Warm in his friendships . . . [he was] bitter
and uncompromising in his hatreds." [15]

Life at Bowdoin in the early 1820's was not particularly gay. Still
under the sober rod of Puritanism, the college frowned upon "any
Bacchanalian conduct disturbing the quietness and dishonorable to
the character of a literary institution," and the authorities were ever
watchful lest some of their charges should fall into such idle and
dangerous habits as card-playing, billiards, disorderly singing, or
"shouting and clapping of hands." Yet, students were known to aber-
rate from the code on occasion, even to the extent of profaning the
Sabbath by "unnecessary walking abroad." Favorite rallying point
for the most refractory of these recusants was Wardsworth's Tavern,
two miles down the road to Bath, where cards and wine could be
dangerously indulged in by the spirited few. Here Hawthorne whiled
away many a perilous hour, and here from time to time during his
senior year came young Pitt Fessenden in search of revelry and relaxation.

A century later, at Bowdoin College's 1923 commencement exercises,
the sober likeness of William Pitt Fessenden was chosen to adorn the
large lapel buttons which were distributed to the assembled members
of the Bowdoin alumni—a fitting tribute to the most illustrious member of that class which had been awarded its degrees an even one
hundred years before. Indeed, this tribute would have been perhaps
even more fitting if Fessenden had actually graduated at the time

supposed. The truth of the matter is, however, that Pitt's name was not among those called when his class was presented for commencement in 1823. The faculty records for that year explain his absence:

Whereas Senior Fessenden was guilty on Monday night, June 30th, of the irregularity of eating and drinking at Wardsworth's tavern without permission, and on Monday night last, during a scene of tumult, when directed by a college officer to proceed to his room, was guilty of disrespectful conduct; and whereas he has today been repeatedly guilty of profane swearing and has indicated a disorganizing spirit; and whereas also, during the great irregularities of this day insults were offered to the members of the Government from one of the windows of said Fessenden's room; Therefore, in the view of these circumstances, and considering his general character and the bad influence of his example, Noted, that he be sent home this day to his Father, and that the Government do not recommend him to the Board of Trustees and Overseers for a degree the present year.[16]

Midway through the following year the Bowdoin fathers relented and awarded to a repentant Pitt his degree in absentia, "after payment of the usual fees." Thus, with the merciful removal of this early blemish from his record, the youth was restored to the realm of academic respectability. Nevertheless, somewhat inauspicious beginnings were these for William Pitt Fessenden of Maine, destined in the course of time to become the foremost spokesman for his state in the arena of national politics.

Getting Set in Law and Politics

AFTER LEAVING Bowdoin in the summer of 1823, young Fessenden moved to the home of his father in Portland and soon after embarked upon the study of law. Since he was then many years short of the required twenty-one for admission to the Cumberland County bar, he felt no press of time and was able to proceed slowly and thoroughly in his preparations—a fact which contributed in no small measure to his later pre-eminence as a lawyer. His first preceptor was Charles Daveis, a Portland attorney of great learning who was at the time of Fessenden's apprenticeship generally accorded top position among the lawyers of the new state of Maine. With Daveis, young Pitt took his first few professional steps, and for the older man Pitt soon acquired a profound respect that would remain with him and influence his opinions for many years to come.

In the spring of 1826, after nearly two years under Daveis' tutelage, young Fessenden left Portland at the behest of his father to continue his study of law in New York City. There, under the direction of his Uncle Thomas, in the prospering firm of Ketchum and Fessenden, he applied himself to learning the mysteries of equity, a branch of law which at that time was still largely undeveloped in Maine. The New York experience proved to be a short one, however, for young Pitt found the city "extremely vexatious," expensive, and wasteful of human labor, and "unless my views much alter I shall certainly have little inclination to remain here." [1] Within four months he was back in Portland, safely deposited in his father's law office on Middle Street, and harboring for his Uncle Tom's metropolis ill feelings which he would never completely shake off. Early in the following year, after a winter's teaching in the nearby town of Gray, William

Pitt Fessenden, then a thin, smooth-faced boy of medium height, somewhat delicate features, and a surprisingly sober disposition, was admitted to the bar of Cumberland County, although still a few months short of his majority.

Meanwhile the young man had succeeded in making a name for himself in the Portland area. As the eldest son of Militia General Samuel Fessenden, who was then a power in city and state politics, Pitt found many opportunities open to him to air his own views before public gatherings, and these opportunities he usually exploited to the fullest. In October of 1825, only a few days before his nineteenth birthday, he gave what was probably his first public speech when he delivered the annual address before the Portland Benevolent Society. After that he seldom missed a chance to speak in public during these early years. Musical or literary societies, patriotic organizations, civic groups—the subject or circumstances were of no particular consequence to him. The important thing to Pitt was that he was becoming known to the public of the Portland area, and at the same time he was being given the opportunity to flex his rhetorical muscles in preparation for that day when he might be called upon to put them to higher use.

Of all his early speeches none was more interesting or important than Pitt's Fourth of July oration delivered in 1827 before "the Young Men of Portland." With this address, admittedly political in nature, he publicly cast his lot with the forces of latter-day Federalism. But more than that, he revealed his thinking on many of the controversial issues of the day—thinking which would change surprisingly little during the years to come. To God, sound banking, moral living, and public schools he pledged his unflinching support. Slavery he deplored, and also intemperance, which he feared was "poisoning our cup of national felicity." Internal improvements were applauded by the speaker as a great good, of prime importance to the future development of the nation. All things considered, Pitt felt that America had reason to be pleased with its accomplishments and growth, but he was deeply disturbed by what he considered an unhealthful lag in manufacturing. The reason for this lag seemed quite clear:

That manufactures have advanced with unequal steps must not be imputed to any physical or intellectual deficiency on our part,

but . . . to certain political causes, or accidents, which have, as
yet, prevented their receiving an equal share of attention.

The answer to manufacturing's woes was, of course, a high protective
tariff. In fact, to Pitt's way of thinking, the higher the tariff, the better. "History will teach us," he proclaimed, "that a nation cannot
fence itself about with too many safeguards." [2] Around such views
was constructed the core of William Pitt Fessenden's political philosophy as expressed a few months before his twenty-first birthday.
To this philosophy the wisdom and circumstances of ensuing years
would bring varying degrees of modulation, but essentially Fessenden
would remain until his final day what he had been when he
addressed the young men of Portland in 1827—a neo-Hamiltonian.
In the autumn of the following year he did the best he could for his
conservative convictions by casting his first presidential vote for John
Quincy Adams.

In the late fall of 1827, a few months after his admission to the
bar, Pitt moved to Bridgeton, a town some thirty miles northwest of
Portland and not far from Fryeburg. There he opened his own law
office, and during his two-year stay in the town the young attorney
showed signs of prospering. "I am getting business here," he wrote
to his lawyer father, "on the ground that I can have your advice,
sent free to my clients. . . ." [3] But it was soon apparent to Pitt that
Bridgeton, despite its profitable clientele, left much to be desired. It
was a small place of little promise, not at all like Portland which now
had nearly thirteen thousand people and was still growing. Furthermore, Pitt disliked being isolated. He felt the need of family and
friends, particularly so after the spring of 1829 when a large measure
of sorrow entered his life. In the opening moments of that year during a visit to Portland, he had culminated a long courtship by becoming engaged to Elizabeth Longfellow, a favorite sister of his poeti-
cal friend of Bowdoin days. Six months later the girl was dead, and
for Pitt there was anguish and despair. In December he returned to
Portland, determined to open his own law office and lose himself in
his work.

But there were giants then in the courts of Cumberland County,
men like Charles Daveis, Samuel Fessenden, and Simon Greenleaf;
and among such titans as these, young Pitt fared badly in the battle

for clients—so badly, in fact, that by October of 1830, after less than ten months in his own office, he was ready to accept his father's invitation to join the established firm of Fessenden and Deblois. And there, in the long shadow of his father, he remained for the next three years. By 1831 time and resiliency had somewhat assuaged his grief, but his despondency was still such that he could describe himself then as "a sober moralizing man, with little care for anything but to win prosperity, deriving absolute enjoyment from nothing but a new 'suit' and a long account of fees with a balance in my favor." [4] Later that year he became engaged to Ellen Deering, youngest daughter of one of Portland's wealthiest merchants.

In the final months of 1831 the capital of Maine was moved from Portland to Augusta at the falls of the Kennebec River. Here the construction of a beautiful new granite State House, designed by the famous Charles Bulfinch of Boston, was nearing completion—"a magnificent edifice" which cost the state well over $100,000 and which, despite its drafty halls and leaky roof, was generally considered "a monument of liberality and patriotism." Among the members of the first Legislature to assemble in the new capitol building in January of the following year was Pitt Fessenden, then barely twenty-five years of age, who was making his political debut as a National Republican representative from the Portland district.

By the time of Fessenden's arrival in Augusta, Maine was strongly Democratic, as it would continue to be with few exceptions until 1856. A predominantly agricultural and seafaring people to whom manufacturing enterprise was an almost total stranger, the common folk of Maine had been shown the light of political and economic reality by the rise of Jacksonian Democracy during the 1820's, and had acted accordingly by turning against their betters and shattering the power of the National Republicans in the state elections of 1830. The National Republican party, which in Maine adopted the name of Whig in the early 1830's, would continue to count in its ranks much of the wealth and influence of the state, but outside of a half-dozen or so commercial centers its hold on the people had been broken by the Jacksonian upheaval, and not until the emergence of Republicanism in the mid-1850's would conservative political opinion in Maine be able to express itself with anything more than sporadic and ephemeral authority. So it was that Fessenden on the occasion of his political baptism in 1832 found himself associated in Augusta with a party on the downgrade, whose golden moment had passed by, and whose future (at least as far as the naked eye could see) held out little promise for an aspiring young politician.

But despite the fact that his party was "in a decided minority here," and despite the fact too that he was the youngest member of the Legislature (or perhaps because of it), Fessenden proved to be surprisingly outspoken on matters large and small during the 1832 session. With the possible exception of Bangor's Edward Kent, he was in fact the most vocal, if not the most effective, of all the members of the Lower House. In long speeches of flawless syntax and precise articulation he assailed the odious practice of dual office-holding, called for the construction of a state hospital with public funds, argued in behalf of a new charter for Portland, and defended fervently Nicholas Biddle's Bank of the United States, then under attack by President Andrew Jackson's Democratic administration. For the most part, though, he could just as profitably have remained silent, for as he explained in disgust to his old mentor Charles Daveis: "If the majority would be content with bearing us down in party questions only, I should be satisfied, but everything proposed by us is voted down, for fear that there may be some trick in it." [5]

In one important matter, however, Fessenden played a significant role. This, the principal issue before the Maine Legislature at the time, was the Northeast boundary affair, which involved conflicting claims of the United States and Great Britain. The controversy centered about a sizable area of land in what is now, for the greater part, northern Maine and western New Brunswick, land which had been left in disputed ownership by the treaty of peace with England in 1783. Several attempts had been made by the two nations, subsequent to the treaty of 1783, to arrive at a satisfactory settlement of the problem, but all had brought disappointing results. Finally, in 1827, the matter was submitted to the King of the Netherlands for arbitration, and four years later the King recommended what amounted essentially to a two-to-one division in Maine's favor of the twelve thousand square miles in contention. All this seemed fair enough to the Jackson administration in Washington, but not so to the people of Maine, especially the National Republicans, who saw in the situation a tailor-made opportunity for embarrassing, and perhaps discrediting, their Democratic opponents.

Particularly vehement against the King's decision and President Jackson's apparent acquiescence was young Pitt Fessenden, who, in a forceful speech delivered before the Legislature in late January of 1832, denounced the national administration for its ready willingness to sacrifice Maine's interests. He proposed on that occasion that the people of the state rise up in loud protest to make known their indignation against all suggestions of surrender.[6] Nor is there any reason to suppose that his remarks were formulated out of anything but the sincerest of convictions. After all, he knew that Maine's cause was a righteous one. Regardless of what the Dutch King had thought of the affair, Mr. Fessenden sensed the real truth. This business about the disputed land was basically a moral issue (as indeed most issues were apt to become when confronted head-on by Fessenden), and in matters of this sort Pitt was confident that he could always (once armed with the facts, of course) distinguish between right and wrong without much trouble. His ability to do so stemmed in part at least from an infallible instinct, and it was a wonderful power to have at his disposal. It had never failed him during all of his twenty-five years, and he knew that it never would. To the sensitive mind of Pitt Fessenden, whose world abounded and always would abound in rights and wrongs, it was comforting to realize that the ability to recognize right, no matter how strangely bedecked or cleverly disguised it might be, would be his abiding genius; to fight in right's behalf, his relentless obligation. And in the matter of the boundary dispute, when right was so clearly on Maine's side, he would of course stand for no compromise or temporizing. A few days before his boundary speech in the Augusta House, Pitt had confided to his friend Daveis his suspicions that Maine's Democratic Governor would attempt to muffle discussion of the affair in the Legislature, "for fear it may affect the prospects of Jacksonism. . . ." But Fessenden and his National Republican friends, for reasons righteous, patriotic, and political, intended to see to it that the issue was brought completely into the open. Public opinion could be an effective weapon, and public opinion must be aroused. "I think," Pitt wrote to the influential Daveis, "that a few spirited touches in the papers, from the right source, might do good." [7]

Scarcely two weeks later the Democratically controlled Maine Legislature bent with the wind by creating a special delegation to present Maine's case in the boundary matter before the lawmakers in Wash-

ington. Either as a recognition of his growing importance or as a convenient means of getting the noisy young man out of Augusta, Fessenden was named a member of the delegation and in early February
left for the nation's capital.

Upon his arrival in Washington, young Pitt set out at once to lobby
for federal backing of his state's claim to the disputed territory. He
soon discovered, however, that the boundary controversy loomed less
large in Washington than in Augusta. Judging from information received from interviews with Congressional leaders, he concluded that
Congress was simply not sufficiently concerned with the affair to adopt
anything resembling a strong stand in Maine's favor. Particularly dis-
heartening to Pitt was his visit with Henry Clay, who insisted that
the dispute as it then stood lay outside the jurisdiction of Congress.
To Fessenden, Clay was merely straining at the proverbial gnat in
order to escape having to act on the issue. More forthright, in Pitt's
opinion, but scarcely more encouraging, was Senator Littleton Tazewell of Virginia, who impressed Pitt most favorably as a man of ability and understanding. At that time chairman of the Foreign Relations Committee, Tazewell confided to his young visitor:

> While I agree with you in most of your abstract propositions,
> and in some of these, probably, go still further than you do, we
> must look at the thing as practical men; we must consider how
> other nations will regard us, and we cannot get rid of the fact that
> the arbiter we agreed to has pronounced against us.[8]

Tazewell, still speaking as a practical man, then urged that Maine
accept the award, rather than run the risk of ending up with something much worse. As matters turned out, however, Senator Tazewell's sound advice went unheeded, and lamentably so, for ultimately, in 1842, Maine would be forced to accept an even thinner
slice of the disputed territory by the terms of the Webster-Ashburton
Treaty.

After his interview with Tazewell and similar visits with Vice-
President John C. Calhoun and Secretary of State Edward Livingston,
Pitt concluded that any speedy solution of the problem was out of
the question. To his colleagues in Augusta he wrote that the affair
would doubtless drag on for weeks, or even months, with the result

that Maine would probably be called upon to cede her claims to the Federal Government before any final settlement could be arranged. In the matter of indemnity from Washington he felt that Maine should hold out for a substantial amount, and he so advised the State Legislature, adding his opinion that "a more ample indemnity could be obtained in land than in money." [9] On the final day of February the Maine Legislature begrudgingly responded to Fessenden's suggestions by resolving that the state open negotiations with the Federal Government for the cession of Maine's claims to the disputed territory. In return the state expected a satisfactory compensation and made it known that no arrangement could be considered final without ratification by the Augusta Legislature. And there, far short of any settlement, matters stood until ten years later when Pitt's friend Daniel Webster and England's Lord Ashburton cut the knot in their own way.

Upon his return to Portland in March of 1832, Pitt could look back with satisfaction to his baptismal performance in politics. He had served his people and party well in Augusta, and for a brief moment he had received a modicum of recognition for his efforts in Maine's behalf on the national scene. If he had profaned the State House by talking too much during his initial session, he had at least talked very well. To his fellow members in Augusta, many of them by background dirt farmers and down-east fishermen, this precise young man with his meticulous syntax must have seemed something of an oddity; yet, few could fail to recognize that here in their midst was a man to be reckoned with. The National Republicans were understandably more than pleased with their new warrior, and before the close of the session there was talk among them of Fessenden for Congress. Pitt shook off all such suggestions, however. He declared himself finished with politics—for a while at least. He was getting along in years, twenty-five now, and he felt the need of becoming more firmly established in his profession, particularly so since he was then on the verge of becoming a family man.

But escaping from the snare of politics was no easy task for Pitt, as is indicated by the fact that after his marriage to Ellen Deering in the month following his return from Washington, he honeymooned his bride back to the national capital where he sat as a Maine delegate in the Young Men's Whig Convention and beat the drum for

Henry Clay. His determination to remain aloof from politics was substantially strengthened in the autumn of that year, however, when an obliging Maine Democracy saw to it that young Fessenden was defeated for re-election to his Augusta seat. "I was never beaten," he remarked to a friend many years later, "except in 1832, when Jacksonism swept everything before it." *

For about a year after this Pitt remained in Portland, working in the law office of Fessenden and Deblois. During this period a son, the first of many, was born to Pitt and Ellen. But while gaining the comfort of a son, Pitt in a sense lost a part of his father, for at this time there arose between him and Samuel a major difference in thought and attitude which would send them down diverging political paths. Although the strong intimate bonds of affection between the two men remained unimpaired, and would continue so, Pitt was grieved to find himself for the first time aligned against his father on an important public issue, an issue which Samuel deemed "one of the holiest and most important in which mortal man ever engaged." By throwing his support behind the rising clamor of abolitionism, a movement which in most areas of the North was as unpopular as it was noisy, General Samuel Fessenden knowingly cut short a most promising political career and alienated not a few of his personal friends. But his conscience left him no choice. "How long! Oh Lord! how long shall Thy vengeance sleep? When shall Thy Soul be avenged on such a nation as this?" [10] By the mid-1830's he had become the recognized leader of the abolitionist movement in Maine, and an unflagging friend of William Lloyd Garrison whom he would idolize until the end of his days. "If I could covet any thing of post-humous fame," he wrote many years later, "it would be the fame which *William Lloyd Garrison* will have as the pioneer in the anti-slavery cause in the United States, and the tried, and constant, and devoted friend of the oppressed." [11]

For Pitt, however, Garrisonism was not the answer, and, whether from reasons of conscience or political ambition, he insisted upon adhering to a "live and let live" attitude toward slavery. "I am not, and never have been, a member of any Abolition Society," he pro-

* Fessenden to James S. Pike, April 9, 1859, in Pike Papers (Calais Free Library, Calais, Maine). Actually Fessenden was also beaten in his bid for Congress in 1850. See below, page 57.

claimed publicly in 1835, "and have made no secret of my unqualified want of confidence in the expediency and beneficial effects of such associations." [12]

By late 1833 Pitt had grown uneasy in his father's office and had once again decided to strike out on his own. This time he moved northward to Bangor, where he arrived not long after a series of anti-Catholic riots had disgraced the town in the autumn of that year. At this time Bangor was still little more than an outpost of northern civilization, with scarcely three thousand inhabitants, but recently a sudden boom in land and timber speculation had transformed the little trading community into one of the fastest growing settlements in the eastern United States. By spring of the following year Bangor, flush with that ebullient frontier prosperity and expansionism that was part and parcel of the early Jacksonian era, could boast of plank sidewalks and a new city charter, and by 1840 it would be able to point with pride to a population tripled in size. Nor did culture fail to keep apace. In the summer of 1834 the new metropolis was honored by a brief visit from Monsieur Canderbeck, celebrated performer on harp and violin, who entertained the citizenry with "specimens of his playing." And for those of less refined tastes—a concert in the First Baptist Meetinghouse by the world-famous Boston Band. Even the Indians were impressed with the wonderful changes going on about them, "those drones who may be seen in scattered groups along the streets." [13]

With the get-rich-quick fever abroad in Bangor, prices and excitement ran high as people continued to pour into the town. On nearly every boat up the Penobscot from Portland and Boston came herds of speculators to profit from the bubble, and close on their heels, sniffing the promise of fees and litigation, came the lawyers, of whom young Pitt Fessenden was one.

Here in this city of strangers Pitt opened his law office in the late days of 1833, and here he remained for the next year and a half. During this period he lived quietly and alone in a grimly respectable boarding-house overlooking Kenduskeague Stream, and registered no great mark or name for himself in the town. All things considered, it was not a happy time for Pitt. The illness of his wife, who had fallen into a semi-invalid condition soon after the birth of her first child, had forced him to undertake the Bangor adventure alone, with the result that while in Bangor young Fessenden frequently found himself weighed down with loneliness and uneasiness. Furthermore, his hopes for success in the law fell far short of realization. By 1834 there were forty lawyers in the city, approximately one for every eighty inhabitants. Among these were a dozen or so well-established, prosperous practitioners, like Charles Stetson, generally considered the shrewdest attorney north of Portland, and popular Edward Kent, Pitt's National Republican colleague of Augusta days who would soon become governor of the state. By such leviathans as these the legal trade in Bangor was customarily sifted, and for the young and unknown of the profession there too frequently remained only the chaff to be battled over. How successful or unsuccessful Pitt Fessenden was in this battle may be indicated by the fact that during his eighteen months in Bangor he argued a scant two dozen cases, and of this number only three were of sufficient scope or importance to reach the county supreme court docket.[14]

In April of 1835, during an unusually high freshet in the log-crowded Penobscot, Pitt closed his Bangor office and returned to Portland, where he arrived just in time to attend the funeral of his Grandmother Sarah, who had lived out her final years under Samuel's care in the old house on India Street. Not long after his return Pitt made one of the most providential moves of his legal career by entering into a law partnership with William Willis, an established attorney some ten years his senior, who preferred the quiet of his office and history books to the turmoil of court appearance. Since Pitt revelled in the excitement of the courtroom, this complementary combination between the two men proved from its very beginning a most happy one, and from that time until the partnership was dissolved by Fessenden's entrance into the United States Senate nearly twenty years later, the firm continued to grow in prestige and prosperity. Court records show, in fact, that by as early as the autumn of 1837 the new firm of Willis and Fessenden had outstripped all competitors, including Fessenden and Deblois, in the number of cases argued before the Cumberland County Supreme Court.[15] And, although the quality of cases and clientele handled by the partnership remained for some time less impressive than their quantity, eventually bigger and better things found their way to the Middle Street offices of Willis and Fes-

senden, until within a few years the young firm was recognized as one
of the top two or three in the Portland area.

Thus with surprising suddenness did professional success come to
Pitt Fessenden after many false starts. Never again in his legal career
would he know the frustrations of another Bangor.

Also Kent and Fessenden

Now, who shall we have for our Governor,
  Governor?
Who? Tell me, who?
Let's have Edward Kent, for he's a team
For Tippecanoe and Tyler too.

IN THE autumn of 1835, Fessenden met Daniel Webster for the first time since "Black Dan" had stood as godfather for him in Fryeburg nearly three decades before. A presidential election year was approaching, and even though Jacksonism still had a seemingly unbreakable hold on the nation, Webster had responded vigorously to the persistent proddings of his fellow New England Whigs and his own political ambitions by declaring his candidacy. Consumed by a desperate desire for the presidency, and apparently undaunted by the general realization that 1836 would not be a Whig year, he had plunged with all his accustomed enthusiasm into the hopeless struggle against the forces of darkness and Jacksonian Democracy. It was, in fact, largely with a view toward enhancing his presidential prospects that Webster had journeyed into Maine during the middle months of 1835.

This first encounter between Fessenden and Webster occurred at Wiscasset, a few miles up the coast from Bath. Here in this small seaboard village the Squire, en route from Bangor to Portland, paused long enough to devour a dinner of steamed clams and visit briefly with his godson, who had come to Wiscasset to argue before the autumn session of the Circuit Court. Little is known of this meeting, save that it was a prelude of sorts to a close personal and political association between the two men. More specifically, for Fessenden it was the beginning of a political fealty toward Webster which, although often strained, would linger on until the Whig Convention of 1852. It was also, this open alliance with the Godlike Daniel, a relationship which would prove in days to come a source of some political prestige and advantage for Pitt among his party colleagues in Maine. As for Squire Webster, the Wiscasset interlude signalled the discovery and baptism of another booster for his persistent presidential aspirations, and, as time would show, a most fervently loyal and diligent booster at that— at least during election years.

During the following year Pitt labored long and hard against heavy Jacksonian odds to create a Webster boom in Maine, but, as the election of that autumn demonstrated, he accomplished little. His efforts did not pass unnoticed by his friend Daniel, however, and when in the spring of 1837 Webster, flush with three thousand dollars of borrowed money and already eyeing the election of 1840, decided upon a goodwill tour of "the West," he wrote to young Fessenden that "it might not be disagreeable to you to be one of our party . . . :

> Our purpose is to set off in such season as to leave Philadelphia on the first of May; to go to Pittsburgh via Harrisburg; thence to descend the river, visit Lexington, Frankfort, Cincinnati, Louisville, etc., etc., arrive at St. Louis about the first of June. From St. Louis our course will be up the Mississippi and Illinois Rivers to Peru, Galena, and other places in that neighborhood, and then across to Lake Michigan and so to Detroit and home by way of Buffalo and Utica.[1]

And so it was that in the spring of 1837 at a time when the initial impacts of the first genuine, full-fledged American depression were just beginning to be felt, William Pitt Fessenden set out on his first and only journey into the untamed West. Leaving Portland in late April, he overtook the Websters at Harrisburg, whence the trip was immediately continued to Pittsburgh. The fact that the journey across Pennsylvania was made "all the way by canal or railroad except eleven miles" was a source of great amazement to Pitt, and a vindication of his Whiggish enthusiasm for internal improvements. A shame that Maine refused to profit from this excellent example of

"enlightened state policy." "When I look upon this great work," he
exclaimed, "and then think of the little, mean, sordid motives which
direct our own State Councils, I get into a perfect rage, and feel with
regard to Maine, as if I could curse it and quit it." To his friend and
law partner, William Willis, he wrote from Pittsburgh:

> I am pleased and gratified thus far, and I trust I shall continue
> to be so. Daniel cannot be said to possess a very good manner, but
> his wife does, and that's something. The people of Pittsburgh have
> invited him to eat, but he declines; says he had a dinner and made
> a speech here four years ago, and should not feel justified in making
> another disturbance. . . .
> The aspect of things, in regard to money, has not seemed to im-
> prove much, as I get farther from home. People talk of nothing here
> but "these cursed hard times." It is confidently said that Van Buren
> has lost Penna., that some of his strongest supporters have sworn
> off and that eyes are fast opening. Self-interest may, after all, be the
> principle that will save the country. If that will not do it, I think,
> at this day, that the battle may be given up.[2]

For the next two months Pitt continued his travels with the Websters, displaying all the while an abiding, albeit somewhat con-
descending, interest in the new sights and places which confronted
him, and seldom failing to notice increasingly ominous signs of "the
hard times." Descending the Ohio in a river-boat from Pittsburgh,
the party stopped over for a time in Wheeling, and thence steamed
down to Maysville, Kentucky, where they left the river behind and
crossed overland to Lexington. There, on the homeground of Henry
Clay, they were entertained lavishly by the area's most prominent
Whigs. Drinking, dancing, gambling, horse-racing—a far cry indeed
from Portland, and although Pitt fancied himself as certainly no
prude (after all, hadn't he been expelled from Bowdoin for lib-
ertinism not so many years before?), nevertheless he found himself
somewhat shocked and a little disgusted by the spectacle of "Clay,
Crittenden, Robinson, and others of that stamp apparently as much
excited, talking as loudly, betting as freely, drinking as deeply, and
swearing as excessively as the jockeys themselves." [3]
During late May and early June the Webster party made its way
down the Ohio and up the Mississippi River as far as St. Louis, stop-

ping off now and then at various settlements along the way. Arriving at St. Louis on June 10, they found the shores lined with cheering spectators, and according to Pitt, the great Daniel was placed in a coach and paraded through the town—"windows lined, handkerchiefs waving, boys huzzaing, dogs barking, noses glowing, with four or five Indian chiefs following in the rear, each of whom seized Mr. Webster in his arms and kissed his cheek, and so ended that lesson." [4] From St. Louis the little group moved northward through the towns of southern Illinois and thence to Peoria and Chicago, where Pitt thankfully said goodbye to the Websters and headed for home. The trip, with its great noise and glory, had become for him progressively more tiresome, and as for Daniel: "So far as gaining friends was concerned, Mr. Webster might well, if not better, have stayed at home and left his fame and public service to speak for him." [5] Thus ended on a note of quasi-tedium Fessenden's trip westward with the Websters in the panic year of 1837. For better or for worse he would never again venture west of Harrisburg.

During the two years following his return from the West, Pitt abstained from political office-holding in order to give as much attention as possible to the law. By the spring of 1839 his children numbered three, all sons with husky appetites, and this fact plus an increasingly lucrative practice helped account for his reluctance to re-enter the political arena. All this does not mean, however, that his support of Maine Whiggery had flagged, for although he himself held no political office during the turbulent years of the late 1830's, he did not hesitate to invest his talents and influence liberally in behalf of his party's policies and candidates. This was particularly true of the gubernatorial contest of 1837 in which Fessenden served tirelessly as campaign-manager for the Whig candidate, Edward Kent of Bangor.

By the autumn of the year Maine was in the throes of hard times. Hundreds of businesses throughout the state had failed; many, if not most, banks had closed their doors or had severely curtailed operations; and unemployment had already assumed frightful proportions. Against such conditions, daily becoming worse, and against what appeared to be a do-nothing attitude on the part of the Democratic administrations in Washington and Augusta, "anti-Locofoco" * sentiment throughout Maine became articulate and rife. "Will Congress

* By the mid-1830's the term "Locofoco" was applied indiscriminately to all Democrats in many areas of the North.

do anything for the relief of the people?" asked the Bangor *Courier*. "We fear not. . . . Mr. Van Buren says naught of relief to a suffering people. Let the people take care of themselves." [6] For the Whigs of Maine the moment was most propitious, and capitalizing on the widespread popular unrest, Campaign-manager Fessenden and his friends managed to accomplish something very unusual. In September of that year they broke the Democratic stranglehold on the state by successfully inserting Kent into the governor's chair. Perhaps even more remarkable was the Whig triumph in capturing the Lower House of the Augusta Legislature. Small wonder that Fessenden was pleased with his first venture into managerial politics. For the first time in the brief history of the state the Democratic party was unhorsed. Whig ascendancy and Mr. Fessenden's gratification were cut suddenly short in the following year, however, when a somewhat resuscitated, but still very shaky, Democratic party regained its traditional hegemony. And there, in the uncertain hands of the Maine Democracy, control of the state still rested when Pitt emerged from his temporary political retirement to take his seat in the State Legislature in January of 1840.

Back in Augusta after an absence of nearly eight years, Pitt was immediately recognized as one of the two or three top leaders of the Whig opposition. His role in the 1840 Legislature was not destined to be a conspicuous one, however, for soon after his arrival in Augusta he was named chairman of a special committee set up to revise the badly antiquated Maine statutes. This was to prove a slow and thankless task and was to consume most of his time during the session, but when the job was finally finished, Mr. Fessenden's legalistic mind was inordinately pleased with what had been accomplished. Years later, long after he had left the Augusta scene for the United States Senate, he would still consider his work on the Maine statutes one of his most significant contributions to the welfare of his state.

There were important matters before the Legislature at this time. Among them none was given more attention by the Whig minority at Augusta than the recent attempts that had been made by the United States Congress to remove bounties then being paid to New England fishermen. Such an action by Congress, it was generally agreed by the Whigs and not a few disgruntled Democrats, could bring only disastrous results for Maine's economy which was already staggering under the weight of the worst depression in the nation's history. There was also concern shown by Fessenden's Whig colleagues over the apparent reluctance of the Federal Government to distribute to states and individuals involved, those funds which had been collected from France pursuant to the spoliations settlement of 1831. A sizable sum was due the people of Maine, particularly the shipping interests, and what better time than the present could be found for payment? Certainly the money would never be needed more desperately than at that very moment.

On both these matters Fessenden gave his wholehearted support to those forces attacking Democratic perfidy and corruption in Washington. His role in the long and heated debates on these issues was, however, a much less active one than might have been expected, probably because of his many absences from the floor, necessitated by the excessive demands made upon his time by the statutes committee. Only once, in fact, during the entire 1840 session did he figure prominently in debate. On that occasion he argued impressively but futilely in favor of a policy of state aid for Maine's colleges. To most of his Whig colleagues the aid suggested by Fessenden fell under the heading of legitimate internal improvements and certainly made good political and economic sense. To the Democratic majority, however, Fessenden's proposal was not only a barefaced scheme to tap the public till, but, worse yet, it was offensively undemocratic. "Colleges are to educate rich men's sons," the Locofoco majority agreed. " We are not in favor of sustaining institutions which educate aristocratic men to come here in the halls of legislation and contend with us who have had no such advantages." [7] As far as the Democrats were concerned, there was already quite enough of patricianism in Augusta. Remarked one, in commenting on the situation to a friend: "Such men as Fessenden, Otis, and Allen, are an honor to any party, but there are some of that party so overbearing and aristocratic in all their feelings, I could never endure them." [8]

Shortly after the close of the 1840 Legislative session, Fessenden accepted the Whig nomination for Congress. He could scarcely have chosen a more turbulent time for his entrance into national politics, for certainly few political contests, if any, in Maine's history can compare in energy and excitement with the famous "hell-bent" election of 1840. From the outset it was clear that the campaign between the Whigs and Democrats would be a no-holds-barred struggle between

two evenly matched giants, each determined to fight it out every inch
of the way. Faced with a strong chance for victory on both the state
and national levels, the Maine Whigs adopted a "turn the rascals
out" platform and, like their Whig colleagues in other states, aimed
their electioneering primarily against the widespread economic unrest
that had plagued the state and the nation since the spring of 1837.
To oppose the Democratic incumbent John Fairfield for the office of
governor, they put their best foot forward by running the popular
Edward Kent of Bangor, the only Whig ever to have won a gubernatorial election in Maine. And in the all-important second Congressional district, it was young Pitt Fessenden of Portland who did battle
for property and respectability against the powerful Maine Democracy.

For aid in his campaign Fessenden called upon the services of Freeman H. Morse of nearby Bath. A carver of figureheads and an artist
of sorts, Morse was recognized throughout Maine as a political manipu-
lator of great skill, and despite his lack of formal education he was
generally conceded to be one of the most brilliant Whig orators in
the state. From this time until the end of Fessenden's life, the rough-
hewn, self-taught Morse would be counted as one of Pitt's staunchest
political friends, and eventually, after Fessenden's accession to national prominence, a fitting place would be found for Morse in the
London consulate. William Pitt Fessenden had his faults, but political
ingratitude was not one of them.

The key to success in the early-bird September election,* Morse
concluded as he viewed the political situation in the second Congressional district, lay in minimizing the influence of the rabidly Jacksonian *Eastern Argus* of Portland—the largest, loudest, and most
powerful newspaper in the state. As far as the other papers in the
district were concerned, there was no real problem involved. Most of
them were outspokenly Whig and could be counted upon to back
Fessenden all the way. But the *Argus* was a host in itself. Never at a
loss for words or strong opinions, it habitually loomed large in shaping
the thinking and attitudes of the Portland area, and its influence was
bound to pose a serious threat to Fessenden's chances.

But, Morse pointed out, there were ways of diminishing this influence. For instance, political journals of a temporary nature might
be published in key spots throughout the district in order to facilitate

* Prior to 1960 Maine's state and Congressional elections were held in September.

the spread of the Whig gospel. As matters turned out, in fact, a few such papers actually did come into being during the spring and summer of 1840, and these served their purpose tolerably well despite the difficulties encountered by their sponsors during this troubled depression year in raising money for their support. To Morse's way of thinking, however, of all the weapons available for battling the *Argus* and generally enhancing Fessenden's chances for success, none would prove half so effective as personal contact with the people of the district. "You must go to them and talk to them," he advised Pitt, and while Fessenden perhaps recognized the wisdom of doing so, he balked at the impropriety of taking to the stump. It was not in the gentlemanly tradition to boast and beg before the people. This was something a Democrat would do, but he was no Democrat and had little disposition to enter into this sort of rabble-rousing. To soften Fessenden's opposition toward stumping was no easy task, but Morse somehow managed to accomplish it, probably by convincing his young friend that there was no other way to win the election.[9] And so in the log cabin and hard cider year of 1840, at a time when Whigs in other sections of the country were emerging from their political cocoons and out-Jacksoning the Jacksonians in selling themselves to the people, Pitt Fessenden somewhat reluctantly fell into step and for the first time in his life took to the stump.

During the summer months he traveled the length and breadth of the district, pausing to speak wherever a few people would gather to listen to him. And always dogging his steps and snapping at his heels was the *Eastern Argus*, warning the voters against:

FALSE ATTACKS UPON DEMOCRATS
FALSE ACCOUNTS OF CHANGES
FALSE REPRESENTATIONS OF THE DOINGS
OF GOVERNMENT
FALSE REPRESENTATIONS OF THE PRINCIPLES
OF DEMOCRACY
FALSEHOODS OF EVERY SHAPE, HUE, AND KIND [10]

As the campaign entered its final days, and as Fessenden and his Jacksonian opponent, "that brawling, wreckless fat boy" Albert Smith, made their last-minute appeals to the voters, the *Argus* in a final fulmination saw fit to alert its readers against:

FABRICATIONS, FALSEHOODS, AND FORGERIES!
which have been and will be promulgated by the British Whigs,
and the LIARS, SCOUNDRELS, etc., and HIRED TOOLS in their
employ—too late to be contradicted—in the shape of FORGED
LETTERS—FORGED CERTIFICATES—FALSE NEWS, etc.[11]

But despite such stern counsel, the election results of that September brought sad tidings to the *Argus* and the Maine Democracy, and
to the Whigs unbounded joy, although their success could hardly be
described as sweeping. As it turned out, the voters had not, as the
Whigs had predicted, gone "hell-bent for Governor Kent," or for
anyone else. In fact, when the smoke of the contest had finally
cleared, it was apparent that the Whig victory had been anything but
a "hell-bent" one. True, the Whigs had captured the State Legislature
by a comfortable enough majority, but of the eight Congressional
seats then belonging to Maine, the Whigs had managed to get nothing
better than an even split. And as for the gubernatorial contest, it
was found that out of a total of nearly ninety-one thousand votes
cast, Kent had nosed out Fairfield by a scant sixty-seven. In the second
Congressional district, however, William Pitt Fessenden with, as the
Argus lamented, "the spirit of Federalism deep-seated in his heart,"
had won more handily than had been expected, and had thus become at the age of thirty-four the first Whig Congressman ever to be
elected from the Portland district. From his Uncle Thomas Fessenden
in Fryeburg came congratulations and advice:

> I congratulate you on your election rather because I believe it
> is gratifying to you than because I believe it will conduce to your
> advantage. I think you will find the navigation difficult as a public
> man—because you will consistently be obliged to suffer the in-
> testine war . . . between conscience and the natural hankering
> after popularity which every man, at least every *youngerly* man has.
> Now, on this point I have only to say, whenever circumstances force
> you to the "impassable point" where conscience or popularity must
> one or the other of them be surrendered, be true to yourself, your
> name and your highest interests and let it be popularity that is
> given up and not conscience.[12]

Mr. Fessenden Takes His Seat

WASHINGTON IN the early 1840's was in no sense of the word an attractive city. At that time fewer than twenty thousand people walked its dirt streets, which were often rutted and spotted with tufts of wild grass. Here and there unattended cows could be noticed wandering aimlessly about near the center of the city, and it was not uncommon to see herds of manacled slaves being driven down Pennsylvania Avenue, which, when it was not a stinking quagmire, was likely to be blanketed with long tan clouds of dust. Charles Dickens, a critical visitor to Washington during this period, saw this city of "tobacco-tinctured saliva" as a place of great emptiness and pathetic pretentiousness:

> Spacious avenues that begin in nothing, and lead nowhere; streets, mile long, that only want houses, roads, and inhabitants; public buildings that need but a public to be complete; and ornaments of great thoroughfares, which only lack thoroughfares to ornament, are its leading features. One might fancy the season over, and most of the houses gone out of town with their masters. . . .[1]

To a capital such as this most Congressmen preferred to come alone, mercifully leaving their families at home. During the day these men sat and declaimed in the none-too-comfortable chambers of the Capitol, working on the job that they had been sent there to do, or at least making noisy gestures in that direction. At night they returned to their respective boarding houses, which were scattered fairly widely

33

throughout the city. In each of these houses generally a half-dozen or more Congressmen, usually from the same party and often from the same state, lodged together and took common mess. And on a clement evening it was not at all extraordinary for foot-loose members of the Massachusetts mess or the New Jersey mess, etc., to be seen making their collective way to one of the city's more fashionable taverns, or heading in the direction of the old Washington Theatre where the great Junius Brutus Booth could be seen in such engaging roles as Sir Giles Overreach, Lear, Othello, and Shylock, provided that Mr. Booth were sober enough to stand.

The Whigs that arrived upon the Washington scene in the spring of 1841 were a jubilant crowd, and with good cause. Seldom has a political party been faced with more promising prospects than were the Whigs as they trickled into the Capital during the last week in May to attend a special "hard times" session of Congress. Carrying with them a seemingly enthusiastic endorsement by the nation's voters in the elections just past, the Whigs had no reason to suppose that they would encounter any significant difficulty in instituting a long-deferred program of economic reform. Indeed, conditions throughout the country seemed to demand immediate action. The depression that had begun in 1837 still hung like a pall over the land, and obviously it would be up to the Whigs to provide a remedy. The only real question concerned the exact nature of the ingredients that should go into making up such a remedy. And it was on this matter that Whiggery foundered during its most golden moment.

In attempting to explain to a friend some years later the chaotic demoralization of the Washington Whigs in 1841, Congressman Caleb Cushing of Massachusetts, himself a onetime Whig, declared: "I have heard of men running their heads against a wall, but this is the first time I ever heard of men building a wall, and squaring it, and clamping it, for the express purpose of knocking out their brains against it." [2] And in a sense it was true that the Whigs were in a large measure responsible for what befell them at this time. By failing to establish adequate discipline within their ranks, by displaying an incredible degree of intra-party peevishness and irascibility, by scrupulously tormenting themselves with sectional suspicions, and by generally acting the role of political amateurs, and second-rate amateurs at that, the Whigs of 1841 contributed generously to their own undoing. But there was luck involved too—or lack of it. In fact, of all the major political parties in the nation's history, none has been more inordinately unlucky than the Whigs. In two decades of national prominence Whiggery was able to elevate but two of its candidates to the presidency, both of whom responded to the honor by dying in office. The first of these, William Henry Harrison, had been in the White House only a month, barely long enough to call a special session of Congress, before going to his reward in April of 1841 and passing on his office and responsibilities to John Tyler of Virginia.

Tyler, often referred to derogatively by his Whig colleagues as "His Accidency," might just as appropriately have been dubbed "His Expediency," for he had been entered into the 1840 contest as Harrison's running-mate for the principal purpose of attracting Southern votes. "We took Harrison," remarked a Southern politician at a later time, "because Tyler was his endorser—and it was known that we would take him on no other condition." [3]

John Tyler was a man of considerable political experience and achievement. He had been governor of his state, and he had served prominently in both Houses of Congress. During most of his political career he had been a devoted Democrat, but the imperiousness of Andrew Jackson had driven him, as it had so many others, from the Democratic fold and cast him in name, if not in spirit, with the forces of Whiggery. As a friend and admirer of the Whig chieftain Henry Clay, Tyler found his new surroundings congenial enough as long as the Democrats retained control of affairs in Washington and the Whigs were able to do little more than make angry noises against Jackson and his disciples. But with Whiggery's smashing victory in 1840, the political situation changed drastically. The Whigs were no longer on the outside looking in. They were now supposedly in a position to get things done, and as a result of the death of President Harrison, Tyler was suddenly and quite unexpectedly called upon to play a conspicuous role in putting Senator Clay's program into operation.

The fact soon became painfully apparent, however, that John Tyler was not the person for the job. Reared in the solid states-rights tradition of his fellow Virginians, Jefferson and John Randolph, the President could not take kindly to the strongly nationalistic implications of the Whig program as envisioned by the legions of Henry Clay. Scarcely had the special session of the twenty-seventh Congress opened for business, in fact, before there began to appear unmistakable signs that all was not well between Tyler and Whig leaders in Congress. During the summer months attempts were made by both sides to patch up the increasingly ominous differences between the views of the President and those of the party that had accidentally put him into power, but to no avail. These differences seemed to the Democratically oriented President to be fundamental, and John Tyler was not a man to compromise on fundamentals. Consequently, by September an open breach had appeared which cast a heavy gloom upon the legislative aspirations of Clay and his supporters, for not only had the President "defected," but also he had taken with him a small but influential group of Congressional Whigs. Contemptuously labelled by Clay as the "Corporal's Guard," these Tyler Whigs, mostly Southerners, represented a split in Whig ranks which could and would prove to be a thorn in the side of the twenty-seventh Congress.

But, as has been indicated, to attribute to Tyler and his "Corporal's Guard" full credit or blame for frustrating the Whigs of the twenty-seventh Congress would be to give the devil more than his due. Even if President Harrison had lived, chances are that Clay and his friends would have encountered more than a little difficulty in attempting to put their full legislative program into effect. Born out of opposition to Jacksonism, the Whig party on the national level was an amorphous affair held together more by common antipathies than by common goals. As long as the party remained out of power it functioned fairly well as a group, but once in control it almost immediately revealed its dangerously eclectic nature. In fact it often appeared that because the Whig party was so many things to so many men, the greater part of Whiggery's time and energy was expended in efforts to circumnavigate potentially explosive issues, such as slavery, lest the party be destroyed by antagonisms from within. Such was clearly the case during the twenty-seventh Congress, and few Whigs were more aware of this situation or more chagrined by it than young Pitt Fessenden of Portland.

The members of the twenty-seventh Congress lost little time in getting down to business, and Fessenden soon discovered that the legislative pace was more rapid and demanding than he had anticipated. "If what I have had is a fair specimen of Congressional life," he wrote to his Portland law partner after only a week in Washington, "then the place is no sinecure." [4] A few days later Pitt was assigned to the House Committee on Naval Affairs, which met regularly in the south wing of the Capitol under the stern eye of Chairman Henry A. Wise of Virginia, soon to defect to the "Corporal's Guard." These meetings would provide Fessenden with his sum total of committee-room experience during the next two years. They also provided him with his first intimate encounter with the Southern mind at work, and what he saw and heard in committee, and to a lesser extent on the floor of the House as well, failed to impress him very favorably. The Southerners as a whole, he concluded with characteristic decisiveness after only a few weeks in Washington, were a pretty inferior breed, and of them all the Virginians were clearly the worst—"selfish, hair-splitting, senseless animals, without consistency and destitute of reason. The President stands at their head and is the weakest of the lot." [5] Never widely known for the malleability of his opinions, Mr. Fessenden during the remainder of his life would see little reason to change his mind on the nature of Southern politicians in general and Virginians in particular.

In the main business of putting Henry Clay's program into operation, Pitt Fessenden was a willing and diligent worker. Plans for the establishment of a new national bank, greater tariff protection, internal improvements, as well as other cherished Whig projects, received his hearty endorsement and support. In fact, with few exceptions he adhered closely during his first and only term in the House of Representatives to the line prescribed by Whig leadership in Congress. Nor was it at all strange that he should do so, for in Fessenden's mind above and beyond all considerations of party policy and harmony was the strong conviction that the path of Whiggery was the shortest and best way to national well-being and progress.

As a freshman member in a body of such notables as the venerable John Quincy Adams, Caleb Cushing, Alexander H. H. Stuart, Millard Fillmore, Joshua Giddings, and Truman Smith, young Fessenden played a less than momentous role in the over-all drama of the twenty-seventh Congress, but his newness upon the Washington scene did not prevent him from engaging actively in many of the debates of the Lower House, sometimes with commendable fluency and effect. In his first major speech, on July 8, Fessenden spoke for half an hour in favor of the Loan Bill, designed to enable a badly harassed federal treasury to borrow a sum of twelve million dollars. Although mindful of the unhealthy state of the Government's finances in general, Pitt was particularly concerned with the necessity of providing immediate funds for defense purposes. The dispute with England over Maine's northeast boundary was still unsettled, and who could say when the whole festering affair would erupt into war with Great Britain? Money must be made available for many things, he agreed, but most especially and most immediately it must be made available for defense. "Should a war arise," he argued, "the people would pronounce it a poor and niggardly policy, which, for fear of asking for the money necessary to be expended, had left them defenseless to their enemies." [6] Old John Quincy Adams noted the speech with some satisfaction and in his diary rated young Fessenden "a fluent but unimpressive speaker." [7]

A week later during debate on the Fortifications Bill, Pitt revealed something of that honest, uncompromising solicitude for the public treasury which would so prominently characterize his later career, and which, incidentally, would not always conduce to his increased popularity with the folks back home. On this occasion he startled his Maine colleagues in the House by opposing an amendment which would have allocated six thousand dollars for repair of the forts in Portland harbor. Calling the House's attention to the fact that a similar appropriation had been made during the last days of the previous Congress, and that since that time there had been no further request for funds, he made it known that "he could not see the propriety of embarrassing an appropriations bill of this character with such amendments, unless imperiously called for. He would vote against all such, let them come from what quarter of the country they might, and he was willing to begin with his own." [8] Understandably, there were those people in the Portland area who found it difficult to comprehend why their Congressman had denied them this gift of six thousand dollars for the protection of his own city while at the same time voting in favor of thirty times that amount for Boston harbor defenses. In a fit of partisan rage the *Eastern Argus* denounced Fessenden for his "ignorance and indifference on this subject," adding indignantly that "Mr. Fessenden puts a far too high estimate upon his common place scurrility and cold insolence. . . ." [9]

During the summer Fessenden kept up a running attack against the "odious" Sub-Treasury Act, a Democratic hard-money measure passed only a year before during President Van Buren's final months in office. Pitt felt that the Sub-Treasury system if actually put into operation would tend to stifle economic recovery and inhibit satisfactory business transactions by relentlessly and very foolishly withdrawing specie from circulation. The repeal of the act in mid-August proved, therefore, a source of gratification and relief for the sober young Whig from Portland. Fessenden's most important speech during this special "hard times" session, however, was that in which he argued for passage of Senator John Henderson's Bankrupt Bill. Early in June, Pitt had written to his partner Willis: "The general impression seems to be that a Bankrupt Law cannot be matured and passed at this session. This is Mr. Clay's opinion." [10] But when President Tyler later declared himself not adverse to such a measure, "carefully guarded against fraudulent practices, and embracing, as far as practicable, all classes of society," [11] it became apparent that summer passage might be realized after all. On August 11 Pitt spoke for an hour in support of the bill. The people of America were in financial distress, he declared, and the Government was largely to blame for their suffering because of the unwise currency policies of past administrations. Now it was clearly the duty of the Government to come to the aid of these depressed people. The proposed bill was emphatically one of relief, and was it not for the purpose of relief that this special session had been called? Fessenden could see no sound reason for opposition to this measure, "called for alike by the feelings of humanity and by the great interests of the community." [12] A week later the Bankrupt Bill, the first of its kind since the long defunct Bankruptcy Act of 1800, passed the Lower House by the narrow margin of four votes and was signed by President Tyler on the following day. In the dimming eyes of John Quincy Adams, who had supported the bill, Fessenden had grown somewhat since his maiden speech of a month before, although it is clear from the following notation in the old man's diary that Pitt still fell far short of "Old Q.'s" standards:

Fessenden, a promising young man from Portland, Maine, made an hour speech in [the bill's] favor. His slender form and pallid face indicate a feeble constitution, ill suited to the latitude of Port-

land. He speaks with great facility, without elegance—plain sound
sense, but without striking thought or imagery, wit or humor—
always grave, always calm, always moderate, never very impressive,
never original in thought or sentiment.[13]

The failure of Whig bank legislation during the latter part of that
summer came as a maddening disappointment to Pitt. There had been
strong indications, however, that President Tyler would not take
kindly to the sort of bank bill that Henry Clay envisaged. As early as
July 4, in fact, Clay had confided to a friend that "Mr. Tyler's opinions
about a bank are giving us great trouble. Indeed, they not only threaten
a defeat on the matter, but endanger the permanency, and the ascendancy of the Whig cause." [14] Later in the month Pitt's friend
Daniel Webster expressed similar concern: "Probably it [the Bank
Bill] may pass both Houses," he wrote to his protégé Edward Everett,
"but whether the President will approve it, is a question which I
hardly dare ask myself. If he should not, I know not what will become
of our administration." [15] And then in August and early September
the lightning struck twice in rapid succession as President Tyler
vetoed two different versions of Whig bank legislation. This deadly
double blow meant more than the end of Whig hopes for a new national banking system. It in effect signalled an open and all-but-com-
plete break between President Tyler and the Whig-dominated Congress. Within a week after the President's second veto, Tyler's entire
cabinet had resigned, save for Secretary of State Webster, and in the
House young Fessenden sat chagrined over "the obstinacy and vanity
of a poor animal [Tyler] who was never worth the snuff of a candle,
or a cheese paring, or a quid of tobacco." [16] Two days later, on September 13, a pained and disgruntled Whig Congress, now irretrievably
alienated from the man whom they had, foolishly perhaps, counted
upon for so much, rang down the curtain on its unhappy special session. "We ought not, after such a victory, to be in so humiliating a
situation," growled Fessenden.[17]

By the time Congress had reconvened in December, Pitt had grown
increasingly anxious over his friend Daniel Webster, who seemed to
be on the verge of being written off by his Whig colleagues as a member of the "Corporal's Guard." Webster, then in the throes of negotiations with the British over the Maine boundary dispute, had remained

in Tyler's cabinet for the sole purpose of seeing the important negotiations through to a successful conclusion—or so he preferred to have
his Whig brethren believe. "I will not," he declared in defending his
decision not to quit his cabinet post, "throw the great foreign con-
cerns of the country into disorder or danger, by any abrupt party
proceeding." [18] This seemed to many a good enough excuse at the
time, but as Webster continued to cling doggedly to his post during
the early months of 1842 while the diplomatic hagglings appeared to
be making little if any progress, even Webster's friends, including Fessenden, began to wonder about the great Daniel's intentions. To his
old preceptor Charles Daveis, Pitt wrote in April of that year: "We
are getting on a little better now. . . . I have, however, lost all hope
of our friend, Mr. W., considering him to be joined to idols." [19]

A further strain was added to the relationship between Fessenden
and Webster by the case of the brig *Creole* in mid-March, an affair
in which, according to Pitt's views, Webster appeared to countenance
the coastwise slave-trade. All of this was too much for young Fessenden, for although no abolitionist, he would not have been his
father's son had he not looked upon slave-trading in any form as a
heinous and detestable practice. Consequently, he found himself for
the first time posed in open opposition to his godfather, and although
he refrained from attacking his friend on the floor, he did feel compelled to register in some manner his disapproval of Webster's stand.
His opportunity came on March 22 when the Lower House voted on a
resolution to censure Joshua Giddings of Ohio for having made some
decidedly unlovely remarks about the Secretary of State. In the censure
vote, Fessenden sided with the nays, thereby announcing by implica-
tion his lack of sympathy with Daniel's behavior. For a time thereafter
Fessenden avoided his old friend, for reasons of honor and delicacy,
but the kindly intervention of Mrs. Webster soon healed the breach,
and by mid-summer Pitt was once again a frequent guest at his godfather's table.

Throughout his freshman term in Congress, young Pitt Fessenden
proved himself an alert and conscientious legislator. From his room
at Mrs. Whitwell's boarding house on Capitol Hill he marched duti-
fully day after day to his seat in the Lower Chamber, seldom missing a
vote or a sitting. During this two-year period he behaved generally as
was expected of a good Northern Whig. In fact, in at least one im-

portant area, that of tariff legislation, he was among the most ardent
and outspoken of the Lower House Whigs—enough so to cause many
of his party colleagues some embarrassment. For not a few of his Whig
brethren, including Clay, tariff protection had lost some of its appeal, but not for Pitt. To him tariff was still a magic word, and the
very marrow of Whiggery. He found it difficult to understand how any
good American could feel otherwise, but it was painfully apparent to
him that many of his Congressional colleagues did not share his feelings on this matter. "The moment the word tariff was mentioned in
the hall," Fessenden noted, "although it was known that the Treasury
was empty, gentlemen seemed to be as much alarmed as if the proposition were brought in to overturn the Government of the United
States." [20]

It was Pitt's affection for tariff protection that accounted in part for
his stand on the controversial Army Appropriations Bill, which cut
across party lines. On May 31, 1842, the first anniversary of his arrival
in Congress, he defended the Army Bill against attempts at retrench-
ment. In what was clearly one of the most outstanding speeches delivered in the Lower House during the entire session, Pitt began by
scolding his fellow-members for their timidity on the issue. Pointing
out that nearly all those who had spoken on the subject, for or against,
had seen fit to preface their remarks by professions of great love for
the army and navy, young Fessenden declared with characteristic
candor:

> For myself, Mr. Chairman, I cannot pretend to any remarkable
> degree of friendship for either the army or the navy. I regard them
> both as necessities, existing by force of our political position, and
> calling for support just so far as they may be essential to the national
> welfare. I could hope, though I cannot expect to see the day when
> both might be dispensed with altogether.[21]

But at the present time the army was, in Pitt's estimation, critically
in need of funds, and as the bill then stood, the provisions seemed no
more than barely adequate. To decrease the amount of the appropriations might very well prove a dangerous error, especially in view of
the fact that the Maine boundary dispute with Britain was still
smouldering. John Quincy Adams, although himself in favor of re-

duction, was genuinely impressed, and Pitt's stock again soared in the old man's busy diary. "Fessenden of Maine," Adams wrote, this time without reservation, "made a very handsome speech against any reduction of the army. . . . It was a spirited and powerful speech." [22] A week later Pitt revealed to his friend Daveis that he had been moved to plead the army's cause by a desire for more than one kind of added protection:

> We are now voting on the Army Bill. Cut down, reduce are the order of the day. It is all very silly in my opinion, but there is no such thing as staying the tide. It will injure our prospects of any such thing as protection in the new Tariff.[23]

When the twenty-seventh Congress closed its final doors in early March of 1843, probably no member was more thoroughly relieved than young Mr. Fessenden of Portland. Since his arrival in the capital city nearly two years before, he had grown increasingly disgusted with the entire Congressional scene. In the ranks of both parties he felt that he had encountered men of the lowest ethical standards, directed by the most contemptible of motives, and void of any apparent concern for the good of their country. "I saw in them," wrote the visiting Charles Dickens about the Congress of Fessenden's day, "the wheels that move the meanest perversion of virtuous Political Machinery . . . :

> It is the game of these men . . . to make the strife of politics so fierce and brutal, and so destructive of all self-respect in worthy men, that sensitive and delicate-minded persons shall be kept aloof, and they, and such as they, be left to battle out their selfish views unchecked.[24]

Less than half-way through his term, Pitt had come to the same conclusion—that Congress was no place for a decent human being. To his family he wrote:

> If you knew how utterly detestable this congressional life is to me, you would entertain no apprehensions of my again becoming a candidate. . . . I am cured, I hope, forever, of all fondness of

public life, and could I do so without forfeiting obligations to others, would gladly resign and come home.[25]

Particularly distressing and disillusioning to Fessenden was the behavior of many members of his own party during this period. From the first it appeared to Pitt that the Whig party in Congress was dominated by the interests of its Southern minority, and in many instances its Northern members seemed to be guided less by conscience and party principles than by fear of offending their Southern brethren. Indeed, it often appeared that the main purpose of Whiggery on the national level was merely that of prolonging its own existence. This philosophy of party-for-party's-sake was nowhere more clearly manifested at this time than in the matter of opposition to the gag rule, a device dating back to 1836 which in effect closed the doors of the Lower House to all petitions and other papers pertaining to slavery. The gag rule was a convenient and effective arrangement for those members, mostly Southerners, who for one reason or another wanted to keep the slavery issue as far away as possible from the floor of Congress. But for others, led by John Quincy Adams, the rule represented a conspiracy of silence designed to deprive American citizens of their constitutional right of protest. During all three sessions of the twenty-seventh Congress Adams fought fiercely and relentlessly against the rule, but to no avail. Even his own Whig colleagues from the North failed to support him, and sometimes lashed out violently against him for endangering party unity. To Fessenden it was sickening to see men of Northern background and interests join in tirades of abuse and ridicule against the venerable Adams for the mean purpose of placating the Southern branch of the Whig family. He would have none of it. He did, in fact, give the old man his constant support, and in late February of 1842 introduced his own resolution to rescind the odious rule. "I am glad to see that you are coming out on the Slavery petitions," his friend Henry Longfellow wrote to him at this time. "All good people in these regions are disgusted with Southern bullying on this subject." [26]

But to the analytical mind of Mr. Fessenden, the gag rule controversy was only one reflection of a painful and fundamental political fact, a fact which Pitt had recognized soon after his arrival in Congress and which would continue to plague him for many years thereafter: The Whig party on the national level was not really a party at all, but an uneasy and perhaps unnatural alliance between groups of increasingly divergent interests, with sectional antagonisms sounding the dominant motif. Where would it all end? Pitt thought he knew the answer. And as the twenty-seventh Congress came to its whimpering close in March of 1843 and a badly disillusioned and disgusted Fessenden prepared to return to Portland and presumably a final retirement from public life, he saw no cause to alter the observation he had made nearly two years before during his first week of Congressional service:

> In my opinion nothing but a strict union and friendly understanding between the north middle and northeast, together with Kentucky and Tennessee, will give strength and consistency to our party. The Southern Whigs are not to be relied on. I think that a union such as I have referred to will be formed. The Western boys are good fellows and ripe for concert and vigor.[27]

All this more than a dozen years before that little group assembled under the oaks in Jackson, Michigan, to proclaim the birth of the Republican party.

V

Portland Again: An Interlude

Often I think of the beautiful town
  That is seated by the sea;
Often in thought go up and down
The pleasant streets of that dear old town
  And my youth comes back to me.

As HE reflected upon it from his Senate seat many years later, the
decade that Pitt spent at home in Portland after his return from Congress in early 1843 seemed the happiest of his life. He remembered
those years as a serene time filled with comfort and contentment, an
unhurried, unambitious time which he enjoyed looking back on as
a respite from Senatorial turmoil. In reality, however, it appears that
these halcyon years existed only in retrospect, in the nostalgic recollections of a lonely man. Actually the period from 1843 to 1854 was
one of intense striving for Fessenden. Driven on by some inner com-
pulsion he could neither control nor understand, he singled out his
special star and followed it with relentless and sometimes almost blind
devotion in the direction of a place he knew only as "success."

Financially, the years of this decade brought to Fessenden and his
family a life of upper middle-class comfort. To the firm of Willis and
Fessenden there came the prestige that accompanies legal triumphs,
and on the heels of this prestige an ever-growing clientele and substantial fees. At the time of his election to the United States Senate
in 1854, "my practice was very large, probably the best in the state,"
Fessenden would recall some years later. "My practice embraced all
branches of the law, in all the state courts, and the Circuit Courts." [1]

46

During the late 1840's Pitt appears to have averaged a net annual income of about three thousand dollars, a figure which, while not excessive, was nonetheless a substantial one for the Portland of that day. Add to this his profits from various real estate transactions and business investments, and it becomes clear that Fessenden's combined earnings during this time were fairly sizable. How sizable may be indicated by the fact that Mr. Fessenden, who was not one to live beyond his means, paid in 1853 a real estate and personal property tax of nearly two hundred dollars, an amount topped by only one hundred of the city's five thousand taxpayers.[2]

In the matter of his profession Fessenden was characteristically intense in his loyalty to the letter of the law. He was not a hard man, but neither was he one of those given to the error of permitting compassion to insinuate itself into matters of a purely legal nature. The law was the law, and to subvert it with ideas of mercy, mitigating circumstances, and what-have-you, was to Fessenden's mind little short of sacrilege. Consequently, once he had ascertained that his client was legally in the right, he customarily pulled no punches in bringing the full and inexorable power of the law to bear down upon all unfortunate adversaries. If, in his professional pursuit of truth and justice, he was forced to operate in a manner which by standards of a later time might seem heartless, or even brutal, at least he had the satisfaction of knowing that he was doing the right thing. After all, if a person would not pay his debts, he was indistinguishable from a robber, and excuses couldn't change the situation one whit. Therefore: "take the body of the Said Debtor and him commit into our Gaol . . . and detain in your custody . . . until he pay the full sum mentioned . . . or be discharged by Said Creditor." [3] And yet in those days of debtors' prisons and unlimited liability the way of the transgressor was hard, and in all fairness to Fessenden it should be assumed that he was scarcely more severe in his coldly legalistic attitude toward the wayward than were many, if not most, of his contemporaries of the Cumberland County bar.

It was during this decade of interlude in Portland that Pitt reached the zenith of his juristic career, when, in 1850, he appeared at the January term of the United States Supreme Court as counsel in the case of *Veazie vs. Williams*. This case, which had had its beginnings in Bangor nearly fifteen years before, not long after Fessenden had

left that town, centered about the questionable sale of two mill sites
on the Penobscot River, a mile or so below Old Town. Involved as
litigants were Nathaniel Williams of Boston, seller of the property,
and General Sam Veazie of Bangor and points north, the hapless
buyer. But the leading actor of the drama was without doubt a Mr.
Head of Bangor, who, as his performance proved, was as enterprising an auctioneer as ever swung a hammer.

When the mill sites were put up for sale on New Year's Day of
1836, Head was employed by Williams' agent as auctioneer, with instructions to accept any amount over $14,500 for the two pieces of
property. Since, however, Head was to receive a percentage of the selling price, it behooved him to part with the sites for as dear a sum as
possible, and this is precisely what he did. When bidding began to
lag at $18,000 and it seemed that the property would go to Veazie
for that price, the auctioneer took matters into his own hands and
began the insertion of false bids by means of accomplices planted
in the crowd. By this process of puffing the bid he gently but irre-
sistibly led Veazie's unsuspecting agent up the ladder until the final
hammer fell at $40,000.

Strangely enough, General Veazie was well pleased with his purchase and for four years thereafter lived in a fool's paradise. The
secret was too good to keep, however, and by mid-1840 the awful truth
had reached Veazie's ears. Understandably upset, the General demanded restitution from Williams, and, receiving none, took his
case to the courts. Because the litigation involved citizens of different
states, the matter in time found its way to the United States Circuit
Court, where in August of 1844 Veazie's claims were considered by
presiding Justice Joseph Story and his Circuit Court colleagues to
be without proper basis.[4]

The General was not one to give in easily, however, especially in
matters involving large sums of money, and by January of 1850 the
case of *Veazie vs. Williams* had reached the docket of the United
States Supreme Court. Here William Pitt Fessenden of Portland and
Daniel Webster, then only a few weeks short of his famous Compromise speech, acted as Veazie's counsel, and the records reveal that,
of the two advocates for the plaintiff, it was Fessenden who scored
the more telling points. Relying, as always, upon cold reason and
his extensive knowledge of the law, Pitt advanced his arguments in

a manner that made his conclusions appear inevitable and inescapable. His performance was characteristically neither colorful nor imaginative, but it was logical and complete, and when his job was through, the earlier ruling of the eminent Justice Story was put aside and Sam Veazie became $20,000 richer. For, as Fessenden had maintained, it was the opinion of the Court that the seller of an article should be held responsible for the acts of his auctioneer and that:

A condition of the contract of auction sale is that the article shall be knocked off to the highest bidder without puffing.[5]

So ended the long case of *Veazie vs. Williams,* with a death-blow for puffing, and a feather for Fessenden's cap.

Although not widely known for his speculative nature, Pitt had by the late 1840's fallen temporary victim to the railroad fever which was then mounting throughout the country. In July of 1847 he took a trip to Montreal as one of a committee of directors to confer with British promoters on the subject of a proposed railroad from Portland to Montreal, by way of New Hampshire and Vermont. The agreement as finally formulated called for simultaneous construction from both ends of the route, with a junction of the two roads in northern Vermont, one hundred and fifty miles from Portland. It was expected, or at least hoped, by Fessenden and his friends that the railroad once completed would permit Portland to tap the abounding riches of the Great Lakes area, and thereby do for Portland, perhaps on a more modest scale, what the Erie Canal had done for New York City. By mid-1851 the eastern end of this new Atlantic and St. Lawrence Railroad had been pushed from its Portland terminus to Gorham, New Hampshire, a distance of more than ninety miles, and, by way of promotion, in July of that year a free excursion train was run over the entire length of the new track for the benefit of the more affluent members of Portland's citizenry. Six months later, however, the promoters of the A. and S.L. were in trouble. Construction had slowed down; costs were mounting rather alarmingly, and uneasiness began to show itself among many of the less intrepid investors, of whom Fessenden was one.[6]

As matters turned out there was never any real reason for consternation on the part of the promoters. After a brief period of unsteadiness, during which sizable bond issues were emitted to the public, the project began to progress happily, and eventually the investors were handsomely rewarded for their risk and enterprise. Not sharing in the profits, however, was Mr. Fessenden, who had been prompted by his characteristic cautiousness in business transactions to unload most of his holdings in the railroad during those anxious months when trouble appeared to be brewing. There is nothing to suggest that Fessenden suffered any substantial financial loss by selling out at an unfavorable time, but in terms of missed opportunity at least (if nothing else) he had good cause to regret his brief plunge into railroad promotion. Fessenden's own comments on the affair indicate, in fact, that his association with the Atlantic and St. Lawrence represented something of a souring experience for the conservative Portland attorney. It is, moreover, not unlikely that this less-than-happy encounter was at least in part responsible for Fessenden's subsequent distrust of railroad enterprises, a smoldering suspicion which in later years would find occasional expression in the Senator's speeches and voting record.

In April of 1844 a musical extravaganza descended upon the city of Portland in the form of a "celebrated band of Ethiopian delineators. . . ."

GREAT NOVELTY!—and Mark—
NO HUMBUG
Great Ethiopian Concert
by the
FIVE ORIGINAL VIRGINIA SERENADERS
at Union Hall.[7]

It is unlikely, however, that Mr. Fessenden joined in attendance or acclaim, for his tastes in entertainment had noticeably mellowed since those ribald undergraduate days in Wardwell's Tavern with his Bowdoin brethren. Now on the verge of forty, he preferred to fill his leisure moments with the comforts of his home and family, which in the early 1840's had been rounded out by the birth of a fourth son, Sam, and a daughter, Mary, who subsequently died of scarlet fever in early childhood. In 1846 Pitt and Ellen and their five children moved

to a larger house on State Street, which had been given them by Ellen's wealthy father. Here in the big house just off Congress Street
on the Ocean side, Fessenden lavished his stern attention and principles upon his brood, and here in a spacious back yard he cultivated
a garden of flowers and vegetables. In later years, long after Ellen
was dead and the boys had gone, it was to this old house on the
crest of State Street hill that Fessenden customarily returned to seek
quiet relief from the strain of his Senatorial duties.

It does not appear that Pitt's life was blessed by a wealth of warm
personal friendships during this period. Indeed, for Fessenden friends
had never been and never would be plentiful. Respect and devotion
he could usually claim in fair measure, but affection generally eluded
him. There was a stern quality of reserve, almost aloofness, about him
which served to keep all but a few of his associates at arm's length.
It was not of his own choosing, this formidable exterior with which
he was forced to face the world. He would have preferred things to
be different, but only on rare occasions could he manage to let his
guard down sufficiently for real friendship to enter his life. Perhaps
he was afraid. Perhaps he feared the candor and intimacy of close personal relationship. After all, there was that indelible stain of bastardy
streaked across his soul, and for a man of Fessenden's pride and sensitivity, the idea of being too closely scrutinized or too deeply probed
was doubtless an uncomfortable one. Whatever the reasons, he was
for a great part of his life a man alone, deprived of the real warmth
and affection that he desperately craved and needed. Even within the
inner circle of his own family there was an inhibiting wall of reserve and formality which, despite his pitifully awkward attempts
to do so, Fessenden was never able to shatter. Thus, for Fessenden
affection was, early and late, a commodity rarely dealt in. He gave
little, and he received little in return.

In 1843 William Pitt Fessenden, who had been expelled from Bowdoin as a bad influence twenty years before, was appointed to the
governing boards of the college, a position he held for the remainder
of his life. Five years later, his eldest son, James, entered Bowdoin,
and after James came William, Francis, and Sam, all within a period
of ten years. Upon each of these boys Pitt impressed the importance
of studious behavior, thrift, abstinence, and other virtues which he

liked to think that he himself exemplified, at least to a modest degree. In a letter to James, sent shortly after the boy's arrival at Bowdoin in the autumn of 1848, Fessenden wrote:

My dear James—

Your mother says you will find the pillow-cases in your trunk. She starts for New York, with Cousin Lizzy, today, and will be absent several weeks.

I am sorry that you and Joseph should have allowed yourselves to give so enormous a price for your room. I trust you will be allowed to retain it, as $26 per year is more, I believe, than the annual room-rent. However, you must, I suppose, pay for your wisdom, and probably calculate to bear a part of the burden yourself. I enclose you $8. The 5 you must make up.

You have not yet sent me the list of furniture, etc., as I requested. I wish you to do so, as soon as possible. Also I wish a list of books received of Joseph. You will, of course, take none but such as you are obliged to use in your studies.

If you have not a good English Dictionary at hand, let me know it, and I will send one. A member of *College* should, at least, know how to spell the word without a superfluous *d*. I trust you will endeavor to avoid such errors, and to improve both the penmanship and style of your letters.

I hope, my dear Son, you will be steady, attentive to your studies, and regular in attendance upon all the exercises and duties prescribed. No effort on my part will be spared for your comfort and improvement. You have my confidence now, and you will, doubtless, think it worth retaining.

If, on further search, your pillow-cases are not found, you had better get the woman who takes care of your room to make you some that are suitable.

We are all pretty well at all the houses, and at home, all send love.

Your aff. father
W. P. Fessenden [8]

For Fessenden, however, the dominant theme of these years was a political one, and despite his earlier resolves, he soon found himself once more enmeshed in the growing party turmoil of the 1840's. Many years after Fessenden's death his son Francis could still count among the recollections of his early childhood vivid impressions of his father at this time, speaking excitedly and waving his arms wildly before large crowds assembled in front of a giant circus tent on a vacant lot off High Street. Indeed, scarcely had Fessenden returned from Congress in 1843 when the resignation of Maine's Reuel Williams from the United States Senate caused Pitt's name to be brought forward as the Whig candidate for the vacant seat. Two years later he was again nominated by his party for the United States Senate, but on each occasion the Democratic machine, with a decided majority in Augusta, had little trouble in conferring the honor upon one of its own members. By early 1845 Fessenden was once more a member of the State Legislature, and there he served intermittently during the next nine years as one of the recognized leaders of the Lower House Whigs.

To the nation at large 1846 was the year of the Oregon settlement and the war with Mexico. To the people of Maine, however, it was also the year of Neal Dow's great frontal assault against the devil drink. Obsessed from his Quaker boyhood by the horrible evils of alcohol, Dow had early set about to impress his abstemious ways upon others. Stern-eyed and sober-faced, the wealthy Dow travelled the state for years, a tower of temperance strength, speaking wherever a few people would assemble to hear him. In 1842 he scored his first major triumph by inducing the majority of his Portland neighbors to vote "No License" for that city, and in the following year, Dow, fired by his homeground success, took the battle to Augusta. At his own expense he caused to be printed and circulated for the people's attention hundreds of petitions which called upon the members of the State Legislature to enact stringent legislation to the effect that "the traffic in intoxicating drinks might be held and adjudged an infamous crime." [9] Undaunted by the recalcitrance of the Legislature at this time, Dow redoubled his efforts and proceeded by tongue, pen, and printing press to build up a tremendous force of public sentiment behind his movement. Later he would claim with good cause that "Maine was made a Prohibition state by sowing it knee deep with Temperance literature." [10] By 1846 it was clear that there could be no staying the tide. Forty thousand petitions had reached the law-

makers at Augusta, and one of these, presented by the prophet himself, was fifty-nine feet long. In late July of that year Neal Dow's
temperance bill became law, notwithstanding the objection and negative vote of Pitt Fessenden, who although a friend of temperance
and not unmindful of the pressures of public opinion favoring the
measure, declared the bill so poorly drawn up as to be worse than
worthless. Aglow with victory, Dow wrote to the Secretary of the
American Temperance Union:

> This is the first instance, I believe, in which the government of
> a civilized and Christian state has declared by statute that there
> shall not be within its borders any traffic in intoxicating liquors
> to be used as a drink. . . .[11]

Within a few months, however, Neal Dow's joy had turned to gloom,
for events had soon demonstrated the wisdom of Fessenden's objections. As a prohibition measure the law of 1846 proved too long on
loopholes and too short on punishment to be of any practical worth,
and it was not until five years later, with the passage of the famous
Maine Law, that Mayor Neal Dow of Portland "with the meekness
of a Christian philanthropist and the firmness of a Roman warrior
. . . [could] stand at his post, discharging daily his important duties
and witnessing the fulfilment of his long cherished hopes. . . ." [12]

In February of 1848 the little war with Mexico was brought to a
profitable close by the signing of the treaty of Guadalupe-Hidalgo.
For the United States the treaty meant the acquisition of a vast new
domain in the West. It also meant the sudden resurrection of the
matter of slavery extension and a concomitant sharpening of sectional
antagonisms. From its beginning in the spring of 1846 many North-
erners, especially New Englanders, had been loudly opposed to the
Mexican War on moral as well as sectional grounds. Like Fessenden
they felt that the United States was doing the devil's work in launch-
ing an obviously unprovoked attack on a poor, weak neighbor, and
this feeling of moral indignation was doubtless strengthened by the
painful realization that the Northeast stood to gain not at all from
the fracas. It was pretty clear, in fact, that the entire trumped-up affair was nothing more than a conspiracy on the part of Southern
slaveholders to obtain more territory in which to plant their per-

nicious institution, a conspiracy in which the Southern Whigs were obviously involved.

To prevent such an extension of slavery along with, of course, a resultant increase in the economic and political power of the South in particular and the Democratic party in general, powerful Northern elements, essentially Whig, had begun attempts shortly after the outbreak of the war to exclude slavery by law from all lands that might be acquired from Mexico. The most famous, or infamous, and persistent of these attempts was the Wilmot Proviso, which in one form or another, seen, heard, or felt, was an almost continuous presence in both Houses of Congress from the time of its introduction in August of 1846 until the passage of the Great Compromise nearly four years later. Here was a statement of principle, unequivocal and devastatingly clear, that to a marked degree cut across party lines and brought the entire question of slavery extension violently and nakedly to the center of the national stage. And in the course of the long debates that followed, the embers of sectional suspicions and moral fanaticisms were roughly raked and bellowed by the mounting passions of angry men.

In the late spring of 1848, only a few months after the end of the war with Mexico, Pitt Fessenden went as a delegate to Philadelphia. There, with the fever of sectionalism running high throughout the nation, Whigs from North and South gathered on July 7 to glower suspiciously at one another and to attempt to restore the semblance of party harmony which had been badly shaken by the Wilmot debates. This they hoped to accomplish by selecting as the Whig champion for that autumn's presidential election, a candidate acceptable to both the Northern and Southern branches of the party. Such a man they found in General Zachary Taylor, a Southerner and hero of the Mexican War, whose past was so conveniently void of any political action or expression, that he had little trouble in receiving the convention's endorsement on the fourth ballot. No platform was adopted. Indeed, in view of the divergent interests within the party, probably none could have been adopted without disrupting the party organization. Support of the old General was to be a matter of party faith rather than political conviction—an obvious attempt to preserve the fiction that national Whiggery was still a solid, going concern.

To many Northern Whigs, including Fessenden who had backed
Webster to the disappointing end, the action of the Northern-con-
trolled Convention was little short of incredible. It was clearly nothing
other than a move to assuage the sectional anxieties of the Southern
branch of the family, a hear-no-evil, see-no-evil bit of temporizing
by the Northern Whigs for the sake of party peace. And this should
not be. At a time such as this, with the day of sectional reckoning
perhaps nearer at hand than any of them liked to think, who could
say how catastrophic the results of such a decision would prove to
be? Far better if the Whig party had faced the issues, especially that
of slavery-extension, honestly and openly. Far better if a man of Northern background and principles had been chosen. Fessenden had, in
fact, nothing but contempt for that band of scheming Northern politicians, like Thurlow Weed of New York, whose selfish machinations
had made possible the nomination of "this great slave-holder, a man
without experience in civil life, but recently known to the country,
with the sword still in his hand and declining to avow any fixed opinions on any one of the great questions of the day." [13] Never widely
known as a good loser, Fessenden returned to Portland later that
month a sorely chagrined Whig. Soon after, however, he made it
known that despite his own personal feelings he would defer to the
wishes of his colleagues and support Taylor's candidacy:

I was a member of the convention and cannot assume to oppose
what a majority of my friends have determined to sustain; for
meanly as I think of the few, the great mass of the honest, patriotic,
and wise men and statesmen of our party have yielded their assent
in view of the present, perilous conditions of affairs.[14]

In view of his opinions on Taylor, Fessenden might well have been
expected to cross over the line to Free-Soilism in the autumn election of that year, as did so many of his Northern Whig colleagues.
It does not appear, however, that Pitt at that time gave serious consideration to such a defection. "The principle of the free-soil movement has my sympathy and respect," he declared in mid-July of that
year. "But I cannot see that it will lead to any practical result other
than the election of [Democratic] General Cass, a calamity to be dep-
recated by all good men." And as a final thought, Fessenden added

a statement which presaged the course of his future political conduct as a moderate statesman: "In these things," he asserted, "we are bound to look at results, rather than to principles alone." [15]

By 1850, however, the gulf between Whiggery and Free-Soilism had noticeably narrowed in some areas of the North, largely as a result of angry reaction on the part of many Northern Whigs to the Great Compromise of that year. This was especially true in Maine, where men like Fessenden, who had bitterly opposed the Compromise of 1850, now flirted openly with the Free-Soil forces, led by Pitt's distinguished father. In fact, in the summer of 1850 a somewhat reluctant Fessenden permitted himself to be put forward as a coalition Whig–Free-Soil candidate for the second district's Congressional seat. "If Mr. Fessenden is elected to Congress," remarked the conservative Portland *Advertiser* shortly after Pitt's unanimous nomination by the Cumberland County Whig Convention, "he will never disgrace himself, his constituents, and the whole North, by any tame, compromising, cowardly abandonment of northern rights and northern *national* principles." [16] But for Fessenden, whose campaign on this occasion was far from spirited or enthusiastic, the time had not yet arrived, for in the final tally of that earlybird September election it was found that out of nearly twelve thousand votes cast in the district, Pitt had lost to his Democratic opponent, Judge Appleton, by a scant thirty-nine.*

The Compromise of 1850, with its partial approval of slavery-extension and its hateful fugitive slave law, proved highly indigestible to many Northern Whigs. In fact, it is probably true that the Great Compromise, together with the long, acrimonious debate which preceded its passage, marked the real beginning of the end for the Whig party. For, not only had the chasm between the Northern and Southern elements of Whiggery now become dangerously wide, but also angry divisions had sprung up within many of the state Whig organizations of the North. While it is true that many of these divisions stemmed from patronage squabbles and other more or less local considerations, certainly the major dissensions resulted from differing attitudes toward sectional issues in general and the Compromise in

---

* In this election there was strong question as to the validity of the final count, but, although urged to do so by his supporters, Fessenden refused to contest the results. See: Portland *Advertiser,* Sept. 16, 1850.

particular. All tended to contribute to the growth of political par-
ticularism at the expense of party solidarity.

Nor was the Whig party the only one to suffer from the centrifugal
forces at work. Indeed, by 1852 in many areas of the North the labels
Whig and Democrat had come to have little meaning unless preceded by at least one modifier. So it was that, with "Straight-Outs,"
"Silver-Greys," "Wooley-Heads," "Hunkers," and "Wildcats" running
rampant, factional coalitions, sometimes of an interparty nature,
tended to come into prominence in several of the splinter-ridden
states of the North. But although party anarchy often threatened to
become the order of the day, there soon began to emerge from the
confusion in most states the hazy outlines of certain political ab-
solutes. First, it was growing increasingly clear that the old issues,
upon which party lines had been drawn for over a generation, were
now being pushed into the background, and slavery with its sectional and moral implications was becoming more and more the
basis for political faction. Second, open flirtations were becoming
more frequent and serious between anti-slavery elements of the two
major parties—a trend which in Maine had been presaged in the
spring of 1850 by Fessenden's open praise of Democratic Senator Hannibal Hamlin for his opposition to the Great Compromise. "I con-
gratulate you on your speech, which is highly spoken of . . . ," Pitt
wrote to his long-time rival. "I like it very much. It gives much better satisfaction to men *of all parties* here than Mr. Webster's." [17]

But although both major parties were severely jolted by the rising
crescendo of mid-century sectionalism, it was Whiggery which was
dealt by far the more staggering blows. Never, on the national level,
much more than a loosely organized league of friendship (or con-
venience), meagerly possessed of the solidarity, discipline, and positive purpose that go into the make-up of any political party worthy
of the name, the Whigs lacked the stamina and resiliency to withstand
the savage attacks of sectionalism and other divisive forces of the day.
Indeed, it would not be far amiss to say that by the time the election
year of 1852 had rolled around, the Whig party, despite the fact
that one of its members was then sitting in the White House, was
already in the advanced stages of disintegration, both on the national
level and within many, if not most, of the states. Yet Whiggery was
sanguine enough, or stubborn enough, to insist upon one last fight.

And so it was that in the presidential election of 1852 the Whigs made their final full-dress appearance on the national stage, even though the more politically astute of its leaders must have realized that they were flogging a dead horse.

In the spring of that year, the Maine Whig Convention met at Augusta and endorsed the candidacy of General Winfield Scott by a unanimous vote. Fessenden was among the state's eight delegates selected to attend the National Convention at Baltimore, and for the first time in two decades he was out to oppose the presidential ambitions of his godfather. He would do so, not because he had any great enthusiasm for Scott, but rather because, like his abolitionist father, Pitt had noticeably cooled on Webster after the Squire's thunderous 7 of March speech in support of the Compromise of 1850. "Pitt goes as a delegate to Baltimore," General Sam Fessenden wrote to Pitt's sister in early June, "I hope, to oppose Webster's nomination. I have no doubt that he will." [18]

At Baltimore the delegates found themselves faced with the problem of having to decide upon one of three well-supported candidates. Southern members of the convention generally favored the avowedly pro-Compromise President Fillmore, while Webster, despite his near-apostasy of two years before, was still considered safe enough on the slavery question (and others) to merit the traditional backing of all New England, except Maine. A decade earlier, while Secretary of State, Webster had brought to an end the long-standing and dangerous Northeast boundary dispute by his not unskillful negotiations with Lord Ashburton of Great Britain. The settlement, although reasonable enough, had been far from what Maine had hoped for, however, and ever since that time many down-easters had never been quite able to shake off the notion that Daniel Webster had sacrificed Maine's interests to the British. Thus, although this particular reason did not loom especially large with Fessenden, the Maine delegation at Baltimore again refused to go along with Webster, just as it had refused on every other occasion since the signing of the infamous treaty. Instead Maine threw its support to General Scott, who, as a supposedly anti-Compromise candidate, was strong in the non-New England North, but not strong enough to muster the number of votes necessary to capture the convention. For a time it appeared that Webster, something of a middle-ground candidate, might be squeezed through between the two more extreme and powerful contenders, and at one point, after a long parade of deadlocked ballots, the psychology of the convention was such that a sudden shift of Maine's vote might well have started a Webster stampede. But there was no such shift, and on the fifty-third ballot General Scott, himself a Southerner, secured a sufficient number of Southern votes to gain control of the convention—though not until after he had agreed to support a platform of adherence to the Compromise.

> The Old men and the Young men—
>   With Scott to lead the fight—
> From hill and dale, from shore and wave,
>   Will rally and unite:
> The Old men and the Young men—
>   With Scott to lead them on—
> Will make the hero of two wars,
>   Their chief at Washington.[19]

Once again Fessenden returned to Portland chagrined over the strange antics of his fellow-Whigs. As a member of the convention's Commmittee on Resolutions, Fessenden had bitterly opposed Scott's eleventh-hour temporizing for the sake of Southern support. But all to no avail. As in 1848, so now four years later, Fessenden felt, the Whigs had sacrificed substance in order to soothe the sensibilities of the South and prolong the empty pretense of party harmony. Well, Maine had wanted Scott. So had the National Whig party. And Scott they got, although as matters turned out, he was hardly the sort of candidate that the Northern branch of Whiggery could support with much political ardor, committed as he was to a platform which was "a thoroughly Hunkerish piece of joiner-work, concocted of Southern pine, and rather awkwardly polished." [20] Later Fessenden made it known that if his hands had not been tied by instructions from home, he would have switched his support to Webster. But no matter, for within six months' time Webster was dead, Scott was a woefully beaten candidate, and the Whig party on the national level was for all intents and purposes nothing but a memory. For a dozen or more years Whiggery had played its not inconsequential role of keeping alive the two-party system in America and bridging the gap from Federalism to Republicanism. But by the mid-century or shortly thereafter, the fact had become eminently clear that National Whiggery had run its course. The old issues upon which it had been founded were now mostly dead or dying, and it obviously lacked the unity and courage to face the new ones. As the somewhat stoical Fessenden remarked by way of obituary as he examined the ruins soon after the humiliating defeat of Scott in early November: "As, since the last election, the Whig party is defunct, we are now all Democrats. . . ." [21]

Back from Elba

WHILE WHIGGERY was backsliding on the national scene during the early 1850's, it received a welcome boost in Maine from an unexpected quarter. By the autumn of 1852 party alignments within the state had been seriously jarred by a sudden resurrection of the temperance issue. Neal Dow's Maine Law, passed amidst much rejoicing in 1851, had failed to wear well with a sizable cross-section of the people. The novelty of abstinence had long since lost its appeal, and forgotten now by many of the thirsty were the vows that had been almost hysterically pronounced a few months before. So it was that during the spring and summer of 1852 there arose throughout the state a strong wet sentiment determined to make itself felt in the coming September elections.

The demon rum being once again in the fore, all other issues paled, and with neither party daring to declare itself opposed to the Maine Law, wet factions soon sprang up in both Whig and Democratic ranks. By the nature of its political creed, however,—stressing as it did the unhampered rights of man—the Democratic party was by far the more seriously affected, and had the Democracy been less solidly entrenched in Maine, it is unlikely that it could have survived the shock of this temperance tempest. As it was, the Maine Law and its subsequent damage to Democratic solidarity were but a preview of a far greater assault to come. For their part, the Whigs managed somewhat better, and in most areas of the state were reasonably successful in holding their numbers behind the Maine Law. Such was the case in Portland, where Fessenden, after a long recess from office-holding, reappeared on the political scene in 1852 as a temperance Whig, seeking a return to his old seat in the Augusta Legislature.

From the election of that September, Maine emerged with its first Whig governor since Edward Kent's "hell-bent" triumph in 1840. The Whigs could hardly have been proud of their achievement, however, for their path to the governor's mansion was at best a tortuous one. In the spring of that year the Democrats had held their usual nominating caucus in Augusta and had chosen as their candidate the incumbent, Governor John Hubbard of Hallowell, an avowed temperance man who had supported and signed the Maine Law. The nomination of Hubbard was a signal for the anti-Maine Law elements of the caucus to bolt and to launch the ephemeral Liberal party which, being soon after joined by a small band of wet Whigs, put forward Anson G. Chandler as their candidate for the governorship. The election that followed, then, involved for all intents and purposes two Democratic contenders, one running dry and the other wet. All other things being equal, the Whigs had good cause to expect victory in the face of their split opposition, but as the campaign wore on, the situation became further complicated by the fact that the Whig candidate, William Crosby, came to be considered by many as only lukewarm on temperance, with the result that several of the more devoted drys among the Whigs, led by Dow himself, deserted the party flag and threw their support to Hubbard.

The final tally revealed that the regular Democratic candidate, Governor Hubbard, had withstood the crossfire and won a plurality, albeit not a majority, of the 93,000 votes cast, with Crosby running a poor second. Since, however, under the state constitution, a majority of the popular vote was necessary for election, the final choice of governor fell to the Maine Legislature which assembled at Augusta on January 5, 1853. Here in Augusta, with Fessenden once again in his old seat, the regular Whigs found themselves in their usual position of minority party, but in the matter of choosing a governor, the Whigs, with their moderately temperate Crosby, appeared less hateful to the disgruntled Liberals than the dry Hubbard. There was little trouble, therefore, in arranging a coalition vote, and in the end William Crosby was duly elevated to the governor's chair amid the understandable protests of the Democracy.[1]

In this session of the Legislature Fessenden played a prominent role. Despite an absence of nearly six years from Augusta, he had become one of the most powerful and respected leaders of Whig opinion in the state. Never a poor man, he had seen his fortune and standing enhanced rapidly by his brilliant success in law during the past decade, and by a substantial inheritance which had fallen to his wife upon the death of her wealthy merchant father in 1851. Although seldom an office-holder since his return from Washington in 1843, Fessenden had never been far removed from politics, and his influence was such that during those years he had gathered about him, purposely or otherwise, an important Whig following, as is indicated by his prominent roles in the National Whig Conventions of 1848 and 1852. Now, once again back in Augusta, he heard his name mentioned frequently by Whig colleagues as a suitable candidate for the Washington seat left vacant by the Democratic James W. Bradbury, who in the previous autumn had declined re-election to the United States Senate. Fessenden could hardly have been deceived on this score, however, for despite Whig strength in the Maine Senate, his party was in a decided minority in the House. Furthermore, after the election of Crosby, time and compromise soon worked their wonders between the Liberal bolters and the regular Democrats to the extent that temporarily at least there was little chance of further Whig-Liberal cooperation. Therefore, in view of the fact that his was a minority standing in his own Chamber, plus the state Constitutional requirement that concurrence by both Houses was needed for the election of a United States Senator, Mr. Fessenden was not beguiled into false hopes.

The regular session of 1853 saw a strengthening of the Maine Law through amendments drawn up by a legislative committee charged with the duty of tightening the language of the law. Fessenden, in accordance with his campaign promises to serve as a friend of temperance, gave his constant support to these measures and protected them successfully against wet schemes to bring about a popular vote on the amendments. To Fessenden's way of thinking, the election had already shown how the people felt on temperance, and to refer the matter to the people again at this time would be nothing more than an act of delay unfriendly to the bill. "If after all this," he argued, "we should send it back to the people as though we did not know what they wanted, they might well say that we are very stupid indeed. . . ." [2]

It was during this session of the Legislature that Maine finally resolved its long-standing problems with Massachusetts on the matter of public lands. In 1825, five years after the beginnings of Maine statehood, the public lands of the two states had been divided in such a manner as to leave Massachusetts in partial control of certain areas within the boundaries of Maine. As Maine grew and prospered and the demand for land became more acute, the existing arrangement with Massachusetts proved highly bothersome. Therefore, at the meeting of the Legislature in 1853, a commission was appointed to negotiate with Massachusetts for the purchase of these lands in question. Among the three commissioners chosen was Mr. Fessenden, and it was ever after a source of great pride with him that this honor had been conferred upon him by a Democratically controlled House. Late in the session, Fessenden and his colleagues on the commission reported the results of their negotiations with the Commonwealth of Massachusetts. Although generally in favor of purchasing the lands at the price set by the negotiations, Fessenden, with characteristic caution, suggested that the Legislature give careful study to the proposal, and urged that ample time be taken to gather all possible information before making a final decision in a matter of such great consequence. He warned too against being unduly swayed by lobbyists. "We have been surrounded by outsiders both for and against purchasing," he growled, "taking every man by the button." Fessenden "distrust[ed] the whole batch of them on both sides." [3] The negotiations were eventually ratified, however, and a contract was entered into by the two states, whereby Massachusetts relinquished its claims in return for a payment of $362,-000. "This act met general approbation . . . ," recalled Fessenden's law partner, William Willis, many years later. "As a pecuniary arrangement [however], the purchase may at best be considered a doubtful one." [4]

While Fessenden was busying himself with matters of temperance and public lands, Hannibal Hamlin sat in Washington as Maine's only member of the United States Senate. Hamlin—big, powerful, and good-natured—was easily the most popular figure in Maine politics. Born in Paris Hill, Maine, not far from Fryeburg, this swarthy champion of Maine Democracy had come to Portland in the early 1830's to make his way in law as best he could. There he was taken into the office of Fessenden and Deblois where he studied under the kind tutelage of General Sam and became well acquainted with the General's brilliant young son Pitt, three years Hannibal's elder. From Portland Hamlin went a few miles north along the coast to the bustling little community of Damariscotta, but soon afterwards he moved to Hampden, a small village five miles down the Penobscot River from Bangor. There he entered the law office of the venerable Charles Stetson and immediately prospered at a time when Pitt was experiencing less good fortune in the nearby city to the north. From a successful law practice Hamlin moved smoothly into the arena of politics, and with his winsome ways and rough-hewn ability, soon climbed the Democratic ladder onto the Washington scene. More politician than statesman, and at times perhaps overly ready to compromise convictions for the sake of party and self, he was, like Henry Clay, more widely loved than trusted. In this respect, as in most others, he was quite the opposite of the man who would eventually be chosen by the Augusta Legislature to sit as his colleague in the United States Senate, and who would one day replace him as the boss of Maine politics.

While Hannibal Hamlin puffed serenely on his beloved cigars in the Senate Chamber, convinced that "this thing of slavery will sooner or later try to subvert the government, but I do not expect it will happen in my day," [5] the Maine Legislature was hopelessly stalled in the matter of choosing a successor to the retired U. S. Senator Bradbury. On January 27, 1853, a nominating caucus of Whig legislators brought forward Fessenden's name by an almost unanimous vote, and midway through the following week his nomination was endorsed, 18–13, by the Whig-controlled Senate. In the Lower House, however, Fessenden fared not so well, for there the Democratic majority insisted upon its own champion, former governor John W. Dana, with the result that a stalemate ensued. Since the session then proceeded to run out with neither House yielding an inch, it was on a note of ill-concealed frustration that the Legislature adjourned on April Fools' Day. Nor did a special session, called for a week during the following September, come any nearer to breaking the deadlock. "It is impossible even to guess what will come out of the present state of things,"

Fessenden complained to the Democratic Hamlin late in the year, "but the prospect is far from encouraging for anything very satisfactory to me. All I can do is stand still and 'let her slide.' . . ." [6]

By the summer of 1853, however, forces were already in motion which would resolve the problem and ultimately change the entire complexion of Maine politics. They represented in a very real sense the beginnings of that revolution which would before long eventuate in the birth of Maine Republicanism. The Democrats, still smarting from their unhappy experience in the previous election, assembled in Bangor in late June to plan their strategy for the coming campaign and choose their candidate for the September gubernatorial contest. Having so recently and painfully suffered the consequences of a party divided, the Democracy now resolved to hold its numbers intact, come what may. To accomplish this would be no mean task, however, since sentiment within the party still ran high on both sides of the Maine Law. Consequently, it was more or less automatically agreed that the Democracy would make no commitment whatever on temperance, and that during the campaign no mention should be made of that explosive issue. The convention then proceeded to nominate Albert G. Pillsbury, a man known to be personally opposed to the Maine Law, but capable of a judicious silence. Commenting on the doings at Bangor, the Democratic *Eastern Argus* of Portland considered the matter of temperance to have been admirably handled: "The convention gave no sign by which it could even be inferred that there was such a thing on the statute books as a liquor law. . . . Consequently all Democrats may unite in giving him [Pillsbury] their cordial support." [7]

But once more the question of liquor proved stronger than party ties, and again the Democracy was seriously jarred by a defection of many of its leading members. This time, however, the roles were reversed, and it became the lot of the dry wing of the party to leave the fold. Dissatisfied with the attitude, or lack of attitude, on the part of the Democracy toward temperance, the drys soon withdrew their support from Pillsbury, and on August 4 met in convention at Portland to proclaim themselves the true Democratic party and to put forward Anson Morill as their candidate. Thus, largely as a result of this temperance bolt, there entered upon the scene the Morrill Democrats, destined to change the shape of Fessenden's future and to serve ulti-

mately as one of the earliest ingredients of that strange political con-
coction that became the Republican party.*

With Governor William Crosby running as Whiggery's candidate,
Maine again found itself faced with a three-way race for the governorship, its second such election in as many years. And once again the
regular Democratic machine survived the shock of defection and
emerged from the September contest with a plurality of the popular
vote. With over 36,000 for Pillsbury, to 27,000 for Crosby, and 11,000
for Anson Morrill, the verdict of the people seemed clear, but lack of
a majority again threw the election into the Legislature, which was
slated to convene on January 4.†

While the Portland populace wept and otherwise emoted over the
miseries of Uncle Tom and Little Eva, as then presented in a great,
new moral drama at the old Civic Museum, William Pitt Fessenden,
thin, grim, and forty-seven, set out in early January of 1854 for his
final session at Augusta. There he and his colleagues were at once
confronted with the difficult chores of selecting a governor and attempting once more to break the apparently unbreakable deadlock in
the Senatorial contest. By February 10, however, scarcely a month
after the Legislature had convened, both these weighty matters had
been settled with surprising ease and speed. For governor, the Whig
incumbent, William Crosby, who had received nearly 10,000 fewer
popular votes than Pillsbury, was named by the Legislature to succeed
himself; while, to serve as United States Senator for the five years remaining of that term, Fessenden of Portland was elected on the first
ballot over his Democratic opponent. So it was that in early 1854 a
Democratic Legislature bestowed its most precious political jewels
upon two old-line Whigs, and well might the stunned majority party
have asked itself how this double-barreled disaster had come about.

The answer, of course, was coalition, just as had been the case in
the preceding year. This much is a matter of record. But the reasons
for the coalition and the means it employed—therein lies a story

* To attribute the Morrill bolt entirely to the temperance question would be to
oversimplify a complex situation. Patronage, anti-slavery feeling, and personal ambition were also factors. However, by far the most important single ingredient in
the sunderance of the Main Democracy at this time was the temperance issue.

† Not unnoticed by Maine political leaders was the fact that nearly 10,000 votes
were cast in this election for Ezekiel Holmes, gubernatorial candidate for the Free-
Soil party.

which has been subject to several interpretations, not all of which are flattering to Fessenden. In later years when recalling the circumstances of his election to the United States Senate in 1854, Senator Fessenden always took great pride in the fact that he had been chosen by a Democratic Legislature, with no bargains made and no pledges given. He had made it clear at the time, he claimed, that he "could not consent to be elected on any other basis," and that he "could give no pledge on any question, but must be left free to act as a Whig on all questions." The coalition which had effected his election, Fessenden maintained, was motivated by an anti-slavery impulse and the subsequent desire to send to Washington a man who would stand firmly opposed to the threat of slavery extension which was then hovering over Congress.[8] Understandably, it is this same view that appears in the family biography of Fessenden, written by his son many years after the Senator's death.[9]

A somewhat different account of the election was given by W. W. Nisston in a letter written to the Senator's son, Francis, nearly a decade after Fessenden's death. According to Nisston, who had been on the Augusta scene at the time, it was true that Fessenden was chosen on a platform of non-extension of slavery. But, claimed Nisston, the driving force behind the coalition which made his election possible was temperance, and therefore temperance rather than the slavery issue must be reckoned as the most significant factor of the election—that is, the most significant factor aside from Fessenden himself. "No other man," remarked Nisston, "could have got together and held together this combination and no other man in the state could have been elected by force of it." As for political bargaining, Nisston confirmed Senator Fessenden's contention that the election had been completely free of it. "No bargain or trade was made," he wrote. "None was needed, none thought of. No pledge was asked and none would have been given if asked. Our common purpose operated upon everybody and that was sufficient." [10]

Less complimentary to Fessenden is the version of Neal Dow which is told in great detail in Dow's published memoirs. According to the father of Maine temperance, soon after the Legislature convened in early January a bargain was struck up between the leaders of the Whig party and Anson Morrill's recalcitrant following, which, although small, controlled the voting balance in both Houses. By the terms of this bargain, Whig votes would be used to elect Morrill governor, and in return the Morrill Democrats would support Fessenden's candidacy for the United States Senate seat. Whether Fessenden actively encouraged the deal then being made in his behalf, Dow could not say, but certainly Fessenden was aware of it. The plan worked well at first. The coalition in the House managed to eliminate the favored Pillsbury from the contest and send to the Senate only the names of Crosby and Morrill, in that order of preference. In the Senate it was arranged that Morrill would receive the nod, with the House later to defer to the Senate's choice by switching its support from Crosby to the maverick Democrat. But at the last moment one Whig senator snapped under the strain and, reverting to type, cast his vote for the Whig Crosby instead of Morrill. Thus, by the narrowest of margins, did the grand scheme run afoul.

After the failure of the Whigs to honor their part of the bargain, the chances for Fessenden appeared slight indeed. As an added inducement for Morrill to return to the regular fold, the Democracy now played their trump card by putting forward as their opponent to Fessenden, Morrill's brother, Lot. But neither the disappointment of defeat nor the enticement of kinship would attract Anson back to his erstwhile associates, and when the choice of United States Senator finally came up on February 10, the Morrill Democrats held fast to their end of the bargain by casting their vote with the Whigs for Pitt Fessenden.[11]

Such were the circumstances of Fessenden's election as recalled by Neal Dow several years later. A certain degree of credibility is given the story by the detail in which it was told by the author, and by the fact that it appears to provide an explanation for the strange manner in which the vote fell. How else can the unexpected strength and near victory of the recusant Anson Morrill in the gubernatorial contest be accounted for? Furthermore, the contemporary reports of the *Eastern Argus* indicate that some such agreement had been reached between the Whigs and Morrill Democrats. On the day following Morrill's defeat for the governorship, the *Argus* commented:

What the next move of the Coalition will now be remains to be seen. Mr. Fessenden of this city wants to be United States Senator.

The result of the Gubernatorial election will disturb the arrangement in this respect.

We are inclined to think that the wire-pullers will have to adopt an entirely new programme, and indeed we much doubt whether the power of the Coalition has not had its back broken by the unexpected action of the Senate.[12]

Whatever the true circumstances surrounding Fessenden's election, however, one fact seems plain. Bargain or no bargain, Fessenden was chosen because the time had been reached in Maine politics when issues had to many people become more important than party, and on the principal issues then affecting the Legislature—temperance and non-extension of slavery—Mr. Fessenden was known to represent majority opinion. On both these matters, in fact, he was considered sounder than his Democratic opponent, and when the moment for final decision arrived, it was perhaps natural that the scales should be tipped in his favor by the Morrill Democrats, who saw many of their own opinions reflected in the Whig candidate. For favors such as these Fessenden was never ungrateful. Upon his arrival in Portland on the day following his election, he wrote to Governor Crosby to remind the Governor that Anson Morrill's Democrats had been instrumental in electing them both. He hoped that this fact would be kept in mind when the time arrived for dealing out patronage. It would be wise to offer them the hand of friendship. "I think I see in the present state of things," wrote the new Senator-elect prophetically, "a fair opportunity yet to build up a strong independent party essentially Whig." [13]

Shortly after noon on February 10, 1854, in the State House at Augusta, "William Pitt Fessenden was declared duly elected Senator, to fill the vacancy now existing in the Senate of the United States from this state. . . ." Later that same day he left Augusta, and upon arriving in Portland on the following morning, immediately began preparations for his journey to Washington, where political storm-clouds of a most ominous nature were gathering over the Kansas-Nebraska Bill. From his minister brother in Rockland, Samuel C. Fessenden, who would at a later time sit beside Pitt in Washington as one of three Fessenden brothers in the famed 37th Congress, came congratulations and blessings. "You are now 'back from Elba.' God give you wisdom and strength to do the cause of Truth and your country good service. I know you have the ability and the will to do so. I hope you will be on in season to give a blow at the Nebraska Bill." [14] And from Pitt's political crony of way down east in Washington County, James S. Pike, at that time Washington correspondent for Greeley's powerful *Tribune*, came a plea for haste:

> [It's] not that the bill is likely to come at once to a vote but that you may get ready and ripe for your duty. Every possible speech is wanted and you are set down for one already. The great object is delay. The bill must be kept in the Senate as long as possible. Meanwhile hell must be raised in the North. The ear of Congress is open. It must be deafened with a roar of condemnation. . . . If you have affairs to arrange, as you must have, come on and see the bill through the Senate and then you can be spared to go back.[15]

But upon Mr. Fessenden there was little need to impress the urgency and gravity of the situation. The Kansas-Nebraska Bill must somehow be blocked, Fessenden realized with fearsome determination. Everything else was secondary to this great main purpose. To his friend Israel Washburn, later war governor of Maine and at that time a member of the Washington House, Pitt wrote: "If my vote would defeat it, I would take the next train to Washington if I left my house on fire." [16]

VII

Storm over Kansas-Nebraska

ON FEBRUARY 23, 1854, less than two weeks after Fessenden's election in Augusta, Hannibal Hamlin presented his new colleague's credentials to the United States Senate. Had he made a deliberate effort to do so, Fessenden could scarcely have come at a more critical time, nor could his arrival have been more heartily welcomed by that small, embattled band of Northern Whigs who now found themselves sorely pressed by the relentless juggernaut called "popular sovereignty." In the thinking of Fessenden and other anti-Nebraska Congressmen, mainly but not exclusively Whigs, the question of slavery in Kansas and Nebraska had been settled once and for all a generation before. Then, in the famous Missouri Compromise of 1820, the South and the North had solemnly agreed that slavery would "forever" be excluded from all territory lying north of the 36°–30' parallel (the new state of Missouri excepted) in that vast Louisiana Purchase area obtained from France in 1803. Now, however, in this insidious Kansas-Nebraska measure being sponsored by "that lying little villain," Democratic Senator Stephen A. Douglas of Illinois, it was proposed that the Missouri Compromise be repealed and that the two territories of Kansas and Nebraska be organized as slave or free in accordance with the desires of the settlers themselves. A great triumph for democratic process was this principle of "popular sovereignty," claimed Douglas, who saw no reason why he and his contemporaries should feel bound to honor the mistakes of an earlier generation. A base betrayal, a breach of honor and decency, responded Douglas' opponents, to whom this proposal to shatter the time-honored Missouri Compromise seemed almost diabolically evil. Here in the Douglas bill was a thing to be abhorred and resisted to the final iota of strength; here was the question of slavery extension reduced to its least common denominator, and here to leaders of a dying Whiggery, essentially Northern now, was a painful lesson to be long remembered and profited from. For out of the shambles and humiliation of the Kansas-Nebraska affair came the seed that ultimately germinated into Republicanism and the shifting of political control to an all-Northern party.

Many years later Charles Sumner, who at the time of the Kansas-Nebraska crisis had been a Free-Soil Senator from Massachusetts and one of the leading figures in the fight against Douglas, recalled the memorable occasion of Fessenden's arrival in the Senate Chamber:

> He came in the midst of that terrible debate on the Kansas and Nebraska Bill by which the country was convulsed to its center, and his arrival had the effect of a reinforcement on the field of battle. . . . One more in our small number was a sensible addition. We were no longer fourteen, but fifteen. . . . There he stood. Not a Senator, loving Freedom, who did not feel on that day that a champion had come.[1]

In little more than a week after his arrival, this new champion took the floor to sound his voice against the Douglas bill. It was during that long night session of March 3, termed by Pitt's friend Longfellow as the *"noche triste* of our history," and Fessenden's speech, delivered in the ebbing hours of the night beneath the blaze of a thousand gas candles, was the last to be made against the measure before its passage by the Senate shortly before dawn of the following day. With neither outline nor note to guide him, the Senator from Maine stood beside his desk, "bold, clear, fluent, and hard as flint," and proceeded to electrify the Senate with what was perhaps the most brilliant speech of the long, bitter debate.[2]

He was somewhat reluctant, Fessenden began, to speak at this time because of his recent arrival in the Senate. He feared that he might be considered presumptuous by some of the members for doing so, and for that very reason he had purposely deferred his remarks until all others had spoken. But since he understood that the bill would soon come to a vote, he felt compelled now to give his views on the measure. Not to do so would be to fail in his duties toward his state and his nation. He thought it unlikely that he could add anything to what had already been said on the subject, but the fact that he had come so recently from the people and was therefore particularly sensitive to their feelings on the matter, would perhaps justify some comments by him on the Douglas bill and the principles involved in it.

Senator Fessenden wanted it understood at the outset that he was speaking not as a "sickly sentimentalist" or "humanity-monger." Although he earnestly deplored slavery in any form, he had no intention of going into the morality of the institution at this time. He preferred to argue his case on the stronger ground of national interest and concern for the common good, and in this respect he could not help but feel that slavery reacted to the detriment of his state, his section, and, indeed, the entire country. Certainly the people of New England were well aware of this fact. "They are a reading and thinking people. They have churches, academies, common schools, newspapers, and all the ordinary resources of moral and mental education." These people could understand what slavery meant to free workers in all sections, and they could understand too how slave labor had retarded the growth and prosperity of those states in which it was allowed to exist. "They have also another idea," Fessenden continued, "and that is that . . . inasmuch as they belong to this country and are a part of the great whole, whatever is injurious to the whole becomes a matter of interest to them. And, sir, they believe that if an institution injuriously affects the prosperity of a part, its evils are felt through the whole system." Feeling as they did on the matter of slavery, the people of his state and section had every reason and right to oppose its extension. "And this right they will exercise."

Senator Fessenden then reviewed in some detail the history of the extension of slavery since the beginnings of nationhood. He felt that, all things considered, the South had no real cause to complain. It had carried its slave system westward with little difficulty until the late 1840's when the Wilmot Proviso suddenly threatened to halt its progress. And even then, Senator Fessenden declared with some distortion, the South had eventually won its demands by threatening to dissolve the Union. The history of slavery extension was, to Fessenden, a long story of Southern success and Northern acquiescence or surrender, and from it all, the North had emerged with only one positive concession—the promise given by the South in 1820 that, Missouri excepted, slavery would be kept forever out of that part of the Louisiana Purchase north of the 36°–30′ parallel. Now it was proposed to snatch away even this single comfort, to break the covenant that had been so solemnly entered into thirty-odd years before and throw the entire area open to slavery and its concomitant evils. Senator Fessenden could not understand how Southern gentlemen, who seemingly placed so much stock in the matter of personal honor, could conceivably lend their support to such an obvious breach of faith. "It is not enough to tell the people of the free States that this was tendered by the North to the South," Fessenden declared in reference to the fact that the bill had been sponsored by a Northerner. "We do not admit the authority of the senator making it . . . to speak for the North. He [Douglas] has no more authority than I have. . . . And allow me to say," continued Fessenden, "that I do not understand that principle of honor . . . which allows that what cannot honorably be taken directly can be grasped with honor when offered by another having no authority to give it."

To Mr. Fessenden the entire affair was almost unbelievable. He had thought that for a time at least after the Compromise of 1850 the matter of slavery extension would have been allowed to rest. But no! Suddenly it had reappeared—and for no apparent reason. Why? "For what purpose has it come? To allay agitation? There was none . . . ," Fessenden asserted with some stretching of the truth. "Was it to establish a principle? Will you set this country in a flame upon a principle?" Fessenden was at a loss to understand the motives behind the Douglas bill, but whatever they were, he felt certain that they would one day be regretted. "I hope if there is agitation," he stated, "if there is excitement, if there is fanaticism . . . in the free States from this time forward, you will just cast your eyes back to those who made it, started it, and gave occasion for it. If you hear the cavilings of the North, coupled with denunciations of slavery at the South, recollect the state of quiet from which you brought it forth."

Well, where would it all end? Mr. Fessenden couldn't say. He only knew that if the North yielded now on this point, there would soon after be another, and another following that—an endless drama of appeasement played to the dull cacophony of Southern threats of secession. By all such talk of dissolution, the Senator admitted, he was frankly bored. It had long since become *vieux jeu* to him and to his Northern colleagues, and Fessenden, for one, was no longer impressed by it in the slightest degree. He felt that even Southern members themselves tended to laugh at it in private.

"Who laugh?" interrupted Democratic Senator Andrew Butler of South Carolina.

"You at the South," answered Fessenden. "You do not carry it seriously into private conversation."

"No, sir," exclaimed Butler. "If your doctrine is carried out, if such sentiments as yours prevail, I want a dissolution right away."

"As has been said before, do not delay it on my account," replied the Senator from Maine.

Do not delay it on account of anybody at the North. I want the gentleman to understand that we do not believe in it. We love the Union as well as you do, and you love it as much as we do; I am willing to allow that. But, sir, if it has come to this, that whenever a question comes up between the free States and the slave States of this Union, we are to be threatened with disunion unless we yield, if that is the only alternative to be considered, it ceases to be a very grave question for honorable men and free men to decide. I do not wish to say anything offensive to gentlemen, but I desire them to understand what I mean. It is that we are ready to meet every question on this floor fairly and honestly; we are willing to be bound by the decision of the majority, as law. If it operates hardly upon us, we will bear it. If it is unconstitutional, we must go to the proper tribunal for a decision, and not threaten each other with what no one of us desires to execute.

Such, sir, are my views in reference to this matter. I have not spoken them so much for the Senate as for the purpose of giving expression to what I believe to be the sentiment of those I have the honor to represent on this floor. Whether right or not, time only can decide, and I am willing to abide that decision.[3]

The reaction in the North to Fessenden's speech was electric. His "do not delay it on my account" reply to Butler immediately caught the imagination of a public long devoted to slogans and pithiness, and literally overnight Senator Fessenden became a figure of national prominence. "Mr. Fessenden the new Whig Senator from Maine made a great speech against the bill last night," commented Ohio's Senator Benjamin Wade who was "sleepy as a hog" after the all-night marathon. "He is a real fire-eater . . . and will bring much strength to the small band of Northern Whigs of the Senate." [4] From Pitt's poet friend, Henry Longfellow, came words of praise and thanks for his "intrepid bearing in the Senate on that dark night. . . ." [5] And from a stranger in New York:

> I have read that speech with deepest interest. I thank God for it and hope and shall expect more from you. You have taken the ground of a *man*. To be a man in these days is a great thing. To be able to withstand what you are called upon to do requires nerves, brains, and a soul. The three I see you possess. May your days be spared, your health continued to a good old age to reap the reward of your noble act.[6]

On the day following his speech, Fessenden reflected on his words of the previous evening. "You will observe that I participated in the debate on the Nebraska Bill," he wrote to his family in Portland. "It was a speech which was made entirely without preparation or memo of any kind at a late hour in the evening. . . . I may have said some things imprudently, but I was resolved to make a clean breast of it. . . ." [7]

At five o'clock in the morning of March 4, only a few hours after Fessenden's speech, the Kansas-Nebraska Bill passed the Senate, and as had been expected, the vote in favor of the measure was an overwhelming one, 37-14, with both Maine Senators voting in the negative. To William H. Seward, acknowledged leader of the Northern Whigs, the results were sad and humiliating. To Thomas Hart Benton, now a member of the Lower House and a confirmed hater of Douglas, the action of the Senate was unspeakable. "The Senate is emasculated, sir," he thundered. "Yes, sir, it is emasculated. A majority do not belong to the masculine gender, sir. No, sir, do not belong to the masculine gender." [8] Fessenden's friends Sumner and Solomon Foot were despondent, as were other opponents of the bill, but their grief was somewhat assuaged by the hope that the measure would meet defeat in the House. Benton assured them that such would be the case. "Yes, sir, the bill will be sent to hell, sir, and its authors will be sent there with it, sir." [9]

During the weeks following the passage of the Douglas bill by the Senate, both camps prepared for the coming struggle in the House. Meanwhile, after casting his vote in favor of Dorothea Dix's relief bill for the indigent insane, Fessenden set out for Maine to attend to matters that had been left hanging at the time of his sudden departure for Washington in February. There he remained from the latter part of April until early June, while Democratic President Franklin Pierce dreamed of annexing Cuba, and Pike's friend Horace Greeley was busy "giving the Nebraska rascals hell in the Tribune." [10]

In Maine, Senator Fessenden soon discovered that, as he had anticipated, the Kansas-Nebraska Bill had thrown Maine politics into a turmoil. Throughout the state, Whigs, Free-Soilers, and not a few Democrats had united in angry conventions to denounce the iniquity of the Douglas measure. The largest and most significant of these meetings had been held in Augusta, only two days before the passage of the bill by the Senate. Here at Augusta were seen unmistakable signs of a new political alliance about to be born out of common revulsion against this most recent slavocratic outrage. Led by Pitt's abolitionist father, and by Democratic Anson Morrill, so recently Pitt's political benefactor, the convention labelled the Nebraska Bill a "gross outrage upon humanity and justice, and a palpable and utterly inexcusable violation of the plighted faith of the nation." Its members then called upon the people of Maine to put aside their political differences and unite in common cause against the further extension of the slave system in the federal territories. Compromise had been repeatedly tried and repeatedly found wanting. Now the time had arrived for bold men of all parties to stand firm for freedom and Northern rights. "We now declare it to be our unalterable purpose," resolved the Augusta convention, "to resist, in every practicable and constitutional way, and to the utmost of our power, the introduction of slavery not only into that territory, but into any and all territory which may now or hereafter be within the jurisdiction of the United States." [11] All this, four months before that austere assemblage under the oaks in Jackson, Michigan, gave birth to the Republican party.

Despite the excitement caused by meetings of this sort, however, the fact soon became clear, after the initial wave of enthusiasm had subsided, that old party ties were in most instances not yet ready to snap. After all, was there really much danger of the bill's ever becoming

law? "We cannot believe," commented the Oxford (Maine) *Democrat,*
stumbling over its editorial syntax, "that this Administration will lend
itself to a scheme which, had the fact been known before the election
of '52, it could never have had existence. We do not believe that this
Administration will thus desert the people." [12] At the same time, Neal
Dow, who now had rum sufficiently trounced to give his attention to
other matters, was "amazed at the supineness of our Maine people in
relation to the Nebraska affair—but the truth is, the measure is so
enormously wicked, that it is supposed to be impossible to pass it." [13]
And then, one day in late May, the impossible suddenly happened,
when by a margin of thirteen votes the Douglas bill passed the House
and was sent along to receive the blessings of the President. Shortly
thereafter, Fessenden packed his valise and made his way to the old
Canal Street Station, where he again boarded the train for Washington.

Once back in the Capitol, Senator Fessenden went about his duties
quietly. During the remainder of the long session, which ended in
early August, he had little to say on any issue of importance, save the
subject of reciprocity with Canada. On this matter, brought before the
Senate in the form of the Marcy-Elgin Treaty, Senator Fessenden took
a position which was clearly displeasing to his Maine constituents and
to many of his party colleagues in Washington. To that ardent apostle
of protection, Horace Greeley, the proposed agreement gave promise
of universal ruin. But, although himself long devoted to tariff protection, Fessenden thought he saw in this measure provisions that would
conduce to the growth and prosperity not only of his own section but
of the rest of the country as well. For this reason, and despite the fact
that the people of Maine were particularly vocal in their opposition
to the idea of duty-free lumber, Fessenden felt compelled to support
the reciprocity treaty, which, the first of its kind for young America,
was finally ratified in the late spring of 1854. In his decision he may
have been influenced by his old friend and political henchman, Freeman Morse of Bath, who reminded the Senator that Maine's forest
supplies were not inexhaustible, and that easy access to Canadian
lumber would certainly prove a boon to the shipyards of New
England.[14]

As Congress dragged on, with Kansas-Nebraska bitterness still hanging heavily in the air and the miserable heat of Washington summer
taking its toll of energy and patience, Senator Fessenden's fragile

constitution longed for the fog of Portland and a cooling stroll through the garden in back of his State Street home. "Perhaps there will be a cherry or two left," he pined. "If not, I must content myself with a cabbage." [15] There was much talk of annexing Cuba during those summer months in Washington, and long debates were entered into over the House bill to grant free homesteads to settlers in the West. Against both proposals Pitt arched his back in opposition. The plan for annexing Cuba was unthinkable—simply one more attempt on the part of the acquisitive South to obtain more territory for slavery. As for homesteads, Mr. Fessenden could not agree with any scheme which, if put into effect, would deprive the federal government of an important source of revenue and at the same time siphon off the labor supply from the more settled areas of the nation. Furthermore, to Fessenden's way of thinking the bestowal of free gifts invariably led to a lamentable shiftlessness of attitude and behavior on the part of the masses. Concerning homesteads, therefore, "I shall vote not to give them to anybody." [16] But no matter, for the time of real decision had not yet arrived for Cuba or homesteads, and in the first week of August, 1854, the famous or infamous Kansas-Nebraska session of the 33rd Congress came to a welcome and somewhat anticlimactic close.

By mid-August a sorely weary Fessenden was again home in Portland. There he immediately turned his attention toward the coming state elections. With the final passage of the Kansas-Nebraska Bill there was no longer much doubt as to the course to be followed. The time had arrived for men of true Northern principles to unite in a solid front of opposition to the encroachments of the South. Earlier in the summer there had appeared upon the scene in many Northern states a third party which called itself the Republican party and pledged itself to eternal opposition to the further extension of slavery in the territories. But, although Fessenden was in general agreement with what the new party stood for, he was not yet quite ready to go so far as to surrender his Whig identity. Instead, he urged political cooperation between Whigs and other anti-Nebraska elements. Essentially he agreed with the sentiments that had been expressed a few weeks earlier by the Bangor *Mercury:*

If the Whigs of this State, as an organization . . . set their backs up stiff and haughty, independent as a hog on ice, they will succeed

in performing about as well as a hog on ice. They will neither go
nor stand. We say to them, be wise, pursue no shadows; go for the
substance; names are nothing; facts are the things.[17]

It was apparent, however, that the idea of cooperation or "fusion"
had failed to impress itself on many of the old-line Whigs. From
John Perry, running for Congress as an anti-Nebraska candidate in
Maine's second district, came the complaint that his fusionist platform was being undermined by the opposition of certain members of
the Whig party. Perry then appealed to Fessenden to use his influence
in putting down this opposition, lest the results be ruinous to what
Perry termed "our new party."

At the same time, reports of similar discord reached Fessenden
from Brunswick and Bangor. To his friend James Pike, Pitt confessed disgust with the behavior of many of his Whig colleagues,
"just when they ought to be very nice boys." Couldn't they realize
that the time had come to unite against the slavocrats? Brunswick, he
felt, was already lost for want of a solid front, and in Penobscot
County it was reported that so-called Whigs were doing their best to
defeat the anti-Nebraska candidate. "Isn't it strange," Fessenden
mused, "that when only united effort can accomplish *any thing*, men
seem most disposed to discussion." [18] Nevertheless, the earlybird
September elections of that year turned out surprisingly well for
the anti-Nebraskans, with fusionists capturing the governorship and
both Houses of the Augusta Legislature by a landslide vote. So it was
that the policy of cooperation among like-thinking elements of all
parties, spelled out political victory in Maine during the autumn of
1854, and in doing so, pointed the way toward greater triumphs to
come.

The short session of the 33rd Congress, which began on December
4, was something of a lull before the coming storm. During this session
Pitt was regular in his attendance and in his support of the Whig
cause, but only rarely did he take to the floor. It was, in fact, characteristic of the man that throughout his career in the Senate, he
shunned talking for talking's sake, and had little patience with those
members who habitually fed their own vanity and wasted the Senate's
precious time with mere words. Still, Fessenden was not slow to take
to his feet if the occasion warranted, and such an occasion presented

itself late in the session when Democratic Senator Isaac Toucey of Connecticut reported out of the judiciary committee a bill to prohibit state courts from hearing cases involving suits against federal officers engaged in the enforcement of federal law. Although not so specifying, the bill was obviously aimed at strengthening the Fugitive Slave Law of 1850, which had been noticeably subverted by the hostile attitude of many of the state courts in the anti-slavery North. A long and heated debate followed the introduction of the Toucey bill, and in this debate Fessenden took an active part, finding himself squared off against his heart's abhorrence, Senator Stephen Douglas of Illinois. To Mr. Fessenden the bill was a shameful thing, designed to deprive the state courts of their vitality and power to protect the rights of their own citizens. It was clearly "an intentional, direct insult to the courts and people of the several states. . . ." Senator Fessenden maintained that he held the laws of the land in high regard, and that he meant to respect them at any and all times, but:

I wish to say still further to gentlemen who give their support to measures of this description, that whenever they are brought forward with such a design, whenever they exhibit such a tendency, whenever they show that our legislation is to be directed, at all times, with reference to this slave power which governs us—for govern us it does—I stand here to oppose them, to make my opposition and protestation against them on all occasions.[19]

Finally, after nearly twelve hours of continuous debate, the Southern-oriented Democratic majority had its way, and, shortly before midnight on February 23, notwithstanding Fessenden's "opposition and protestation," the Toucey judiciary bill passed the Senate by a one-sided vote, only to die later from lack of attention in the House.

Following the adjournment of the 33rd Congress in early March of 1855, Pitt returned to Portland. Not long after his arrival he again became engaged in his law practice, which soon involved him in the April session of the Cumberland County Supreme Court, and during the late spring found him cast in the role of defense counsel in the strange case of the *People vs. Neal Dow*. By 1855 Maine had become cork dry, so dry, in fact, that in early June Mayor Dow saw fit to import from Massachusetts a sizable shipment of liquor to be used for medical purposes. The affair was to be handled quietly, and the liquor stored in the cellar of the City Hall, to be dispensed as necessity warranted. But word of the transaction leaked out, and the news soon spread that Neal Dow, the father of Maine temperance, was secretly caching liquor in his own basement.

Almost at once broadsides denouncing Dow and temperance appeared throughout the city, and in the mid-morning of June 2 a crowd began to form about the City Hall. At first only idly curious, the crowd grew more turbulent as the day wore on, and by evening had degenerated into an angry mob. The police were called out by Mayor Dow, but were soon put to flight by stones and other well-directed missiles. Finally, when all else had failed, the militia was unleashed and ordered to march upon the mob. In the subsequent melee one rioter was killed and four others wounded, with the result that Dow's political enemies attempted to press manslaughter charges against the hapless Mayor. Failing in this, they settled for an indictment against Dow charging him with violating his own Maine Law. The case that followed was significant, aside from its ironical aspects, only because of the appearance of the prominent Democratic jurist Nathan Clifford as prosecutor and Mr. Fessenden as defense counsel— the latter a United States Senator, the former a onetime United States Attorney-General and at the time of Dow's trial only two years shy of appointment to the nation's Supreme Court. For Dow and Fessenden victory proved simple enough, and the Mayor was in time duly acquitted, although not without much bantering publicity and considerable injury to his abstemious dignity.

Fessenden's main attention during this recess from his Washington duties, however, was given to the matter of state politics. By this time he had become convinced that the only answer to encroachments by the South would be found in the development of a strong third party based upon and motivated by Northern principles. So it was that in the summer of 1855 Pitt Fessenden, without much fuss or fanfare, crossed over the line from Whiggery to Republicanism, and began directing his influence and energies to the promotion of the new organization. Actually the birth of the Republican party in Maine had been officially proclaimed a few months before while Pitt was still in Washington, so it can not be said that Fessenden was a charter member, despite his early sympathy for the movement. Nevertheless, there

can be no denying that once committed to the new party Fessenden
played a highly significant role in shaping the infant organization
into a powerful, well-disciplined machine. In July Fessenden travelled
up the coast a few miles to address the citizens of Damariscotta. Here
in an admittedly political Fourth of July speech, he denounced the
principle of popular sovereignty and called upon his listeners to unite
in opposition to the further extension of slavery in the territories.
From many Democrats and old-line Whigs of the area came complaints that the speaker was sullying the patriotic meaning of the day
by dealing in politics, but to Fessenden the struggle for freedom belonged as much to the present as to the past. And for this cause of
freedom he was ready to welcome every man of every party. He made
it clear to his audience that he was no abolitionist, but, to his mind,
if the country were to be subjected to the slave interests, then free
government had failed.[20]

Scarcely had he returned home from Damariscotta when Senator
Fessenden joined in preparations for a monster Republican rally to
be held in Portland during mid-August. Meeting-halls were arranged
for, half-fare agreements were reached with many of Maine's railroad
companies, and invitations were sent to prominent politicians of other
states, urging them to appear before the convention.* To Benjamin
Wade of Ohio, then high in Fessenden's esteem, went Pitt's personal
appeal for help, and from Wade came the promise that he would be
on hand when the time came, although he feared he might not do
well before an Eastern audience. On August 14 at the call of Governor
Anson Morrill, former Democrat now contemptuously dubbed "that
figure-head of fusion" by the *Eastern Argus,* the first state-wide Republican convention assembled in Portland. Beginning in the early
morning, Portland was thronged with people of all political shapes
and sizes, including fifty carloads who had been brought there at half-
fare from all sections of the state, and as the day wore on, members
of the new party continued to pour into the churning city by the
hundreds. They were, according to the disgusted *Argus,* "temperance
men, Know-Nothings, Know-Somethings, Free-Soilers, Abolitionists,

---

* Among those invited were Truman Smith (Connecticut), Benjamin F. Butler
and Nathaniel P. Banks (Massachusetts), John A. Dix (New York), John P. Hale
(New Hampshire), and Benjamin Wade (Ohio). The Democrats Butler and Dix did
not attend, however. See *Eastern Argus,* August 4–14, 1855.

Whigs who had forgotten their names, Democrats who had forgotten their principles . . . all on the 14th [lying] down in the same political trundle bed." [21] Throughout the day and into the evening, meetings were held in various sections of the city and in nearby Deering. On hand to address these gatherings were such out-of-state notables as Wade, Nathaniel P. Banks of Massachusetts, and the old Free-Soiler, John P. Hale of New Hampshire. And supporting these imported attractions were many of Maine's own political leaders, including Governor Morrill, Edward Kent, and William Pitt Fessenden, appearing on the same political platform with his distinguished abolitionist father. "As to the speeches, they were just what was to be expected," commented the *Argus*. "Nebraska! Nebraska, and nothing else." [22]

In terms of political interest and audience turn-out the Portland "half-fare convention" provided the new Republicans with good cause for rejoicing. But the Democracy soon demonstrated that votes were the thing, when less than a month later the regular Democratic ticket headed by Judge Samuel Wells and aided in many instances by the support of die-hard Whigs, scored a substantial victory in the September elections. For all its enthusiasm and promise, Maine Republicanism had proved a slow starter, and no one was more disappointed by the results than Mr. Fessenden—disappointed but not despondent. "I did hope," he wrote to a relative soon after the election, "that Maine would have placed herself in the front rank of that great Northern movement which I believe to be essential to the future welfare of the country, and which lies, therefore, nearest my heart. . . . As it is, the end is not yet." [23]

Senator Fessenden, Republican

By the time of Senator Fessenden's return to Washington for the opening of the 34th Congress in December of 1855, affairs in Kansas had taken an ugly turn. The Kansas-Nebraska Act of the year before, with its provision for letting the settlers themselves decide upon the matter of slavery in the two areas, had had little effect one way or the other on Nebraska, which was by nature obviously unsuited for slavery. But for Kansas, where nature was benign enough perhaps to permit slavery to be profitably established, the Kansas-Nebraska Act had meant the sudden beginnings of a great and ominous race to people the territory and gain control of the territorial government. From Missouri and other parts of the South armed bands had poured across the border, determined to claim the area for slavery; while from Northern states hundreds of settlers had flocked into the territory, equally determined that Kansas should be free. By the late autumn of 1855 opposing governments had been set up within the territory, and with each passing day Kansas, urged on by outside friends, drew nearer to wholesale violence. "Money is now being raised for Kansas," wrote Charles Dana of the *Tribune* to Pitt's friend, James S. Pike. "Boston has furnished $5500 for Sharp's rifles and Colt's revolvers, and $2500 is wanted here [New York]. I suppose I may put you down for $50 at least. The guns have gone forward and one of these days we shall certainly have a good fight there." [1]

On January 24, 1856, Fessenden's former college-mate, President Franklin Pierce, sent a special message to Congress in which he denounced the free government of Kansas as a revolutionary body. This message was soon followed by another on February 11, which, although condemning rowdyism on both sides, left little doubt of where the President's sympathies lay. Almost at once several Northern members of the Senate, including Fessenden, openly accused Pierce of willfully presenting only a partial picture of the Kansas affair, and when on March 17 Senator Douglas reported from his Committee on Territories an enabling bill endorsing the pro-slavery legislature in Kansas, the stage was set for the thunderous debate of 1856. In the fierce encounter that followed, however, the anti-Douglas forces were for a greater part of the time without the services of the Senator from Maine, for by early April Fessenden's health had become so precarious that he was compelled to return home. And there in Portland, plagued by political and personal anxieties, he remained until the first week of June.

Before his illness forced him to leave for Maine, Fessenden had taken a prominent part in the heated discussions arising out of growing differences with England. These differences stemmed in part from Britain's unfortunate insistence upon encouraging the enlistment of American citizens for England's Crimean armies. But a far greater source of irritation was a situation that had evolved out of conflicting interpretations given the Clayton-Bulwer Treaty, an arrangement which pledged both nations to a strict "hands-off" policy in regard to Central America. In a word, it was felt by many in Washington that the provisions of the Clayton-Bulwer Treaty were meant to be retroactive and that Britain was breaking faith with America by insisting upon continuing her past policy of protection over certain areas of Central America, particularly the Mosquito Coast.

While negotiations were in progress between the two governments, certain Senators of both parties, especially Seward of New York and Lewis Cass of Michigan, saw fit to bring the matter into the political arena of the Senate. Impelled by patriotism, politics, and the understandable desire to divert attention from Kansas, eloquent Solons harangued against the contemptible behavior of the British with angry words which could scarcely fail to raise a jingoistic fever in many sections of the nation. From his seat in the Senate Fessenden watched the proceedings with grave misgivings. "The whole affair is 'Bunkum,'" he wrote home in January, "and in my judgment ought not to be meddled with; but if it runs along into a general debate, there is no knowing what may befall in the way of talking." [2] By late

March the matter had reached perilous proportions, and on April 2, as a final act before leaving for Portland, Senator Fessenden took the floor to urge moderation.

In what was one of the longest speeches of his national career, the Senator from Maine began by questioning the wisdom of bringing this issue before Congress at a time when the negotiations were still in progress. "Discussions upon such subjects in legislative bodies, before their actual interference becomes necessary," he declared, "are very apt to be more productive of evil than good." Mr. Fessenden made it clear that he had no sympathy with England's enlistment practices or her policy on the Isthmus, but he felt that debate on the affair at this time was both injudicious and dangerous. "Heat on this side of the water has produced heat on the other," he noted. "Speeches made in the Senate have been responded to in the British Parliament, and with equal warmth." Why not leave the settlement of these difficulties to the proper department of the government and refrain from interfering until the matter should become one of legitimate concern to the Senate? As for the allegation made by some of his colleagues, including Fessenden's friend Solomon Foot of Vermont, that whatever might be said or done, Great Britain would not fight, "well, sir, if she will not fight, and we are quite certain of that fact, it is hardly a proof of our courage or magnanimity to threaten or intimate that we will declare war if she does not yield to our demands." [3] Fessenden's speech had the ring of good sense to many of his fellow Senators, but his words were soon proved superfluous; for by mid-April the problem of Anglo-American relations had been crowded harmlessly into the background by the mounting crisis in Kansas, and England was left free to settle the Isthmian matter at her leisure.

Since the beginning of the session, Fessenden had been active with his anti-Nebraska colleagues of the Senate in laying plans for the coming presidential campaign. On a night in early February a dozen Northern Senators and Congressmen had met secretly at the H Street home of New York's junior Senator, Hamilton Fish, to decide upon the fate of the Whig party in national politics. The immediate question before the group was whether or not the Whigs should call a national convention that year. Senator Fessenden, already committed to the new Republican party, thought not. He then proceeded to paint a gloomy picture for Whig hopes. In the East the Whigs had become hag-ridden by Know-Nothingism, and in the West their ranks were falling rapidly before the new Republicanism. To think of entering a Whig candidate in the 1856 presidential election would be worse than folly. It would be outright surrender to the Democracy. There were those at the meeting, including Fish himself, who were not yet ready to accept Fessenden's view of things, who could not yet bear to break their ancient political ties. But the majority of those present agreed that the time had come to give up the Whig ghost, and for all intents and purposes it appears that there on H Street in early February of 1856 national Whiggery was quietly consigned to its final rest.[4]

Back in Portland in early April, an ailing Fessenden kept a sharp eye fixed on the coming Republican convention, to be held at Philadelphia in mid-June. For some time it had seemed likely that the new party would choose for its first presidential candidate either the popular pathfinder, John C. Fremont, or the more politically wise Judge John McLean of Ohio, aged member of the United States Supreme Court. As late as mid-April the scales appeared tipped somewhat in favor of the latter, but Fremont's stock was soaring rapidly. From Fessenden's friend Ben Wade in Washington came the report that "Fremont is growing very fast in the public estimation. I find that his name takes in Ohio like tinder. I think he will distance all others, and if he is nominated, he will be elected. *Mark that.*" [5]

As the day of the convention approached, all outward indications were that Fremont had outrun his rival and would secure the nomination. "I tell you Fremont is the man for us to beat with and the only one," Charles Dana exclaimed enthusiastically to his co-worker Pike. "Besides *he is the true metal*, that I'll swear to, and more than that, if he is elected, *his cabinet will be made up of our sort of men.* With McLean we are all at sea and besides he can't be elected." [6] Fessenden, however, viewed the coming convention with the more analytical and guarded eye of a practiced politician. To his friend and former law-partner William Willis, a member of Maine's delegation to the Philadelphia convention, he wrote:

If the Americans [Know-Nothings] will take Fremont and will not take McLean, they will, undoubtedly, determine the question in favor of the former. What gave McLean the appearance of strength was a positive assurance that he could carry Penna. and Fremont could not. This is now doubted. But you will undoubtedly be able to decide what is best to be done. I still adhere to the opinion that Fremont would be the best Pres't, if we can elect one, and that he is the best candidate for New England—but I am content, let who will be the nominee. I hope Maine will vote as a unit.*

Concerning the vice-presidential candidate, Fessenden felt that Hannibal Hamlin must be considered as a strong contender. Only a few days before the Republican convention, Hamlin, convinced finally that the Democracy had been swallowed up by the slave-interests, had crossed over the gulf to Republicanism in a sufficiently bizarre manner to recommend himself strongly to the leaders of the new party. In regard to the possible selection of Hamlin, however, Fessenden held certain reservations:

I think H's nomination would be a good one for Maine—and perhaps it might help us, and it is all important to the cause that Maine should be carried in the fall. Hamlin is much respected, well-known, and I think his nomination would meet with general acceptance.

If, however, Fremont [former Democrat] is nominated, we must have a Whig—that is . . . a Republican who was neither abolitionist nor free-Soiler, but a Whig. This, I think, will be absolutely necessary, on account of the old Whigs, of which there are many.

Who it is will not be of much consequence. . . . I think Foot of Vermont would be the best nominee, all things considered. If he is presented, I hope he will be brought forth as the candidate of New England.[7]

* Fessenden to William Willis, June 15, 1856, in Willis Collection (Maine Historical Society). The American or Know-Nothing party was an important factor in the politics of the 1850's. Although originally composed almost entirely of anti-foreign elements and characterized by nativist attitudes, by the mid-1850's the Know-Nothing party had become something of a grab-bag assortment of political malcontents, including many die-hard Whigs, and was powerful enough to be deferred to by both major parties.

There had in fact been some mention of Fessenden himself for second place on the Republican ticket. "Suppose Fremont should be nominated, from the Extreme West," wrote a friend from Boston, "your name would be an excellent one from the Extreme East—to sail in the same ship. That could not be styled as sectional nomination, as the candidates would live farther apart than any two have ever yet lived." [8] But Fessenden gave no serious thought to such a possibility. His chosen place was in the Senate, and there he proposed to remain, at least until his present term expired in 1859.

During the spring and summer of 1856 the spectre of Kansas hung heavily over the land. Opposing governments continued to vie with one another in Kansas, and the failure of Congress to provide a solution or palliative for the explosive situation seemed to serve as an open invitation for violence to consume the territory. In late May full-fledged civil war broke out in Kansas Territory, and Northern newspapers reported in detail to thousands, if not millions, of readers the horrors of "bleeding Kansas." For Senator Fessenden the Kansas affair now took on a new and painfully personal meaning, for shortly after his return to Washington in early June, he received word that his youngest son, Sam, then a boy of no more than fifteen, had run away from home to strike a blow for freedom in Kansas. To a relative the Senator wrote of his despair a few weeks later:

I do not hear a word from Sam. I know not what will become of the poor misguided boy—but I fear the worst. Only a miracle can save him, but I do not know what to do. I have written to Kansas, but such is the disturbed state of things there, that all intelligence is difficult, and he may not be there. I hope he went north. He would not go south unless he is perfectly crazy. [9]

Not until mid-autumn was Sam's whereabouts discovered. After working his way to Kansas, the boy had joined a group of Free-Soilers who had the misfortune to fall afoul of a band of "border ruffians." In deference to his youth, Sam was gently but firmly deposited onto an eastbound flat-boat which took him to the Mississippi, and eventually to southern Illinois. There, he was ultimately reached by the long arm of his father's powerful friend, Judge Lyman Trumbull, and shortly thereafter an unharmed but infinitely wiser Sam began the long journey back to Portland. Years later, after Sam, still a boy, had been killed at Second Manassas, the Senator liked to recall his son's Kansas adventure in the summer of 1856, and to read to friends an account of the experience Sam himself had written following his return to Portland. It was a good literary composition, Mr. Fessenden thought. The boy had shown great promise.

From another quarter also the Kansas turmoil brought a large measure of personal grief to Senator Fessenden. Although time and political differences would one day wither their friendship, there was in 1856 no member of the Senate, with the possible exception of Jacob Collamer of Vermont, for whom Fessenden had a stronger personal regard than he had for Charles Sumner. They were close then—"my dear Sumner" and "my dear Fessenden"—and it was not an uncommon sight to see them walking arm-in-arm into the Senate chamber. Even at that time, however, the two men differed widely in the intensity of their views on slavery, and Fessenden often confessed to members of his family that he suspected his friend of being "quite insane" on the question of slavery. Indeed, there was really no secret about the fact that Charles Sumner was almost fanatically opposed to slavery in any form, and that he had long been spoiling for a showdown battle with his slave-holding colleagues in the Senate. "For a long time my desire has been to make an issue with the Slave Oligarchy," he had written to H. J. Raymond of the *New York Daily Times* earlier in the year, "and provided this can be had, I am indifferent to the special point selected. Of course, at this moment Kansas is the inevitable point." [10]

On May 19–20, while Mr. Fessenden was still convalescing in Portland, his friend Sumner seized upon this "inevitable point" and took the floor to deliver his intemperate "Crime Against Kansas" speech, an exceedingly bitter attack against the South, and particularly against the person of Senator Andrew Butler of South Carolina. Two days later, on May 22, Preston Brooks, a member of the Lower House and a kinsman of Butler, entered the Senate chamber and administered a merciless caning to Sumner while the Massachusetts Senator sat defenseless at his desk. Following this nearly fatal beating, Sumner was carried bleeding and unconscious out of the hall, and with the exception of a few brief and scattered appearances, the towering form of Charles Sumner would not be seen again in the Senate chamber

until December of 1859—three and a half years after the Brooks assault. And even then there were those who felt that only a part of
the man had returned. "He calls himself well," Fessenden confided
to his friend Hamilton Fish soon after Sumner's return in 1859, "but
there is a change in him which strikes me unpleasantly, but which is
more easily felt than described. There is a lack of his old alertness,
which, perhaps, may be accounted for on other grounds than bodily
infirmity." [11]

Whatever else may be said of the Brooks attack on Sumner, the
fact seems clear that here was grist for the anti-slavery mill, and a
matter which would not go unmentioned in the coming presidential
campaign. In this sense it may perhaps be safely said that Senator
Sumner's greatest contribution to pre-war Republicanism lay in receiving rather than giving, for there can be no denying that the unfortunate Brooks episode reacted to the great detriment of the Southern-oriented Democratic party. It was believed by some, in fact, that
the attack on Sumner cost the Democratic presidential candidate,
James Buchanan, 200,000 votes in the election of that autumn. By
the time of Fessenden's return to Washington in mid-June, the excitement had died down somewhat, but the Senator from Maine was
conscious of "a strong ground-swell":

> The Brooks affair has done our adversaries much harm, and I
> do not think a similar outrage will be attempted, as much, per-
> haps, for the reason that it has shocked all honorable feeling as
> because it is well understood that nothing of the kind can be done
> with impunity. I think that Northern men have made up their
> minds not to be beaten to death without making such an experi-
> ment dangerous.[12]

During the two months following Senator Fessenden's return to
Washington, Congress remained at a stand-still on the Kansas affair,
with each House insisting upon its own solution to the ugly issue.
On July 8 the Douglas bill, pointing the way toward the eventual admission of Kansas as a slave state, passed the Senate over the noisy
protests of Fessenden and his Northern friends, but later failed to
meet a favorable response in the House. In turn, the House bill of
July 3, favoring the Topeka (Free-Soil) bid for statehood, soon came

to an inglorious end in the Senate. From that time until the end of the session in mid-August, the Kansas issue dominated the action in the Senate, with few notable results, save for the harvesting of harsh words. Night sessions were frequent, and Senator Fessenden's health again began to fail under the strain. He seldom left the chamber during those days and was frequently forced to relieve his fatigue by taking naps doubled up on a window seat in the rear of the Senate hall. From time to time he entered into the endless round of debates, although he sometimes wondered if it were in any way worth the bother. And all the while there was Sam somewhere in Kansas, dead for all Mr. Fessenden knew. And from Boston the reports on Charles Sumner were all bad. "May God confound the villains."

On July 9 Senator Fessenden was drawn into one of his many angry clashes with Douglas. Of all the members of Congress, there were no two more mutually antagonistic than Fessenden and the diminutive Senator from Illinois, and when the one spoke, the other seemed to rise almost automatically in opposition. Later, not long before his death, Douglas recalled the great speakers of the Senate with whom he had been associated. "Henry Clay was the most fascinating," he declared, "Daniel Webster the most powerful orator, John C. Calhoun the logician of the Senate, [but] William Pitt Fessenden [was] the readiest and ablest debater." [13] Of a somewhat different, but not entirely uncomplimentary nature, was Senator Fessenden's estimation of Douglas. "I have for such men as Douglas," he remarked to his Republican friend, Senator Lyman Trumbull of Illinois, "the same sort of respect which we entertain for an open, bold highwayman, who meets you in broad daylight, and bids you stand and deliver." [14] In his speech of July 9 Fessenden felt compelled to denounce the Democratic Douglas for the latter's lack of common courtesy toward the minority, but although Pitt's words proved gratifying enough to his Northern colleagues, they made little lasting impression upon the "snarling insolence" of Mr. Douglas. In fact, after more than two years in the Senate and a series of similar angry encounters with Douglas, Senator Fessenden was about ready to agree with what his Republican friends had long maintained—that Stephen Douglas was impervious and that to talk against him was to talk against a stone wall. Still, Fessenden had no intention of allowing Douglas to act the bully with impunity. As long as Pitt Fessenden was in the

United States Senate, Douglas could expect retaliation for his transgressions.

On August 18 the first session of the 34th Congress adjourned,
with the Kansas situation still very much unsettled. Fessenden was
again in a state of near exhaustion, and he found himself unable to
attend the ten-day special session which convened on August 21 to
consider the Army Appropriations Bill. Instead, he set out at once
for Maine, and upon arriving at his home in Portland, he immediately applied himself to the business of regaining his health. For a
time he was content to rest, and revel in his garden, and breathe the
cool ocean air he had so often dreamed about during those hot,
sleepless nights in Washington. But perhaps his friend James Pike
was right in thinking of him as "the man who never lays his armor
off," for even as Fessenden convalesced in the quiet of his State Street
home, he could not rid himself of great anxieties concerning the approaching elections. To him the presidential election of 1856 promised
to be an all-important one. Earlier that summer the Republican
National Convention had selected the popular John C. Fremont as
the new party's presidential candidate to run on a platform of opposition to the further extension of slavery in the federal territories.
Now, for the first time, the people of the United States would be allowed to express themselves nationally on the subject of Kansas and
the larger issue of Senator Douglas' popular sovereignty. And upon
their decision might well depend the continued existence of the infant Republican party.

Senator Fessenden yearned to take an active part in the campaign
of that autumn, but the condition of his health remained such that
he was forced to refuse all invitations to speak out of state, and to
limit his activities mainly to correspondence and occasional speeches
in the Portland area. Meanwhile, however, his political friends were
not idle. Realizing that Maine's example in the early September elections would be likely to exert a powerful influence on the presidential
contest to follow, Republican leaders of the state determined to carry
Maine by as large a majority as possible. To help accomplish this
they put forward the recently converted Senator Hannibal Hamlin
as the new party's candidate for governor, while tacitly agreeing that
temperance, still a bugbear in Maine politics, should be left carefully unmentioned. With the popular Hamlin heading the Republi-

can ticket, there was from the beginning little doubt as to the eventual outcome of the contest, but the margin of his victory astounded even the most sanguine of his supporters. Harvesting a total of nearly seventy thousand votes, Senator Hamlin literally ran away with the gubernatorial race, and behind him, overwhelming Republican majorities captured both Houses of the Augusta Legislature. At his home in Portland the ailing Fessenden received the news with great elation. "In Maine we are of course exultant," he wrote somewhat later to his friend Lyman Trumbull. "At present, there is hardly such a thing as modern democracy, and it is one of our chief points of gratification that men who professed to be with us in sentiment, but were traitorous at heart, have been obliged to strip off their cloaks." *

Less gratifying to Fessenden and his Republican colleagues, however, were the results of the presidential contest two months later; for when the final tally had been taken, it was discovered that although Fremont had carried Maine by a healthy majority, he had in the national total been out-distanced by Buchanan by an emphatic half-million votes. Commented an anguished friend of the Senator:

> Well, it has turned out as expected. Slavery at the polls is stronger than freedom, though I blush to say it. I have long thought that the only way to arrest the extension of slavery and ruffianism in this country is by *force*. Argument and appeal are all in vain, and the time is coming . . . when the battle of liberty will be fought over again—and *strength* alone decide the contest.[15]

But for Senator Fessenden there was solace even in defeat. "We are beaten," he grumbled, "but we have frightened the rascals awfully. They cannot help seeing what their doom must inevitably be, unless they abandon their unrighteous ways. I am grieved that we could do no more, but surprised that we accomplished so much in so short a time." [16]

---

* Fessenden to Trumbull, November 16, 1856, in Trumbull Papers (L.C.). Fessenden refers here to certain old-line Whigs who had fraternized with the Democrats.

Kansas Again,
and Rising Republicanism

WHEN FESSENDEN returned to Washington in December of 1856 for the short session of the 34th Congress, he moved into the National Hotel on the corner of 6th Street and Pennsylvania Avenue, where Henry Clay had breathed his last not so many years before. There in the old corner building which had been constructed during the administration of John Quincy Adams and would remain a Washington landmark until its demolition in 1942, the Senator took a "large pleasant room"—not so handsome perhaps, but comfortable, with a good bed, a long sofa, and soft-coal heat. This last he considered a special blessing since his rheumatism was once again causing him some trouble. Scarcely had he grown accustomed to his surroundings, however, when his health appeared to take a turn for the worse, and suspecting that the "miasma" of his new quarters was at least partially to blame, Fessenden thought it advisable to move. To his friend Sumner he wrote in early February:

> I have taken possession of your rooms this morning as your "locum tenens." I am in such miserable health, that getting away from the National [Hotel] became a matter of absolute necessity. The pleasure of seeing you sufficiently restored to be with us again would remunerate me, a thousand fold, for the inconvenience of finding a new place. In the meantime, nothing of yours shall be disturbed by me, though I will not swear not to open some of your books. I only wish that the place and its associations could give me something of my predecessor's spirit and power.[1]

On December 2, President Pierce's last annual message was read to both Houses of Congress, and a most incendiary message it proved to be. In it the President took the stand that individuals in the North, encouraged in some instances by Northern state governments, had embarked upon a deliberate policy of agitation against the South and Southern interests. They had outrageously violated the Fugitive Slave Act of 1850; they had stirred up unrest over the repeal of the Missouri Compromise; and they had lent their support to the furtherance of violence in Kansas. Recently, as a capstone to this agitation, they had organized a political party which in the election just past had openly attempted to "marshal in hostile array towards each other, the different parts of the country. . . ." He hoped, now that the will of the people had been registered at the polls, that the nation would return to a less inflamed state of mind. With the furor of the election behind them and peace now restored to Kansas by Federal troops, President Pierce urged that members of Congress once again dedicate themselves to calm legislation and wise counsel.

Two days later an aroused Fessenden was on his feet to reply to the President's message. He had found it almost unbelievable. What the President had done, in effect, was to label as Abolitionists all those people in the North who had voted for the Republican ticket. Senator Fessenden had never felt that the Senate chamber was a proper place for name-calling or harsh words, but in this instance he wanted to go on record as saying that "the Chief Magistrate, in my judgment, has . . . in this message studiously misrepresented facts; he has sedulously endeavored to fix upon a very large portion of the people of this country associations which he knows to be applicable to but few."

Well, came the question, could the Senator from Maine deny that the Abolitionists had supported Fremont?

Fessenden saw no reason to deny it. "That individuals of that party voted for the Republican candidates may be true; but how does that prove that more than one million of men who voted for John C. Fremont are actuated by the same principles? Is a party responsible for the principles of every man who chooses to act with it. . . ?" For his part, Senator Fessenden had supported the Republican candidates, and he certainly didn't consider himself an Abolitionist. "What I mean to say for myself is that if a slaveholder had been presented as a candidate for the Presidency who avowed, and was

ready to maintain, the sentiments of the Republican party, of opposition to the extension of slavery over free territory, I would have voted
for him just as soon . . . as for any man of the Free States. . . ."

But the Republicans *had* geen guilty of agitation, someone inter-
jected.

Well, they had made it a point, Fessenden replied, to stand up for
their convictions. Were they to be condemned for this? "Sir, of what
stuff do you suppose we are made? If we are disposed to be quiet,
you call us craven, we are afraid to speak, we have not spirit enough
to protect or defend ourselves. If we speak out, we are agitators and
desire to rake open the coals of discord throughout this great country."

From that point the proceedings almost automatically degenerated
into another angry exchange over the larger issue of slavery extension,
a forensic free-for-all characterized mainly by a reiteration of the same
phrases and sentiments that had been voiced all too frequently during the preceding three years. There was, however, one very significant
aspect of the controversy that Senator Fessenden wished to mention
at this time, a point which he felt had been largely overlooked in the
past—namely, that not only the North but the South as well had a
large stake in the exclusion of slavery from the territories. Fessenden
often wondered if there were anything at all but slavery in the South.
Apparently not, for it was obvious that slavery, and slavery alone,
steered the thinking and actions of the Southern Congressmen. But
what of those people in the South who owned no slaves, the great
majority of the South's inhabitants for whom no one bothered to
speak in the legislative halls? Would not Free-Soilism in the territories ultimately react to their advantage also? "For their benefit,
as well as ours," Senator Fessenden declared, "I would open these
territories to freedom, and hold them consecrated to freedom forever." [2]

Although it is unlikely that Fessenden's remarks had much effect
upon Franklin Pierce and his Southern friends, his speech of December 4 certainly didn't injure his own standing among his anti-extension colleagues. He had taken the true ground. He had shown no
fear or hesitation in defining the position of the new Republican
party and in expressing the views of himself and his Northern friends,
even to the extent of labeling the President of the United States

a premeditated liar. "In my bed I have read your speech, and its many interjections and your felicitous responses," wrote Pitt's friend Sumner a week later. "And [I] have been happy that you are there, so ready and able. I wish that I were with you. You are the best debater on the floor of the Senate, and you must make them all confess it." [3]

To this Fessenden responded:

The speech, such as it is, was a sudden affair, and that, I feel is its only claim to any part of the commendation bestowed upon it.

I miss you very much, my dear Sumner, and so do we all, looking forward impatiently, to the time when we can again have the aid of your great powers. But let not your own impatient ardor disappoint us. Be sure that your physical vigor is well restored before plunging again into this whirlpool of abominations.

We are a power *now*, as you will readily perceive from the altered tone of certain people. . . . There is no lack of zeal anywhere.[4]

A few days earlier Senator Fessenden had written of his December 4 speech to his favorite Cousin "Lizzy" Warriner. "It was really accidental," he declared, "but my friends profess to be very much pleased. They profess to think that an unpremeditated fight is particularly in my line. Perhaps it is so, although I would much rather not fight at all." [5]

During the remainder of the short session, which ended on March 3, Fessenden was a frequent figure in debate, speaking on matters ranging from codfish bounties for New England fishermen to disputed elections in Iowa and Indiana. On one major issue, however, the Senator from Maine was conspicuously silent. This was the Democratically sponsored proposal to effect a revision downward of American tariff rates to a virtually free-trade level. In fact, the absence of his name from the various roll calls taken at this time, including that of February 26 on the final passage of the bill by the Senate, suggests that Fessenden was only infrequently present in the Chamber during the last few days of February. Had he been on hand to cast his vote, he would have been faced with something of an unpleasant choice. On the one hand there was his own traditional and abiding affection for tariff protection to be taken into account; while on the other was the fact that by the late 1850's New England had reached the level of industrial development which seemed to render the protective tariff much less attractive than Daniel Webster had considered it a generation before. It was, indeed, indicative of a major economic shift when only two of New England's Senators cast their votes against the Tariff of 1857, and the ailing Charles Sumner, from the nation's erstwhile citadel of protection, momentarily interrupted his long convalescence to take his Senate seat and vote in favor of tariff reduction.

On March 5 the Senate met for a special ten-day session to consider matters of contested seats and the reorganization of its standing committees. Soon after this special session had adjourned, Senator Fessenden set out for his home in Maine. From the mid-1850's until his death in 1869, the Senator was almost continuously in a state of poor health while in Washington, and he customarily lost little time in leaving the Capital after his work had been completed. Once back in Maine, his headaches seemed always to grow less severe and his body appeared to take on new strength from the cool air of his city by the sea. "Pitt . . . has not today been quite as well as for the last week," Fessenden's father noted soon after the Senator's return to Portland in March of 1857. "It seems to be somewhat of a serious task to eradicate the miasma of Washington from his system. This is not strange. That atmosphere is all poison." [6] How poisonous, however, not even General Sam could have known at the time; for it now seems very probable that during the last fifteen years of his life Pitt was an almost constant sufferer from malaria. Small wonder that Fessenden, never a robust person, actually hated Washington and frequently found the Congressional pace to be almost beyond his poor physical powers.

While the Senate was assembled in its brief special session in March of 1857, a bombshell suddenly rocked the nation. On March 6 Chief Justice Roger Taney handed down the findings of the United States Supreme Court in the case of *Scott vs. Sandford*. By declaring, in effect, that Congress did not have and had never had any Constitutional authority to exclude slavery from the federal territories, the Court seemed to have placed itself in open alliance with the slave interests against the free-soil aspirations of the North. Now, finally, the entire national domain appeared to have been thrown open to the extension of chattel slavery. Throughout many sections of the

North feeling against the Dred Scott decision ran dangerously high and in some areas assumed almost hysterical proportions. "This decision," snarled Greeley's *Tribune*, "is entitled to just so much moral weight as would be the judgment of a majority of those congregated in any Washington bar-room. . . ." [7] In somewhat more refined language Mr. Fessenden voiced the same sentiments. "Whether or not this decision," he commented, "is to be considered a pure emanation of the judicial mind, uninfluenced by sectional or party prejudice, the people will decide." [8]

To Senator Fessenden the action of the Court in this instance was beyond all comprehension. Since his arrival in the Senate in the winter of 1854, he had frequently had occasion to plead cases before the nation's highest tribunal, and for the dignity of its members and their station he had always maintained the greatest respect. Only two years before he had, in fact, eulogized this same body of judges in a speech on the floor of the Senate. But now——. With august and authoritative phrases the nation's highest tribunal had disclaimed federal court jurisdiction in the Dred Scott case because in the opinion of the Court the plaintiff Scott, a Negro, was not and could not become a federal citizen. And yet, with phrases just as august and authoritative this same Court, which had so emphatically disqualified the federal courts from deciding upon the issue at hand, had with its very next judical breath issued those extraordinary ex-cathedra pronouncements designed to throw open all federal territories to the uninhibited spread of slavery. To the organizers of a public protest meeting slated to be held in New York City, Senator Fessenden wrote at this time, declaring his belief that "while the mandate of that court within the range of its constitutional authority must be submitted to, the opinions of its members, more especially when extra judicial, are open to examination, and will stand or fall according as they oppose themselves to the public mind." [9] Less reserved in his views, and probably more representative of Northern feeling, was Pitt's friend, J. A. Ware, who wrote from Chicago:

From what I have seen of that outrageous Dred Scott decision, I am inclined to think that it is the best thing that could happen for the Republican party, for as I understand the decision, it is thoroughly pro-slavery. Now you know we can't stand that sort of thing. When they go systematically to getting everything on their side even to the judiciary, why then we will wake up and look about us to some purpose.[10]

And from his *Tribune* office Greeley agreed, loudly and bitterly. "This judgment," he proclaimed, "annihilates all Compromise and brings us face to face with the great issue in the right shape." [11]

During the summer of 1857 indignation over the Dred Scott decision gradually waned, and in late August the entire matter of slavery extension was temporarily pushed into the background by a sharp financial shock which for a time seemed to threaten the economic health of the nation. To Fessenden, however, the summer of 1857 would prove memorable for another reason, for in late July his invalid wife Ellen passed away in the old house on State Street where she and Pitt and the boys had lived for the past decade. She had hung on barely long enough to observe the twenty-fifth anniversary of her marriage to Pitt in 1832, and now after so long a time, Senator Fessenden, half a century old and broken in health, was again a man alone. From his Uncle Joseph Fessenden in Bridgeton came condolences: "On looking over our Temperance Journal last evening we saw with deep sorrow of heart a notice of the decease on the 23rd ult. of your amiable and excellent wife. . . . You have indeed sustained a loss which you can not hope to have repaired." [12]

It was a despondent Senator Fessenden who returned to Washington for the convening of the 35th Congress in early December. "The prospect is not very delightful," he mused. "What is to become of me if I live to old age? It is to be hoped that I shall not. But it is useless to anticipate. I will meet the events and changes of life as well as I can, and try to retain my manhood until the curtain falls." [13] Fessenden's grief was soon made more bearable, however, by the mounting pressures of his Congressional responsibilities, which now for the first time included membership on the much-harassed finance committee. Fortunately or otherwise, from early in the session until adjournment in mid-June of 1858, the demands upon his time and energy would be so great that Senator Fessenden would find few leisure moments for brooding.

Political power in Washington still rested securely in the hands of the Democrats as the 35th Congress convened in the final month of

1857. In the presidency was the ineffectual but thoroughly reliable Democratic regular James Buchanan of Pennsylvania who had succeeded his party colleague Franklin Pierce to the nation's highest office in the spring of that year. In the Upper House of Congress the Democrats, with thirty-seven seats, still possessed a sizable majority, even though the Republicans had boosted their total strength to twenty members, an increase of five over the previous Congress. Among the new faces in the Republican ranks were those of Senators James Dixon of Connecticut, Simon Cameron of Pennsylvania, and Zachariah Chandler, who had helped father the young party in Michigan only a few years before. For their part, the Democrats could now count upon the estimable services of Jefferson Davis of Mississippi, who had reappeared in his Senate seat after a four-year stint in President Pierce's cabinet; and from Tennessee had come a new man by the name of Andrew Johnson. In the Lower House also the Democrats could point to a convincing majority, although their margin there was much less impressive than that held by them in the Senate. Furthermore, in addition to their numerical control of both Houses, the Democrats boasted the advantage of position and prestige by being able to claim for their organization a national character. For although by now predominantly Southern in orientation and policy, the Democracy could still count among its Congressional ranks a substantial Northern membership. The Republicans, on the other hand, were clearly a sectional party, with all of their twenty members in the Senate representing Northern states, eleven of them hailing from New England. The story of what befell the nation politically during the three years following the convening of the 35th Congress in December of 1857, can be told largely in terms of Democratic failure to preserve the national character of their organization in the face of a rampant spirit of sectionalism, nourished mainly by conflicting opinions on the matter of slavery extension.

The stage for the meeting of the 35th Congress had been set by events in Kansas during the autumn months of 1857. In late October and early November leaders of the pro-slavery settlers in the Kansas territory had assembled in an unauthorized convention at Lecompton and had drawn up a state constitution as an intended final step in the process of qualifying for admission into the Union. These activities, highly irregular if not actually extra-legal, had been carried on under the almost exclusive auspices of pro-Southern elements who refused to allow their Free-Soil neighbors any real voice in the convention proceedings or in the subsequent ratification of the resultant pro-slavery constitution. Immediately the Lecompton affair was recognized as an outrageous fraud and angrily denounced as a slaveholders' swindle throughout many, if not most, areas of the North. Therefore, when in his first annual message to Congress on December 4 President Buchanan made known his sympathy with the Lecompton proceedings, the reaction among Republican ranks was about what might have been expected. "Now, sir, I undertake to say that this Lecompton convention was not a legitimate convention," declared Senator Lyman Trumbull in voicing Republican protest; "that it possessed no authority whatever, and that all its enactments which it has undertaken to carry into effect . . . are void." [14] Far more significant, however, than the expected opposition from Republican spokesmen, was the refusal of Senator Douglas to go along with the pro-Southern Administration in its views on the Lecompton affair. For Douglas, father of the Kansas–Nebraska Act and tireless champion of popular sovereignty, events had taken an ugly turn, for it seemed to him that the principle of popular sovereignty had become a travesty in the hands of the Lecompton people. So it was that the leading figure of the Northern Democracy felt compelled to give notice that "I totally dissent from all that portion of the [President's] message which may fairly be construed as approving of the proceedings of the Lecompton convention." [15] Thus were heard in December of 1857 the early rumblings of sunderance soon to befall the Democratic party.

The debate on the Lecompton Constitution did not break into full flower until early February, however, when the document was formally submitted to the Senate for its approval. In the meantime, Fessenden and his colleagues had become embroiled in long discussion on the matter of an Administration bill to increase the size of the Federal army from 18,000 to 25,000. Ostensibly the purpose of the measure was to provide greater protection for the nation's far-flung frontiers against hostile Indians, and to ward off the Mormon menace in the Far West. Many of the Republican members of the Senate were not convinced of the necessity of such an increase, however, and secretly feared that these additional troops would in some way be used to support the advance of slavery into the territories. When on January 26, 1858, Senator Jefferson Davis reported the bill from committee, Fessenden almost immediately rose in protest. The proposed measure, so far as he could determine, had no satisfactory reason for being. At least, the members of the Senate had not been furnished with adequate information to convince them that a larger army was needed at this time. Such an increase would involve expenditures of from five to twelve million dollars, and it was scarcely a secret that the Treasury was in no condition to meet any such demand. These were hard times. The financial panic of the previous summer had taken its toll, and as a member of the finance committee he could assure his Senate colleagues that the nation was dangerously near the brink of bankruptcy. To Fessenden it seemed that much stronger causes than had already been given must be brought forward to justify an action of this sort at such a critical moment. "It strikes me. . . ," he declared, "that when a proposition of this kind is made in a peaceful day, and with a bankrupt Government which has not money wherewith to meet its expenses, and does not know where to get it, some exceedingly good reasons should be given for this increase of our expenditures." [16] By early February it was apparent that Senator Fessenden's argument of economy had prevailed, and that a sufficient number of Democratic votes would be won over to prevent passage of the measure. "I think the Army bill will be defeated. . . ," Fessenden wrote to his friend Pike. "Seward, I understand, is to make a speech for the bill. He is perfectly bewildered. He will vote alone, so far as the Repubs are concerned, but he thinks himself wiser than all of us." [17] To Pike all this came as no surprise. "As to Seward," he replied somewhat later, "you know his weakness as well as anybody. . . . I never knew the time when Seward did not vote on the stealing side. It seems as though it was our luck to be cursed with leading men having one damned rascally weakness or other." [18]

In mid-January of 1858 President Buchanan confided to a friend that "the Kansas question, from present appearances, will not be one of much difficulty. . . . If what we have heard be true, there will be an end of it speedily." [19] Three weeks later, however, following a special message to Congress in which he called for admission of Kansas under the Lecompton Constitution, the President began to learn how badly he had misjudged the temper and strength of Northern opposition. For from that moment until late in the session the Lecompton matter with its many ramifications dominated the action of both Houses.

In the Senate during this time Mr. Fessenden frequently became involved in bitter rounds of debate on the Kansas issue, the most notable of which, insofar as Fessenden was concerned, occurred on February 8 when the gentleman from Maine delivered a brilliant and impassioned speech against the President's Lecompton message. Clearly, Senator Fessenden maintained, the Kansas pro-slavery constitution was a wholly bogus affair, fashioned by a convention that was neither representative nor legitimate. The entire proceedings of the convention had in no way been sanctioned by any authority higher than that claimed by the participants themselves, and must therefore be considered as flagrantly rebellious. However, Senator Fessenden continued, even if all this were not so, even if the document were to come before Congress in a legal and proper form and it could be demonstrated to him that the constitution met with the overwhelming approval of the people of Kansas, he would still oppose it. Four years before, during the great debate on the Kansas–Nebraska Bill, he had expressed his sentiments on the extension of slavery into this area, and he had since found no cause to alter those views.

Years later, long after the matter of slavery had been put to final rest, Lyman Trumbull's friend and biographer, Horace White, who in early 1858 had been a Washington newsman, would recall the furious Lecompton debate in the United States Senate. "The best speech on the Republican side," White remarked, "was made by Fessenden of Maine, than whom a more consummate debater or more knightly character and presence has not graced the Senate chamber in my time, if ever." [20]

On March 23 the bill to admit Kansas to the Union under the provisions of the Lecompton Constitution passed the Senate by a comfortable vote of 33–25. The success of the bill in the Upper House came as no real surprise, but as that polished politician James G. Blaine later noted:

In view of the events of the preceding four years, it was a significant spectacle in the Senate when Douglas voted . . . against the political associations of a life-time. It meant, to the far-seeing, more than a temporary estrangement, and it foretold results in the political field more important than any which had been developed since the formation of the Republican party.[21]

Shortly thereafter, the fact became plain that the Kansas Bill could not hope to pass the House, and in a subsequent attempt to break the ensuing deadlock an Administration compromise measure, championed by Democratic Representative William H. English of Indiana, was brought before both Houses on April 23. Briefly described, the English Bill provided for an open and fair vote on the Lecompton Constitution by all eligible members of the Kansas community, be they free-soil or pro-slavery settlers. Should the constitution fail to be ratified, the matter of admission for Kansas would then be indefinitely postponed.* If, on the other hand, the settlers of the territory accepted the Lecompton Constitution, Kansas would be immediately admitted into the Union as a slave state and in addition would be generously rewarded with sizable grants of public lands. Although angrily denounced by the Republicans as an out-and-out bribe, the English Bill passed both houses of Congress on April 30 and was signed by the President a few days later. Commented Fessenden: "The whole thing is disgraceful to all concerned. The South has lost all claim to honor, and the Democratic North never had any." [22] At the same time, however, Senator Fessenden wondered if the bill might not, after all, prove ultimately to be a victory for the anti-extension forces. "If the Kansas bill had passed in its original shape," he wrote home in early May, "Kansas could only have been delivered from slavery by a civil war. As it is, the deliverance of that people is in their own hands. It only remains to be seen whether, after having resisted successfully both force and fraud, they will yield to cajolery." [23] On August 2 the people of Kansas supplied Fessenden and the nation with their answer to the English Bill, when by a vote of more than five to one they rejected the Lecompton Constitution and its attendant bonus of public lands.

---

* At this time Kansas had a population of about 35,000, far below that generally required for admission into the Union. By the terms of the English Bill, if the Lecompton Constitution were rejected, Kansas must then wait until its population reached approximately 93,000 before again applying for admission.

During the remainder of the session much of Fessenden's time was taken up by financial measures, mainly of an appropriations nature, to which he was forced to give a good deal of his attention both in committee and on the floor. In the course of his work on the finance committee he had occasion to meet for the first time, in early May, President Buchanan and his cabinet officers. To his father, Pitt later confided his impressions:

> A more inferior looking set of men, including their chief, I never saw together. Most of them are not only ordinary, but positively ugly. They are, in fact, very mean men, having a very small degree of talent among them, and I fear very little integrity. . . . It will not do for them to appear much in public. The people are taken with good looks, and it will not do for men in high positions to fall below the ordinary standard.[24]

Immediately after adjournment of the first session of the 35th Congress in mid-June of 1858, Senator Fessenden returned to Portland. There he soon involved himself in the business of state politics, with a view to getting Maine Republicanism in shape for the September elections. In this task he was given additional incentive by his own personal stake in the outcome; for Mr. Fessenden's term in the United States Senate was about to run out, and upon continued Republican control of the Augusta Legislature depended his chances of re-election. During the summer months the Senator labored tirelessly in the Portland area to raise campaign funds for the meagre treasury of the young party, although he sometimes wondered if his efforts were not being unfairly exploited. "The State Committee . . . have taken the liberty to assess me $500 more," he wrote to his friend Pike who had returned from his Washington news job to direct the campaign in down-east Washington County. "I have already paid more than $1000, which they conceded to be pretty strong. All the money raised here so far has gone out of the District and *our* battle is to be the hardest." [25]

A few weeks before the election, Fessenden took to stumping the areas adjoining the Portland district, some of which were considered rather "shaky" by party prophets. "We do not look so safe in this region as I could wish," he wrote to Pike in late August. "We learn that our adversaries are making a rush upon all the close Rep. districts in this quarter, and have some hopes of checkmating us in the House." [26] Of particular concern to Senator Fessenden and his Republican colleagues was nearby York County, and in early September Fessenden and his friend Anson Morrill invaded the area to begin "pursuing game through the pastures of *the dear people of York County. . . .* " [27] Soon after, the State Committee saw to it that they were given powerful reinforcements in the person of crowd-pleasing Hannibal Hamlin—all of which caused the Democratic *Argus* to ask:

> How happens it, that whereas ten years ago these gentlemen [Fessenden and Hamlin] agreed on *no* points of political policy, *they now agree in all respects!* They both prove, very convincingly, that they have never changed a particle, and yet the people see them now on the same platform.[28]

When the final results of the early September elections were made known, it was discovered that Maine Republicanism had scored a resounding victory. From John Bigelow of the New York *Evening Post* came a letter to Fessenden, asking that the Senator reveal the secret formula that had brought Maine such glorious success. Perhaps it could be used to similar advantage in the coming New York State elections. "I told him," Fessenden wrote to Pike, "that our great secret was unity of action—thinking nothing of men or cliques, and uniting for success." [29] A few weeks earlier Senator Fessenden had expressed much the same sentiment somewhat less delicately when he declared in an electioneering speech: "I would vote for a dog if he were the candidate of my party." [30]

X

Senator Fessenden

on the Eve of Conflict

THE SLENDER, erect figure of William Pitt Fessenden was a familiar and impressive sight to Washingtonians of the late 1850's as he walked among them on his daily trips to and from the Capitol. In appearance Fessenden was at this time, as always, a striking figure. Although slight of frame and of average height, his bearing was such as to suggest that here indeed was a man who merited attention. With his quick step and precise physical mannerisms he fairly bristled with dignity, and even during his casual Sunday strolls through the city, which he customarily took for reasons of health and relaxation, his walking stick never missed its proper mark. His dress was at all times immaculate and, although inclined to be somber, was invariably in good taste. In his long black jacket with the velvet lapels, and his stick-up collar gathered about the neck by a tie of fine black silk, he was regarded by many of his colleagues as the best-dressed member of the Senate. Facially, the man was handsome. His features considered separately were, save for the eyes, ordinary enough, but taken altogether they amounted to a cold, classical type of beauty that seemed to grow richer with age. The abundant hair and the narrow, cropped beard which framed his long face were by this time graying, but not yet gray, and in the lot not a strand was out of place. The eyes of the man are a story in themselves. They were intense and searching eyes, and there was a remorseless, almost fierce quality about them which seemed to suggest in their level stare something akin to cold disdain—or even hatred.

In his public life and in many of his private relationships, Mr. Fessenden's demeanor was too often in accord with his imperious appearance. To all but those who knew him best he seemed a cold and haughty person, thoroughly convinced of his own infallibility and easily triggered to anger against those who dared question or oppose him. As he grew older his disposition, never notably sunny, became progressively worse, a consequence perhaps of the almost constant suffering imposed upon him by long, nagging periods of ill health, and he came to be looked upon by many of his colleagues as querulous and ill-tempered. And yet, while all of these things were true, while it was undeniable that he was on many occasions patently irascible, that he tended to be arbitrary and severe in his judgments and to spare little sympathy or understanding for his adversaries, he was, nonetheless, capable of a great feeling for humanity, as was attested to by all those who knew him intimately. Although by nature reserved and undemonstrative in his relations with others, even those closest to him, he was a man of many mercies and compassions, and his good-will and generosity toward mankind were profuse and unabating. Something of Fessenden's character may be suggested by the fact that his closest friends among his Senatorial colleagues were Jacob Collamer and Solomon Foot of Vermont, Hamilton Fish of New York, and James Grimes of Iowa, all recognized as men of the highest calibre and discriminating tastes.

Nowhere perhaps are the inner feelings of Senator Fessenden during this time more clearly revealed than in his letters to friends and relatives. These invariably show him to have been an essentially lonely and unhappy person, who wished that things might have been otherwise but realized that he had travelled too far to change his course or turn back. To his friend Fish he confessed, upon his return to Congress in late 1858, his weariness with the Washington scene:

> . . . I feel much more comfortable in the ease and idleness of home than anywhere else, although, since the death of my wife, many of its hours are sad and wearisome. But for this, I should little care to continue in public life. . . . But what can I do? The few years left to me may as well be spent in one way as another. So that I may as well spend one half the year in quarreling, and the other in regaining my equanimity.[1]

Somewhat later he wrote home to Portland:

As I grow older, I attach more importance to the cultivation of
the heart. We are too apt, in youth and early manhood, to think
too much of intellectual attainments. Perhaps I should have been
a happy man and done my duty better had I cultivated the affec-
tions more.[2]

And to his favorite Cousin Lizzy, Senator Fessenden wrote on the eve
of the Civil War:

My way of life is very much the same as last winter. I breakfast
about 9. Occupy myself with business until 4½ when I dine. Dinner
through, it is twilight, and then I get into dressing gown and slip-
pers, and think and dream away the time until 7. It is then that the
past, and absent friends come before me with almost the face of
reality, and you always come with them, a prominent figure in that
group of pleasant faces. Then, too, sometimes, I send messages, and
almost fancy they are received and answered. Strange fancies these
for a man over fifty. . . .
I hope, Dear Lizzy, that after all you do not feel very sorry to
have such a cousin as I am; faulty as I am. It is a very bad sign, I
know, that I cling so closely to my errors, and they are very numerous; but want of love for my friends is not one of them, and I
wish to feel sure that they make all the excuses for me they can,
and if they do not love my faults, at least, love me none the less on
their account.[3]

Upon his return to Washington in early December of 1858, Fessenden took over the quarters formerly occupied by his friend Foot
in Mrs. Carter's boarding house on Capitol Hill. At this time the
Capitol building was being remodeled, and Senator Fessenden tended
to look upon the proceedings somewhat askance. To Hamilton Fish,
who was then in Europe, he complained that the "ornamenting" was
going on to the satisfaction of no one but Jefferson Davis. The Representatives' Hall Fessenden thought glaring and vulgar, and the Senate
chamber little better. "The latter is not yet finished," he wrote, "and
I shall not be obliged to sit in it, unless reelected, as my term will

expire in March. Nothing, however, can prevent my reelection, but death, or my own misconduct." [4] Early in the following month Fessenden received word that he had been reelected to his seat in the United States Senate by a unanimous vote of his party in the Augusta Legislature. Soon after this he wrote to his son William:

> I am exceedingly gratified at the good feeling and unanimity. I am doubly bound to serve the people honestly and desirous to justify their confidence. I can say with truth that I have never either sacrificed any political principle or even concealed an opinion, and I have never sought a nomination to office. I have not the shame of recollecting that I owe my success to unworthy means. For many years I struggled on in a hopeless minority [at Augusta], content, as far as I was individually concerned, to remain there, retaining a clear conscience and my own self-respect. I trust that all my sons will ever be guided by the same rule, as they may be certain that no honor can ever repay them for the loss of their own esteem.[5]

The short session of the 35th Congress passed quickly, with Cuba as its dominant theme. In early February a bill was introduced by Democratic Senator John Slidell of Louisiana to authorize President Buchanan the necessary funds to enter into negotiations with Spain for the purchase of Cuba. Fessenden, who was hardly in sympathy with this projected addition of potential slave territory to the national domain, realized that the measure had majority support in the Senate. Consequently, he resolved that the Slidell bill must not be permitted to come to a vote. Upon his Republican colleagues he urged verbosity and other dilatory devices, since legislative heel-dragging seemed the most likely way of preventing the Slidell measure from passing the Senate before the March 3 adjournment date. From the Democracy came anguished cries and harsh words against the Fabian tactics of Fessenden and his friends, but in reply to a savage tirade by Senator Robert Toombs of Georgia, Fessenden declared that he and his Republican colleagues would neither be scolded nor threatened into precipitous action. They intended to take their own time under the rules of the Senate. On February 27, four days before adjournment, Senator Slidell yielded to the inevitable and announced that he would forego further attempts to have the bill passed at the present session.

Delay had triumphed. Writing home, Fessenden noted jubilantly: "We compelled them to beat a most ignominious retreat in the Cuba matter. . . . We shall have the fight over again next year, but our hands will then be strengthened in both Houses." [6]

Earlier in the session Fessenden had spoken at some length against an Administration request that Congress grant armed protection to United States citizens crossing the Central American isthmus. Senator Fessenden, who by this time was seeing Southern conspiracies under every bush, had opposed the measure out of fear that the proposal was designed as a ruse to secure a military foothold in that area and thereby acquire territory for the further extension of slavery. Of greater interest, however, and somewhat surprising in view of his party's proclivities, was Senator Fessenden's stand on a bill to provide for construction of a railroad to the Pacific Coast. Although in sympathy with the idea of a transcontinental railway, the Senator considered this particular measure a bad bill, principally because it provided for construction of the road by private capital. This should not be, argued Fessenden, mindful perhaps of the lessons he had learned from his own unhappy experiences with private railroad enterprise in Portland a decade before. The railroad should be built by the Government with public funds and should remain in control of the Government, Fessenden declared in a speech that would have gladdened the heart of Henry Clay and other internal improvements enthusiasts. It should be a great national work belonging to the American people, and should not be allowed to fall into the hands of any private corporation. For these reasons he could not allow himself to support the bill, and on January 27 he lent his vote to its defeat. A few years later, during the war, when the Republicans pushed through the Pacific Railroad bills of 1862 and 1864, Fessenden still clung to these same views, and from the respective lists of those Senators voting in favor of the measures, his name was conspicuously missing.

Back in Maine by mid-March of 1859, Fessenden was again forced to devote himself to rest and quiet. On the orders of his physician he did little during the spring and early summer, save tend to his correspondence and care for his beloved garden. The weather that year in Portland was not particularly conducive to rapid convalescence or high spirits. For weeks in May and June the city was covered by a cold blanket of wet fog which permeated Mr. Fessenden's rheumatic joints, but it appeared to bear no ill effects upon the Senator's garden, "and I have hopes that July will give us plenty of sunshine and roses, and the fall a reasonable supply of grapes, and such pears as you like." [7] During this time he was visited for a few days by his friend James Pike, who had come up from his home in Calais on behalf of Greeley's *Tribune* to report the arrival of the new British leviathan ship, *The Great Eastern,* in Portland harbor. Here indeed was a strange friendship between men of strikingly different temperaments, the one an austere, reserved person of high intellectual polish, and the other an impulsive, colorful down-East Yankee who swore too much and called his great friend "Pitt." Although noticeably ill-equipped with anything resembling formal learning, Pike was possessed of a native keenness that sometimes bordered on brilliance. A long-time newsman, he had come to the notice of Horace Greeley in the late 1840's and was subsequently sent to Washington as the *Tribune's* Congressional correspondent. There, while wielding an alert and powerful pen, he renewed with Fessenden an acquaintance which dated back to the early days in Augusta. Meanwhile, by the mid-1850's Pike had become a controlling factor in the political destiny of down-East Washington County, and in the turbulent years that followed, it was Pike who proved himself Senator Fessenden's most trusted and valuable lieutenant in the arena of state politics.

During the summer of 1859 the two men corresponded frequently on political matters. With Maine now safely committed to the Republican camp, and with no real fears concerning the coming September elections, they naturally turned their interest to the matter of Republican chances in the 1860 presidential contest. The important thing was, of course, the proper choice of candidate, and who that candidate would be was anybody's guess. Both agreed that Seward's stock had slipped somewhat over the past few months, although he still appeared to be the strongest contender. Salmon P. Chase of Ohio and Nathaniel Banks of Massachusetts would bear watching, however, and then there was always the aging Judge John McLean, who as a Supreme Court justice had recently endeared himself to Republican hearts by dissenting from the Dred Scott decision. But in the maze of speculation one point was clear to both Fessenden and Pike. Whoever the nominee might be, "we should," in the words of Pike, "have a Conservative Republican, good against stealing, for a 'judicious

tariff,' and not obnoxious to the K[now] N[othing]'s." Concerning the
probable Democratic candidate, Pike felt certain that Douglas would
lead the pack, "but how the devil is he going to get two-thirds of the
Charleston Convention?" Perhaps he wouldn't have to, Pike concluded prophetically. "The Democrats *may* run two candidates and
one of them be Douglas." [8]

During the early part of the summer of 1859 Senator Fessenden
continued to be plagued by poor health. As late as the final week of
July he complained: "I am yet lounging about home, trying to get in
better condition, but my success is not very flattering as yet." [9] At this
point the ever-obliging Pike came forward with suggestions for an
August fishing trip as a proposed palliative for his friend's ills. "I can
plan a trip that will do you good," he wrote from Calais. "It is to
come here and go up the river with me in an Indian canoe and camp
out for a week. . . . A weeks course of this, with its paddling and
fishing and shooting on streams and lakes, would set you up amazingly." [10]

For Fessenden the offer was a pleasantly tempting one, for there
were few things in the world that the Senator prized more highly than
trout fishing. Throughout his adult life it was his only abiding diver-
sion, and whenever possible he would seek respite from his political
and legal labors by packing into the wilds of Northern Maine in pursuit of the speckled trout:

> . . . you arrive at a dark, deep pool, where all is still and quiet.
> There you softly steal along, and gently thrusting your rod between
> an opening in the bushes, touch the surface lightly with your
> tempting fly, gently moving it to and fro. In a moment all is life
> and animation. The pool is stirred to its lowest depths. The fly dis-
> appears from the surface and the rod vibrates like a reed. Soon,
> however, the contest is over. The fish is in the basket, and the sports-
> man's eye glistens with satisfaction.[11]

But in this instance fishing was a luxury that Senator Fessenden
felt he could not permit himself. There were too many things against
his going. His legal work had piled up during his illness, including
commitments to argue cases before the District and Cumberland
County Courts in August and early September. Then too, with the

crucial presidential election of 1860 not much more than a year away and the Republican Nominating Convention even nearer, there were important political fences that had to be tended to and meaningful winds that had to be sniffed, both within the state and elsewhere.

With the upcoming national elections of 1860 very much on his mind, a convalescing Senator Fessenden left Portland in late August to compare political notes with his Republican colleagues in nearby states. His two-week excursion took him as far west as Saratoga, New York, where he conferred with Republican leaders of the area and visited for a time with the Empire State's junior United States Senator, Preston King. On his return trip to Maine, Fessenden stopped over for a time at the home of his friend Senator Solomon Foot in Rutland, Vermont, where he found the air "electric with Republicanism." From opinions expressed by party leaders he met along the way, Fessenden gathered that Seward, Banks, and Chase were conceded little chance of getting the Republican nomination, and that the party would probably settle for Judge McLean or some new man. On the matter of Seward, however, Senator Fessenden still couldn't be sure. "You [the *Tribune*] and Pennsylvania may become reconciled to Seward yet," he wrote to Pike upon his return to Portland, "and then I shall expect to see him elected." [12]

When the 36th Congress opened its doors in the first week of December, 1859, the Republicans could count a substantial increase in their membership. Although the Senate was still strongly in control of the Democracy, Fessenden and his friends had added to their strength in that body by four seats, and in the House the new party now claimed a plurality of eight votes over their Democratic opponents. The presence of twenty-six Know-Nothings in the House of Representatives complicated the situation, however, and was partly responsible for the failure of the Lower House to organize until after several weeks of the session had passed. In the Senate, proceedings immediately got off to an angry start when on the first day of the session Senator James Mason of Virginia presented a resolution calling for an investigation of the John Brown affair. Nearly two months before, the fanatical Brown and a small band of followers had invaded the town of Harpers Ferry, Virginia, with the ostensible purpose of instigating a slave uprising. Although of pathetically inadequate proportions and completely unsuccessful in its aims, the raid had

created something akin to panic in the South, causing a Yankee wit
to remark:

There's a flutter in the Southland, a tremor in the air;
For the rice-plains are invaded, the cotton fields laid bare;
And the cry of "Help" and "Treason" rings aloud from tongue
    and pen—
John Brown has crossed the border with a host of fifteen men.[13]

The purpose of the Mason resolution was to set up a committee to
ascertain to what extent Brown had received aid and encouragement
from members of the Republican party. In the debate that followed
Senator Fessenden made it clear that he thought the whole affair
rather senseless, but if the Southern members wanted an investigation, let them proceed with it. For his part, if anyone were to ask
him if he were involved in the Brown raid, he would refuse to answer. After all, he was a United States Senator. He had taken an oath
to uphold the laws of the land, and by such an insinuating question
Fessenden would feel as much insulted as would Senator Mason if he
were charged with complicity in the slave trade. "The debate on
Mason's resolution was rather tame," Fessenden wrote to his son a few
days later, "and has had no other effect than to satisfy us of its party
aim. Democratic policy is to play the old game of dissolving the Union
harder than ever, with a view to political capital at the North." [14]

The John Brown matter came up again in late January, however,
when Senator Douglas reiterated the charge of Republican complicity
in the Harpers Ferry raid and accused the Republican party of
making open war upon Southern institutions. To this, Senator Fessenden rose to reply on January 23. The Senator from Illinois, he declared, had spoken at great length about threats to Southern institutions. But what about national institutions? What about the Constitution itself? It seemed to Fessenden that in this direction lay the real
threat. Republicans had been told that if they elected a president on
their platform in the coming autumn, the Union would be dissolved.
Was not this the supreme threat? As for himself, however, he was not
particularly frightened by such talk, for if the election of a president
by a majority of the American people was to be considered cause for
dissolving the Union, then the sooner the matter was settled the bet-

ter. Senator Fessenden had no desire to live under a government that permitted the majority of its citizens to be bullied and dictated to by a self-centered minority. If, indeed, the time had been reached when one set of men refused to abide by the provisions of the Constitution, then disunion was already in progress, and Mr. Fessenden supposed that another set of men could be found who would see to it that the Union would not be destroyed and that the people would not be deprived of their constitutional rights. Needless to say, Fessenden's reply to Douglas was enthusiastically cheered by his Republican colleagues and by the party press. Less exuberant was the Democratic Portland *Argus,* which, ironically enough, leased its site from that substantial Portland property-holder, William Pitt Fessenden. To the *Argus* the speech had seemed "diffuse and tautological. . . . Perhaps the difficulty of the subject, a defense of the Republican party, was the cause of this." [15]

During the remainder of the first session, which ended on June 28, 1860, angry clashes occurred almost daily between the two opposing parties. Little, if anything at all, of a constructive nature was accomplished. In fact, the time for constructive legislation had long since passed. Now all was passion and bitterness. In these incessant squabbles Fessenden was often involved, frequently finding himself squared off against the fiery Jefferson Davis of Mississippi and the immovably defiant Robert Toombs of Georgia. In questions concerning appropriations Senator Fessenden was particularly vocal, since as leading minority member of the finance committee he felt it incumbent upon him to speak out for Republican interests in the matter of expenditures. Although he doubtless little realized it at the time, during the spring and early summer of 1860 Fessenden was exchanging final words with some of his Southern colleagues, for by the time Congress reconvened in the following December, parts of the South would have already set out upon the road to secession, and in the Senate chamber there would be seats conspicuously unoccupied. This tempestuous first session of the 36th Congress did, in fact, for all intents and purposes mark the last bona fide meeting between North and South in national council before the tragic parting of the way.

As time was running out in Washington, the attention of the American people became focused upon the nominating conventions of the two major parties. First to meet were the Democrats, who assembled in Charleston, South Carolina, in late April. "We are anxiously awaiting the result of the Charleston convention," wrote Harvard Professor Emory Washburn to Senator Fessenden, "and devoutly praying for confusion upon their councils. . . ." [16] By the end of the month it appeared that the Professor's prayers had been answered. Although by far the leading figure of the Democracy and the darling of the Northern Democrats, Stephen A. Douglas, with his stubborn adherence to the principle of popular sovereignty and his narrowly unenthusiastic endorsement of the Dred Scott decision, was clearly unacceptable to the extreme pro-slavery elements in the party. What these extremists wanted, and what Douglas was not willing to give them, was a platform calling for the unqualified protection of slavery in all of the federal territories. As a result, despite the fact that Douglas controlled a majority of the delegates at Charleston and was strong enough to push through his own platform, he was unable to secure the two-thirds majority necessary to achieve the nomination, and after a ten-day deadlock the convention was forced to recess in bitterness and despair. Two months later the adjourned session met at Baltimore, and there in the last week of June, 1860, the disruption of the Democratic party, so long threatened, finally occurred, when the Southern extremists bolted the convention and chose their own candidate, John C. Breckinridge of Kentucky. And so, as if to invite victory for their hated Republican opponents, the Democrats in 1860 put forward two candidates for the presidency, Douglas and Breckinridge, each claiming to be the true defender of the faith.

Meanwhile, the Republicans were busy choosing a candidate of their own. When the delegates of the young party arrived at Chicago in mid-May, they found the nomination was still very much an open affair, although, contrary to traditional accounts, many of the party leaders were already thinking in terms of victory for Mr. Lincoln of Illinois. Indeed, who else was there? Edward Bates, former Know-Nothing of Missouri, had been killed off by the opposition of the large German vote in Missouri and Wisconsin. Salmon P. Chase of Ohio was too radical on the question of slavery. McLean was too old and vacillating. And Banks and Wade could count on little support outside of their own respective states. As for Seward, great efforts had been made by the conservative wing of the party to secure his nomination, but it was generally felt that he would prove a poor vote-getter.

"After all," remarked Charles Dana of Greeley's *Tribune*, "there remains this one hard fact against Seward's nomination, and I can't believe the Convention can get over it, namely, that he can't carry Connecticut, Pennsylvania, N. Jersey, Indiana, or Illinois. I don't see how in spite of all the fanaticism wh. can be brought to bear he can be nominated in the face of that." [17]

Of course there was Fessenden, whose political popularity among the moderate Republican element was well recognized, but he had on several occasions positively refused to allow his name to be introduced at the convention. Had he not so declined, he might conceivably have gone on to capture the convention and subsequently the Presidency of the United States; for Mr. Fessenden's name had frequently been mentioned for the nomination, and he was not without a considerable measure of support, both among the leaders and the rank and file of the Eastern wing of his party. He had the advantage of hailing from a strongly Republican state, and his conspicuous performance in the Senate during the past half-dozen years had gained for him a national reputation. Furthermore, Fessenden's political views fitted in well with those of the proposed Republican platform, for although he was known to be refractory on the matter of a privately constructed transcontinental railroad, he was generally regarded as safe on the tariff and homesteads.* Most important, however, was the fact that by being unalterably opposed to the further extension of the slave system, while at the same time avoiding the anti-slavery fanaticism of a Chase or a Wade, Fessenden stood just right on the most vital issue of the day.

There was no question of home-state support for Senator Fessenden. Even long after the Senator had made it known that he would not consider being a candidate for the nomination, sentiment had continued to run strongly in his favor throughout Maine. When Republican leaders of the state had met in convention at Augusta during the first week of March to select their delegates for the national meet-

---

* Although Fessenden had originally opposed free homesteads (see above, p. 81), he had by 1860 come to favor the view of many of his colleagues that small homesteads would serve as an obstacle to the spread of slavery in the territories. As for the tariff, despite a temporary lack of enthusiasm during the middle and late 1850's, by 1860 Fessenden and most of his New England colleagues were willing to follow Pennsylvania's lead in calling for greater protection. See Chapter XI.

ing, the mention of Fessenden's name had set off a wild demonstration. "It was difficult in the convention to keep a resolution specifically recommending you from being offered," wrote young James Blaine, who had recently become chairman of the State Republican Committee, "and it was only upon the assurance that you would not desire it that the movement was suppressed." [18] Two weeks earlier Blaine had given even more convincing evidence of the Senator's strength in his home state when he wrote to Fessenden: "If you have any wishes in regard to gentlemen [delegates] to be chosen, it is of course only necessary to have you indicate them in order to have them respected and complied with." [19]

But Senator Fessenden's support was not confined to Maine alone. Had he at any time openly declared himself a candidate for the nomination, he could almost certainly have counted upon substantial backing from New Hampshire, Vermont, and Massachusetts, and had his candidacy been announced early enough it is not improbable that he would have been brought forward at the Chicago convention as the candidate of all New England. How great his strength was outside of his own section was a matter of conjecture, but three months before the opening of the national convention, Blaine, who had been corresponding furiously with Republican leaders in other states, had concluded that of all those party luminaries prominently mentioned for the Republican nomination, Fessenden was the only one thoroughly acceptable to the powerful Pennsylvania contingent.

To Fessenden, however, all this meant little. As early as December of the preceding year he had written from Washington to his Cousin Lizzy:

> They say here that my chances are much better than those of anybody else. But do not be alarmed. I am not deceived, or elated in the least. *Positively* I do not wish for it, and tell everybody that no one can do me so much injury in any way as by mentioning my name, and I believe that people are satisfied of my sincerity. The truth is, I am tired of all such subjects, and sometimes feel as if I would resign and go home.[20]

So it was that Senator Fessenden's name, which might have proved an important factor at the Chicago convention, was left carefully unmentioned, and in the end New England received its due recognition when Pitt's colleague Hannibal Hamlin was selected as Abraham Lincoln's running-mate. Concerning the choice of Hamlin, Senator Fessenden was especially gratified. Now, for four years at least, his most serious rival for control of the Republican machine in Maine would be reduced to little more than a political ornament. "Hamlin's nomination is very fitting and proper and occasions no surprise to me," Fessenden commented a few days later. "It will save me a good deal of hard work in Maine, and some worry. I am heartily rejoiced at it, for many and various reasons." 21

When Fessenden arrived back in Portland after the adjournment of Congress in late June of 1860, his health was again in a delicate condition, and for six weeks following his return he devoted himself almost entirely to rest and relaxation. By late August, however, he was once more in the political arena, lending his powerful support to the Republican state campaign. To Fessenden and his friends it seemed all-important that the young party make its best possible showing in the early September elections, for Maine's performance would certainly be productive of a great influence upon the later elections in other states, and most especially, it was believed, upon the presidential contest. "We are a sensitive community to political ideas in Maine," noted Pike, "and a good political barometer. If the [Democratic] humbug don't work here I shall believe it is a no go." 22

In early September Fessenden took to stumping up the Penobscot River, although somewhat reluctantly because of the precarious condition of his health. He had intended to confine his speaking to the Portland area, but when it was learned only a few days prior to election that Pike's brother Fred, a candidate for Congress from the sixth district, was meeting strong opposition in Hancock County, Senator Fessenden "took the boat Friday night, and spoke there on Saturday, doing what I could, outside, by coaxing and swearing." On the following day in Bangor, Fessenden fell ill but managed to reach home before having to take to bed. "The truth is," he wrote to Pike a few days later, "I was not in a condition to take any part in the campaign, but nobody would believe it." 23

Two days after his return to Portland, Senator Fessenden, confined to his room in the old house on State Street, learned the happy results of the Maine elections, and was gratified. "We are covered all

over with glory," he exclaimed. "Our great success must cure me . . .
if there is a spark of vitality left." [24] Less than two months later
Abraham Lincoln was elected President of the United States, and Mr.
Fessenden's Republican cup overflowed with partisan joy.

Fessenden at War

By the time the final session of the 36th Congress had assembled in early December of 1860, the die had been cast. The election of Lincoln in the preceding month had furnished the spark for the mighty holocaust of secession which soon after began its rapid sweep through the Lower South. "Pray enlighten me. What is to be the issue of the present agitation?" wrote Hamilton Fish to Fessenden in mid-December. "I have never witnessed as much anxiety and aggressiveness as prevail at the present time." [1] To this Senator Fessenden replied:

> I have long been convinced that we can have no peace with the Slave power, until the utter folly of this long continued threat of disunion shall have been demonstrated by actual experiment. The people of the South are led captive by ignorance and pride. They must be *left* to learn their own weakness, and then the cure will be speedy and certain. If we arrest them in their course of folly, by yielding to their demands, the delusion will remain, and break out in similar excesses whenever the honor and interests of the nation require a course offensive to their sectional objects and views. I am for seeing the worst of it *now*. [2]

True to his convictions, Fessenden gave little support to the various compromise measures that were formulated during the winter months of 1860–61. In fact, although he was chosen as one of Maine's delegates to the unofficial Peace Convention which was held at Willard's Hotel during most of the month of February, Fessenden refused to attend. For him, the time for compromise had passed, and he made no secret of his lack of sympathy for all such attempts to postpone the inevitable. From his uncle, the Reverend Joseph Fessenden, then on his death bed in Bridgeton, Maine, came a final warning against the ways of temptation. "Artful politicians, rich merchants and speculators, whose god is money, will counsel peace, regardless of principle," the old man admonished. "See that you yield not to their solicitations. . . . Whatever others may do, I beseech you William, to resist by your voice and your vote, any encroachments upon this [Free-Soil] platform. . . . *Beware of Critenden's* [sic] *or any other compromise."* [3] On March 2 Fessenden cast his vote against the Crittenden Compromise, a complicated package arrangement which called for, among other things, a division of the national domain between slavery and free soil along the line of the 36°-30′ parallel. Earlier on the same day, the Senator from Maine had refused to participate in the vote upon a proposed Constitutional amendment, brought forth as a sop to the South by his old Whig friend Tom Corwin of Ohio, whereby Southern states would be guaranteed perpetual immunity from Congressional interference with their domestic institutions. "I am told that I have the reputation of being the most determined adversary of compromise in the ranks of the Republican party," Fessenden wrote to his son William in mid-February. "The Charleston Mercury represents me as the most dangerous man in the country. You see, therefore, how bad a character your father has." [4]

During the winter of 1860–61, while Congress labored with little success and seemingly little purpose, and President Buchanan remained transfixed in a state of confused inactivity, the attention of the nation focused itself on the coming change of administrations. For Fessenden and his friends a subject of prime importance was Lincoln's choice of Cabinet officers, and upon this matter there were many conflicting opinions among Republican leaders. On one point, however, there appeared to be something approaching a unanimity of feeling: Senator Simon Cameron of Pennsylvania, for all his political strength, must not be given a place in Lincoln's official family. To Fessenden the elevation of a man of Cameron's reputation to cabinet level would prove "injurious," even "disastrous," for not only was the Senator from Pennsylvania flagrantly corrupt, but he was also sadly lacking in understanding and ability. When, therefore, it was learned in early January that Cameron was being considered for the post of Secretary of the Treasury, Senator Fessenden felt compelled to urge the President-elect against such an appointment:

> I will say . . . for myself, that I have been associated with him during this and the preceding Congress, on the Committee of Finance, and consider him utterly incompetent to discharge the duties of a Cabinet officer, in any position. Such is also the opinion of other Senators in whom you would place confidence. My belief is, though I have not conversed with all, that there are not three members of the Senate, on our side, to whom the appointment referred to would not be a matter of deep regret.[5]

As matters turned out, Fessenden's advice went unheeded, and the Pennsylvania Senator was given the post of Secretary of War in Lincoln's Cabinet, an office which he proceeded to degrade shamefully during his nine months of tenure.

In view of Fessenden's strong feelings against Simon Cameron at the time of Cameron's appointment, the subsequent behavior of the Senator from Maine in matters concerning the Pennsylvania boss was somewhat puzzling. Soon after his forced resignation from the war office in January of 1862, Cameron was appointed by Lincoln to serve as United States Minister to Russia. In voting for Cameron's confirmation Fessenden surprised and disappointed many of his Senate colleagues, who felt that by his vote Fessenden was helping to whitewash a notoriously corrupt character. Perhaps, however, Senator Fessenden's strange conduct on this occasion resulted from a reluctance on his part to cause further embarrassment to an already harassed administration, or perhaps his feelings toward the former Secretary had been softened somewhat by the fact that only a few weeks after the outbreak of hostilities Cameron had personally intervened to obtain a captaincy for Fessenden's eldest son James.[6]

By the time the 36th Congress adjourned on March 2, 1861, Washington had become a busily apprehensive place of comings and goings, of great anxiety and excitement. Long-time residents of the Capital, Southern in their sympathies and fearful of what lay ahead, were leaving in great number for the South, and from the North multitudes of newcomers were pouring into the city to fill the void many times over. Among them was Abraham Lincoln, who on March 4 ascended

to the Presidency of the United States and in a moving inaugural
address appealed to the recently seceded states to change their minds
before it was too late. Throughout March peace continued to hang
by a frayed thread, while on Capitol Hill the Senate sat in a special
business session during most of the month. By then all but a few of
the Southern seats in the Senate were empty, and with the Republicans in safe control of things, the special session proceeded smoothly
enough to permit Fessenden to devote much of his time to matters of
patronage. For Senator Fessenden, in fact, the relative calm of this
extra session was disturbed only temporarily mid-way through the
month by another angry interchange with Stephen Douglas, brought
on by charges from the Illinois Democrat that the Republicans were
willing to throw the nation into war for the sake of party gain. Interrupted frequently by Fessenden during his anti-Republican tirade,
Senator Douglas finally ran out of patience and lashed out against his
long-time antagonist with a vicious personal assault in which he berated Fessenden for his vanity and intolerable conceit. "He has been
trying to pick a quarrel with me for some time . . . ," Fessenden
wrote to his Cousin Lizzy two days later. "He found no occasion and
therefore made one. Fortunately he did not succeed in throwing me
off my guard, and *people say* that he got awfully drubbed. Even his
partisans in the gallery laughed at him." [7] Although Fessenden could
hardly have realized it at the time, his reply to Douglas on March 15,
1861, was by way of a last farewell to the Little Giant. By the time the
new Congress assembled early in the following July, the diminutive
Senator from Illinois would have answered his final roll call.

The election of Lincoln in the preceding autumn had caused an
imposing army of office-seekers to descend upon the Capital during
the early months of 1861. Now for the first time the hungry party
faithful could hope for their reward, and for Fessenden and other
Republicans in high station there would be little rest until the last
ounce of patronage had been dispensed. "I am not alone in my room,
from breakfast to bedtime five minutes in the course of the day,"
Senator Fessenden complained shortly after Lincoln's inauguration:

It is one constant stream of office-hunters. I could dispose of the
Maine people well enough, but I am beset with letters of introduc-

tion and solicitation from all quarters of the country. . . . Everything in the way of office goes west. We shall hardly get the paring of a toe-nail in New England, and many people feel badly about it, but I am *secretly* rather pleased, though there are a few good fellows I would like to see rewarded.[8]

Foremost among these "good fellows" on Fessenden's list were his home-state political cronies Freeman Morse and James S. Pike. Given a strong assist by newly appointed Secretary of State Seward, Fessenden experienced little trouble in getting Pike named United States Minister to the Netherlands. As for Morse, however, there was some difficulty in obtaining for him the desired position of consul in London, since President Lincoln had already picked out his own man for that much-coveted spot. In the end, though, the President graciously acquiesced, noting on his desk pad that "he [Fessenden] says that when he first mentioned Mr. Morse's name for that place, I said it was the first application." [9] Never one to take his patronage lightly, Fessenden constantly maintained a jealous watch over what he considered his just share; and if in fighting for his rights he were forced to square off against the President himself, he seldom hesitated to do so. On one such occasion toward the end of the war, the Senator from Maine, usually the very soul of decorum, lost his temper during a discussion with the easy-going Lincoln over a question of patronage distribution, and fell into a fit of unrestrained swearing. The President waited patiently until Fessenden's fury had been spent and then:

"You are an Episcopalian, aren't you, Senator?"

"Yes, sir. I belong to that church."

"I thought so. You Episcopalians all swear alike." [10]

Before the famed 37th Congress opened its doors in special session on July 4, 1861, the storm had broken in the South, and President Lincoln had exercised his emergency powers to set the wheels of war in motion. With Congress in recess at the time of the assault upon Fort Sumter, the President had taken it upon himself to call out the militias of the various states, to proclaim a blockade of Southern ports, to suspend the writ of habeas corpus in certain vital areas, and insofar as possible to effect all other measures necessary for putting the nation on a war footing. "It is to be presumed that what they have done thus far is to be submitted to Congress, and confirmation requested," Fessenden had written to his friend Senator Grimes of Iowa a month earlier:

> There may be some doubts whether Congress will not limit the government, but after all in the present excited state of public feeling there is more danger of error upon the other side. I confess that were I in Lincoln's place a small scruple would not detain me from doing what was needful.[11]

Later, when certain of his colleagues in the Senate made known their disapproval of what they considered a usurpation of power by the Executive, Fessenden defended President Lincoln's action, declaring that he approved of it "without crossing a t or dotting an i." [12]

When the 37th Congress met for the first time in special session during the early summer of 1861, the Upper House was clearly dominated by its New England membership. In fact, of the twenty-two standing committees in that body, eleven were placed under the direction of New England Senators. To Fessenden was given the powerful Senate Finance Committee, and the chairmanship of this committee he held, save for his few months in Lincoln's Cabinet, until he chose to resign the position in 1867. To Senator Fessenden, then, fell much of the responsibility of raising money for carrying on the war, and that he proved equal to this tremendous task, both in ability and in his capacity for hard work, has been amply attested to by the record of history and the praise of his contemporaries. So demanding were his duties in this area that he was forced to give himself almost entirely during the war years to problems of finance. In committee-room he labored tirelessly to meet the ever-increasing demands of the Northern war machine, and on the floor of the Senate he assumed personal leadership in championing those measures reported from his committee. Matters of revenue alone would have proved sufficiently burdensome under the trying conditions imposed upon the country by a great civil upheaval. Add to this, however, the fact that at this time appropriations measures were still being channeled through the Finance Committee, and the immensity of Fessenden's responsibility becomes even more apparent. Letters written by the Senator during this period tell of long hours of toil, of fatigue, and great apprehension over the financial prospects for the nation. "When a man feels as if he could cut everybody's throat and that everybody could cut his," Senator Fessenden wrote home early in the war, "he is in pretty bad condition. . . . The truth is that nobody can be found that is equal to this crisis in any branch of the government." [13]

The special session of the 37th Congress in the summer of 1861 lasted for slightly more than a month. During that time Senator Fessenden reported from his committee several measures affecting appropriations and revenue. On July 9 he brought in a bill for the cancellation of duties on arms and other war materials imported by the various states. Two weeks later he called up from the Lower House a new tariff bill, which he soon after reported with amendments to the Senate. Since the panic of 1857, which was thought in some quarters to have resulted from a lowering of the tariff rates earlier that same year, many of Fessenden's New England colleagues had grown less complacent on the matter of tariff protection. In fact, there had been little protest when the Republican party had pledged itself to a policy of higher tariff in the presidential campaign of 1860. This pledge the Republicans proceeded to honor by the passage of a series of tariff measures during the following four years which raised the general average of rates from the 19% level of 1857 to 47% by the act of 1864. The first of these revisions, sponsored by Vermont Congressman Justin Morrill, had gone into effect during the waning days of President Buchanan's administration, after the departure of Southern members had left Congress in Republican control. Although moderate enough, the Morrill Tariff appeared to answer most of the immediate demands of the protectionists, but as a revenue measure it soon proved most unrealistic for a nation at war. So it was that the bill reported by Senator Fessenden in late July of 1861 proposed to alter the Morrill Act in such a way as to provide for a substantial increase in customs receipts.

Fessenden's attempt at tariff revision met with some opposition in the Senate, particularly from Charles Sumner who feared that the measure would prove offensive to European nations. To this Fessenden replied: "I am willing to take all the risk of the righteous indignation of people abroad who think they do not make quite so much money out of us as they ought." [14] There was never much question of the measure's eventual success, however, and on August 5 the new tariff

bill was enacted into law. Insofar as government revenue was concerned, this and subsequent tariff adjustments made during the war
were desperately important affairs, for it was the yield of the customs
houses that provided the nation with its principal and practically
only source of specie during the long period of hostilities. And upon
this thin trickle of gold there came to be based an eminently successful, albeit somewhat fantastic structure of paper currency.

Incorporated into this same act was an amendment sponsored by
Senator James F. Simmons of Rhode Island to increase wartime rev-
enues still further by levying a tax upon individual incomes. In its
final form the amendment called for a tax of three per cent on all incomes in excess of $800, a rate which would be substantially increased
by subsequent legislation in 1862 and 1865. To Senator Simmon's
amendment Fessenden lent his hearty approval, believing, as he did,
that the people of the nation were ready and willing to open their
purses to the government, and that the war should be conducted insofar as possible on a pay-as-you-go basis. In this respect, however,
Senator Fessenden was clearly out of step with majority opinion in
Congress. For despite the passage of the Simmons amendment and
subsequent internal revenue measures of a similarly mild nature, the
level of taxation during the war would remain surprisingly low. It
was, in fact, apparent from the outset that the financing of the Civil
War would be based upon the general principle that the generation
which fought the war should not be made to pay for it. Thus, by the
time of General Lee's surrender in the spring of 1865, the Federal
Government had floated war loans to the amount of $2,622,000,000,
while during the same period it had collected scarcely more than
$667,000,000 in taxes, nearly half of which had come through the
customs houses.[15]

The most urgent piece of legislation to pass through Fessenden's
committee during the special session of 1861 was the Administration
Loan Bill, which was brought up from the Lower House on July 11
and passed by the Senate with few amendments and little opposition
four days later. The purpose of this measure was to authorize Secretary of the Treasury Chase to borrow up to $250,000,000, for which
he was to issue coupon and registered bonds, and treasury notes, "in
such proportions of each as he might deem advisable." The bonds,
usually referred to as "the 81's," were to bear interest not exceeding

seven per cent, payable semi-annually, and were to be redeemable at the pleasure of the government after twenty years.* The treasury notes were of various types, the most attractive being the 7.30 per cent three-year notes, popularly called "the seven-thirties," which subsequently played so significant a role in financing the war. Although Senate passage of the bill was never in question, Fessenden was frequently compelled to take the floor to defend the measure from the ravages of amendment and delay; and the fact that the bill was passed at an early hour and in essentially the same shape as when it had left the committee-room, was something of a tribute to Senator Fessenden's tenacity.

Two weeks before the adjournment of the special session in early August, Fessenden had occasion to express his sentiments on the matter of war aims. Soon after the Lower House had passed the Crittenden Resolution by an almost unanimous vote on July 22, Senator Andrew Johnson of Tennessee introduced into the Senate a similar resolution, which stated in effect that the Government's purpose in prosecuting the war was solely to uphold the Constitution and that it had no intention of subjugating Southern States or interfering with their domestic institutions. Obviously designed to allay the fears of the border states, the resolution met with ready favor in the Senate and was adopted by a vote of 30–5 on July 25. Commenting on Johnson's resolution shortly before giving it his vote, Fessenden remarked:

> I do not want to carry on this war for the purpose of subjugating the people of any State in any shape or form, and it is a false idea gotten up by bad men for bad purposes that it has ever been the purpose of any portion of the people of this country. I am willing therefore to meet them face to face and say that I never had that purpose, and have it not now. But . . . we have a purpose, and that is to defend the Constitution and the laws of the country, and to put down this revolt at any hazard; and it is for them to say whether it is necessary for us in the course of accomplishing a legitimate and proper object to subjugate them in order to do it.[16]

* The maximum interest rate on the 81's was soon after lowered to six per cent by an act of August 5, 1861. See: *Statues at Large . . . of the United States of America*, XII, 313–14. For the original measure, as enacted into law on July 17, 1861, see 12 *Statutes* 259–61.

Only three days before this, Senator Fessenden had voted with the majority in favor of a bill authorizing the confiscation of Confederate property being used "for insurrectionary purposes."

In late July while Congress was still sitting in special session, the North was stunned by the ignominious rout of Union troops at Bull Run. "We are filled with shame and confusion in view of yesterday's battle," Senator Fessenden wrote home on the following day. Meanwhile, as Federal soldiers stampeded back to the Capital, the rumor spread in Washington that Confederate General Beauregard was about to move against the city. But Fessenden gave little thought to packing his trunks. He was too old to run, and besides, nobody seemed to know from which direction Beauregard would come.[17] Senator Fessenden had little trouble in accounting for the causes of the debacle. "The fight at Bull Run . . . ," he wrote to his friend Pike, now United States Minister at The Hague, "was unquestionably brought on prematurely by the Press, and by self appointed Generals. I was not one of the latter, though I confess to having felt that Gen. Scott was behind the times." Foremost among these self-appointed generals, according to Fessenden, were his old friends Trumbull and Wade:

> Our friend Wade, completely upset by having been nominated in the Tribune for Major General, was loud, furious and impudent, denouncing everybody civil and military as incompetent or treacherous. He openly declared, not a week before the battle, that with ten thousand men he would march to Richmond and take it in a week.
>
> Trumbull brought resolutions into our caucus, for the purpose of adoption in the Senate, declaring that it was the duty of the Gov't to march on Richmond and occupy it before the 21st [July], and it was pushed by him and Wade and some others not only strenuously but insultingly towards those who doubted its propriety. I happened to be one of the doubters.

But who could say? Perhaps things had turned out for the best after all. "We had the fight and the lesson. It has done much good; taught the Government the necessity of greater activity; taught Gen'l Scott that he must not expect to monopolize all the glory; and taught Senators that they had better attend to their appropriate duties. . . ." [18]

In the mid-summer of 1861 while the nation recovered slowly from the shock of Bull Run and Congress labored manfully to set the war machine in motion, Senator Fessenden's youngest son Sam graduated from Bowdoin. The Senator had hoped to be on hand for the exercises, but when it became apparent that he would be unable to break away from his Washington duties, he instructed his son William to make the necessary arrangements for the somewhat impetuous, high-spirited Sam. "You must provide for Sam's bills," he wrote to William in Portland. "He has written with regard to an entertainment, and I am willing he should have a reasonable one, but not that he should provide a large quantity of liquors and have a spree. You may look out for it, but on a scale as economical as is consistent with the necessary gentility." [19] Shortly after his genteel celebration, Sam followed the example of his older brothers James and Frank by accepting a commission in the Union army, and by early 1862 three of the Senator's four sons were in the line. "I will hope . . . to meet you all again before I die, and in better times for the country," wrote a despondent Fessenden to his son Frank in the autumn of 1861. "What remains for us all is that each should do his duty in the sphere of action assigned to him, and wait patiently for the developments of time." [20]

Immediately after the adjournment of the special session in early August, Senator Fessenden left the Capital for Portland, where he spent the remainder of the summer "living quietly, taking little part in what is going on around me . . . , and hard pressed to dispose of time after I get it." [21] Meanwhile, the outlook for Northern arms failed to grow any brighter. After the humiliating defeat at Bull Run and the consequent discrediting of General Irvin McDowell, a promising new military figure had come to the fore in the person of young General George B. McClellan. But still there was no indication of approaching Union action against the rebel forces. "Inertia! Inertia! Everything is defensive," grumbled the strange old Polish expatriate, Adam Gurowski, one-time revolutionist and now sporadic Washington reporter for the *Tribune*. And in Portland, Fessenden's patience, a commodity with which he had never been bountifully endowed, was fast running out. "I do so long to hear something creditable to our army," he wrote to his friend Grimes in late September. "When is it to be? If this state of things shall continue much longer I shall join the grumblers." [22]

For a brief moment in late August and early September, Northern hopes were given a substantial boost by the publication of General John C. Fremont's celebrated confiscation order. This decree placed Fremont's military district in Missouri under martial law and proclaimed the confiscation of all property belonging to persons resisting the authority of the United States Government. More important, however, was the declaration in the General's order that the slaves of all people in rebellion in his district should thereafter be considered freemen, a provision which gave to Fremont's proclamation a character of emancipation and caused an immediate flurry of excitement throughout the impatient North. "You have no idea of its electric effect upon all parts of the country," Fessenden wrote to Pike a week after the decree was issued. "Men feel now as if there was something tangible and real in this contest. F[remont] is showing great qualities as a soldier, but this proclamation has shown him to be a statesman." [23] Particularly warm in its praise of General Fremont's proclamation was the avidly pro-Fessenden Portland *Advertiser,* which had until recently been edited by the exacting hand of Fessenden's young friend, James G. Blaine. "There is no reason why the rebels should be allowed to take the field, and have their slaves at home to till the lands and provide them with food . . . ," commented the *Advertiser.* "We see no reason why the bottom should not be knocked out of secession, by setting free the slaves of the armed rebels." [24] Meanwhile, the impact of General Fremont's edict had been felt as far away as St. Petersburg, Russia. "We are all here for Fremont's position in his proclamation," wrote United States Minister Cassius Clay to his friend Senator James Doolittle, "and we trust Congress will enable 'honest old Abe' to take that step this winter. It is surely the true ground." [25]

The elation of Fessenden and his friends, at home and abroad, proved to be short-lived, however; for President Lincoln, always sensitive to the pro-slavery feelings of the border states, quickly disavowed Fremont's action, and when the General countered with an attitude of defiance, Lincoln removed the popular Fremont from his command in early November. To Senator Fessenden, the President's removal of Fremont was "cruel" and "inexcusable," and by his disavowal of the General's emancipation order, "the President has lost ground amazingly. It was a weak and unjustifiable concession to the Union men of the border States. . . ." [26] But, then again, there in Portland during the long, impatient autumn of 1861 Fessenden was beginning to wonder if the nation could expect anything better from a person of Lincoln's calibre. Writing in early September, soon after the off-year elections in Maine, he confided to his friend Pike: "So far as the Repub party is concerned, the war is a godsend. In ordinary times we should have been whipped out of sight, the intense selfishness of the President and Cabinet having disgusted everybody." [27] And in Washington, meanwhile, querulous old Count Gurowski pondered the course of the future:

I still hope, perhaps against hope, that if Lincoln is what the masses believe him to be, a strong mind, then all may come out well. Strong minds, lifted by events into elevated regions, expand more and more; their "mind's eye" pierces through clouds, and even through rocks; they become inspired and inspiration compensates the deficiency or want of information acquired by studies. Weak minds, when transformed into higher regions, become confused and dizzy. Which of the two will be Mr. Lincoln's fate? [28]

Impatience and Preparations

SENATOR FESSENDEN left Portland during the final week of November to return to Washington for the opening of the second session of the 37th Congress. On the way he stopped over for a few days in Boston to call on friends and to confer with Massachusetts financier and philanthropist, J. M. Forbes, upon matters affecting the national economy. "Chase needs advice from practical men, and I am more in need of it than he is," he confessed to Forbes.[1] After his Boston visit, Fessenden continued on to the Capital, where he took a room at Mrs. Shipman's boarding house on Seventh Street. And there in the congenial company of his friends Grimes and Foot, together with Congressmen Justin Morrill of Vermont and Maine-born Elihu Washburne of Illinois, Senator Fessenden resided for the remainder of the long session. Also moving into Mrs. Shipman's in early December of 1861 was Horace White, Washington correspondent for Joseph Medill's Chicago *Tribune* and a young man for whom Fessenden soon developed a lasting affection.

By the time Congress reconvened on December 2, Fessenden and many, if not most, of his Republican colleagues were in an agitated frame of mind. The Fremont affair still rankled, and during the past month the nation had blundered perilously close to war with England as a result of a Union warship's cavalier treatment of the British mail packet, *Trent*. Worst of all, however, was the lack of activity on the part of the administration in putting down the rebellion. The war had been going on for the better part of a year now, and still no significant move had been made against the South. "Lives and treasures without stint have been placed at the disposal of the government," Hamilton Fish complained to Fessenden in January of the following year. "But the earnestness of the people has not been met by energy on the part of those entrusted with the conduct of the war." [2] Or, as one of Senator Fessenden's constituents asserted somewhat more bluntly, "We want our army to kill somebody. . . ." [3] Writing home in mid-December, Fessenden told of "a general feeling of dissatisfaction in Congress. . . . The Cabinet are unpopular, and [Secretary of State] Seward is almost odious through the belief that all this inaction is his work, and his policy. . . . The President has lost all hold upon Congress, though no one doubts his personal integrity. We must wait and see what comes of all this." [4]

Soon after convening, Congress gave expression to its discontent by serving notice upon the administration that it did not intend to sit idly by and see the war conducted in a haphazard manner. On December 5 Zachariah Chandler of Michigan introduced into the Senate a resolution calling for the naming of a joint committee to investigate the causes of the military disasters at Bull Run and Edward's Ferry. Kansas Senator James Lane proposed that the resolution be amended to include the battles of Wilson Creek and Lexington as well. Fessenden's friend Grimes thought that Belmont and Big Bethel should also be added to the list. In fact, why not, suggested Grimes, set up a committee to investigate the causes of all those disasters that had attended Northern arms, or for that matter, a committee to inquire into the general conduct of the war? Senator Fessenden hesitated to support his friend's proposal. He declared himself "not precisely satisfied at the moment with the expediency of passing this resolution." He wanted to think about it over the weekend. [5]

By the following Monday Fessenden had concluded that there might well be merit in Grimes' plan. Certainly, Fessenden declared on the Senate floor, the type of committee envisaged couldn't do much harm. In fact, by exposing military matters to Congressional review, such a committee might be productive of great good.

But, inquired Senator Lafayette Foster of Connecticut, if a committee of this sort were set up, wouldn't Congress be guilty of meddling with the President's powers as commander-in-chief?

Not necessarily, replied the Senator from Maine. After all, Congress had a stake in this war too. Concerning his own part, for example, Fessenden certainly wouldn't consider himself a meddler

simply because he wished to see to it that funds provided for by his
committee were expended only in the proper manner:

> I hold it to be our bounden duty, impressed upon us by our posi-
> tion here, to keep an anxious, watchful eye over all the execu-
> tive agents who are carrying on the war at the direction of the
> people, whom we represent and whom we are bound to protect in
> relation to this matter. . . . Sir, we are not under the command of
> the military of this country. They are under ours as a Congress;
> and I stand here to maintain it.[6]

Later on the same day, December 9, the Grimes resolution passed the
Senate by a vote of 33–3, and thus with Fessenden's blessing was
launched the famous or infamous Committee on the Conduct of the
War.

Early in the following month Senator Fessenden again had occasion
to lend his hand to strengthening the war effort. Upon the resignation of Simon Cameron from the war office, President Lincoln named
Edwin Stanton, short-term attorney-general during the Buchanan administration, to fill the Cabinet vacancy. Since Stanton's Democratic
antecedents were well remembered, his appointment caused a flurry
of suspicion among many of Fessenden's colleagues, some of whom
felt that in choosing Stanton, Lincoln was deliberately swinging toward a policy of peace. For this reason Fessenden felt obliged to ask
that Senate confirmation of the appointment be withheld until he
might have an opportunity to "sound out" the new appointee. On
the evening of January 15 Secretary of the Treasury Chase, acting
in the role of intermediary, sent his carriage to Mrs. Shipman's boarding house, along with a note informing Senator Fessenden that Stanton would welcome an interview with him that same evening. Returning to his quarters after the meeting with Stanton, Fessenden noted
on the back of Chase's message: "I had a long interview with Mr.
Stanton, and found that we agreed perfectly on all points. If he acts
up to his promises, he will be just the man for Secry of War."[7] Two
days later the Senator wrote home to his son William:

> Our new Secretary of War inspires great hopes. He is a man of
> vigor and energy, and is said to be a man of the highest character.

I had a long interview with him before he was confirmed, and, if a truthful man, he is just what we want. I have no reason to doubt him, and he impressed me forcibly and favorably.[8]

During the long session of the 37th Congress, discontent continued to mount in Washington and elsewhere against President Lincoln and his administration. In a letter written from Portland in mid-January, Pitt's aged father, now almost totally blind, confessed to the Senator his fears that the country was surely going to pieces. Why weren't the armies moving? What about slavery? Something had to be done, and soon, or the people would lose what little confidence they had left in Republican leadership. "I have no doubt that the President has a strong desire to restore the Union," commented the old General, "but with it to restore slavery, with all its power to curse and destroy the Union. . . . He hitherto has been fighting with a view to preserve the system as sacred in his view as to restore the Union." [9]

Although less avid in his anti-slavery attitudes than his abolitionist father, Fessenden could not help but agree with the old man that President Lincoln's "mustn't touch" slavery policy was proving to be most unfortunate for the Northern cause. Especially disturbing to the Senator was Lincoln's refusal to permit the use of escaped or captured slaves as troops in the Union army. Such a prohibition was, to Fessenden's way of thinking, a serious hindrance to the the successful prosecution of the war. As Senator Fessenden's good friend Israel Washburn, then governor of Maine, asked somewhat rhetorically:

> Why is it that while Maine has sent 20,000 men to the Army and Navy to save the Govt, and more are called for, and while the lives and property of her loyal men are being devoted to the Union, the salvation of the Union is put in jeopardy by a strange and shocking fear to weaken the rebellion by the employment of the slaves . . . ?
>
> These questions, so often asked, may do injustice to those who are in authority, but they certainly interfere grievously with the ready recruitment of men for the war.[10]

On a Sunday in mid-April the seven-man joint Committee on the Conduct of the War assembled in Stanton's office to talk matters over with the Secretary of War. Included on the Committee from the Senate were Wade, Chandler, and Andrew Johnson, while for the House the Speaker had designated John Covode of Pennsylvania, G. W. Julian of Indiana, D. W. Gooch of Massachusetts, and Moses Odell of New York. Since the purpose of the meeting was ostensibly to discuss matters of war policy, the chairmen of the finance and military committees of both Houses had also been invited to attend. These included Fessenden and Henry Wilson of Massachusetts on behalf of the Senate, and Thaddeus Stevens and Frank Blair from the Lower House. Within a short time what had begun as a policy meeting had degenerated into an indignant complaint session, with members vying with one another in their denunciation of the administration and its prosecution of the war. General McClellan was roundly condemned for his stalling tactics on the Peninsula and over-all lack of energy, while Secretary Stanton listened attentively behind his meagre eye-glasses and tremendous beard. Bitter old Thaddeus Stevens, chairman of the Ways and Means Committee and a power in the Lower House, harangued mercilessly against the Lincoln regime, asserting with his customary bluntness and profanity that there wasn't a single member of the Cabinet fit to hold his seat, except Stanton. Meanwhile, Frank Blair, whose brother was Lincoln's Postmaster-General, shifted his weight uneasily in his chair and said nothing. Fessenden, for his part, declared himself distressed by the President's timid policy toward slavery, particularly as it applied to fugitives. He could see no reason why the army should descend to slave-catching, why fugitive negroes should be sent back into enemy territory. Recently he had heard of a case in which a fugitive had come to Union lines bearing valuable information, only to be turned back. Most of those present at the meeting readily agreed that the war effort was being badly bungled, but when the session broke up, the great questions still remained unresolved: Who would bell the cat, what cat, and how? The time for action had obviously not yet arrived.[11]

Despite Senator Fessenden's ill-concealed disgust with the manner in which the war was being conducted, it would be wrong to consider him as having belonged to that growing group of Radicals within the Republican party who were by the spring of 1862 beating the drum loudly in favor of such drastic measures as general emancipation and confiscation of enemy property. True, the Senator from

Maine favored the use of Negro troops, and he had also endorsed the ideas expressed in Fremont's emancipation policy of the previous summer; but his reasons were those of military practicality rather than idealism. It is true too that he was one of the staunchest supporters of the bill to abolish slavery in the District of Columbia, which passed the Senate on April 3. He realized, however, that the path to general emancipation was fraught with great difficulties, not the least of which were those arising from questions of constitutionality. He had, in fact, little patience with those of his Congressional colleagues, like Sumner and Stevens, who were apparently attempting to make of the war a holy crusade. "Gentlemen are . . . so much engaged in 'abolishing slavery under the war power,' in 'confiscating the property of rebels,' and . . . purchasing negroes in the border states," Fessenden noted in early March, "that practical measures have lost their interest. I am getting to be considered a 'conservative'; pretty soon I shall be a pro-slavery member." [12] And as if to confirm Fessenden's observations, Thaddeus Stevens said of the Senator from Maine a few months later: "He has too much of that vile ingredient called Conservatism, which is worse than secession. He is not so great as at one time I had hoped he would prove." [13]

Nowhere, perhaps, was Fessenden's reluctance to go all the way with the Radicals more clearly manifested in 1862 than in his attitude toward the confiscation bill which was introduced into the Senate early in the session. This measure, much broader than the original confiscation bill passed during the special session, called for harsh punishment of convicted traitors, and proposed to render all property within the insurrectionary states liable to confiscation. The bill furthermore provided that the slaves of all persons supporting the rebellion should be "forever free of their servitude, and not again held as slaves." This final provision meant in effect that Negroes escaping to Union lines would no longer be turned back, and since this policy would seemingly conduce to the advantage of Northern arms, it proved especially gratifying to Fessenden. On the question of confiscation of property, however, Senator Fessenden had his doubts as to the advisability and wisdom of such action. At a meeting of the Republican caucus in mid-March he urged that the matter be referred to a special committee for careful study of all facets of the problem, and that a new bill then be drawn up which would be more acceptable to the moderate members of the Senate. In this attempt he was defeated, however.[14]

When the time arrived for final consideration of the confiscation bill in mid-July, Senator Fessenden was still unconvinced of the wisdom of the measure. With his friend Collamer he had striven with some success to "tone down" the more radical features of the bill, but he still hesitated to give his unqualified support to what he considered "the most important measure that [has] been brought before . . . Congress since I [have] been a member of it." In general he favored confiscation, but only within constitutional limits. "I am in favor of confiscating the property of rebels," Fessenden had declared on the Senate floor in early May. "I am in favor of doing it, and of doing it to just that extent, and no further, that I judge the good of the country requires." And to Lyman Trumbull and others who chose to berate him for being faint-hearted in his attitude toward the bill, Senator Fessenden snapped back: "I have a right to be and no man has a right to call me to account for it. No man has a right to question my motives or my opinions, and no man has a right to speak for the people, to threaten me with the judgment of the people, or to talk about the disappointments of the people." [15] Later, after Fessenden had somewhat reluctantly voted with the majority for passage of the bill on July 12, he confided to the moderate Senator Orville Browning of Illinois that he thought "it would have been better not to legislate upon the subject of confiscation at all." [16]

Soon after the passage of the Second Confiscation Bill by Congress, there arose strong suspicions that President Lincoln would not take kindly to the measure. "I fear that the Prest. will be mad enough to veto the Confiscation Bill," Fessenden wrote to Hamilton Fish three days after the Senate had given its approval to the bill. "Such an act will disappoint, and I fear will dishearten the country. He seems to be very much in the hands of the Philistines. Well, we have what we bargained for, a Splitter of rails, and have no right to complain." [17] Fearing the unfortunate impact of such a veto upon Republican ranks and Republican chances in the elections of that coming autumn, Senator Fessenden took it upon himself to visit the White House and discuss the bill personally with the President. During the interview Lincoln made known his principal objections to the measure, and declared that he was in particular disagreement with that provision of the bill which would extend forfeitures of property "beyond the lives of the guilty parties." Fessenden noted these objections carefully and returned soon after to the Senate with President Lincoln's suggestions. For a time feeling among the more radical members ran high against the President and to a lesser degree against Fessenden himself. Wade was especially upset and proceeded to harangue loudly against the President, while berating Senator Fessenden for "mousing around" the White House. In the end, however, Congress rushed through a hastily drawn-up explanatory resolution to the effect that forfeiture would not extend beyond the life of the accused, and President Lincoln responded by giving his unenthusiastic approval to the Second Confiscation Bill.

The financial outlook with which the nation was confronted when Congress assembled in December of 1861 was anything but a cheerful one, as is indicated by the fact that on the first day of the following month the National Treasury was compelled to suspend specie payments. Acting under the authority given him by the Loan Act of the previous July, Secretary of the Treasury Chase had arranged for the emission of a quarter of a billion dollars worth of securities and treasury notes. By early 1862, however, the Secretary was once again in desperate need of funds and was forced to call upon Congress for a second Loan Act which authorized him to issue various types of public paper totaling over $700,000,000. The principal feature of this act, signed by the President on February 25, 1862, was its provision for the emission of $500,000,000 in long term six per cent bonds, redeemable in not less than five or more than twenty years. More noteworthy, however, was that section of the act which provided for the issuance of $150,000,000 worth of legal-tender notes, thereby launching the federal government upon its first experiment with irredeemable paper.

When the bill reached the Senate from the Lower House, it was subjected to a thorough working-over by Fessenden's Finance Committee. In the first place, Fessenden immediately recognized the advisability of stipulating that the interest on the new "five-twenty" bonds should be paid in specie. In that way the bonds would prove a greater attraction and consequently claim a higher market value. Second, he took exception to that part of the bill which would allow customs duties to be paid with treasury notes, redeemable or otherwise. Although designed as a means of stabilizing paper currency, this policy would in Fessenden's estimation have the disastrous effect of drying up the meagre flow of specie through the customs houses and thereby cut off the government's only major source of gold. But unquestionably, Fessenden's greatest objection to the Loan Bill was found in his abhorrence of the entire idea of legal-tender notes, although he realized that the tide of public opinion was decidedly against him.[18]

In the debate on the Senate floor Fessenden convinced his colleagues of the desirability of specie interest payments, and of the danger in accepting paper at the customs houses. "It is but truth to say," noted the Portland *Advertiser* a few days after the Loan Bill became law, "that to no man does this country owe so much, as to Hon. Wm. Pitt Fessenden, for these most important provisions." [19] Less successful, however, was the Senator's attack upon the legal-tender clause of the bill. In Fessenden's judgment, the issuance of "greenbacks" would be nothing other than "a confession of bankruptcy. We . . . go out to the country with a declaration that we are unable to pay or borrow, and such a confession is not calculated to increase our credit." Furthermore, he felt that:

> . . . it is bad faith and encourages bad morality both public and private. Going to the extent that it does, to say that notes thus issued shall be receivable in payment of all private obligations is, in its very essence, a wrong, for it compels one man to take from his neighbor in payment of a debt, that which he would not otherwise receive or be obliged to receive, and what is not probably full payment.[20]

Nevertheless, when the motion was made by Senator Collamer on February 13 to strike out the "greenback" clause, the Senate refused to concur by a count of 17–23, Fessenden voting with the minority in favor of Collamer's amendment. Later on the same day, however, Mr. Fessenden felt compelled to bite his tongue and vote for passage of the Loan Bill despite its retention of the hateful legal-tender provision. "The *legal tender* was odious to me," Fessenden wrote later to Pike, "and I considered it unnecessary. I voted against it, but sustained the bill. The specie for interest saved it, people say, and *that* was mine. Mr. Chase and I do not agree. I think he lacks both system and courage, sometimes." [21]

Despite his occasional doubts as to the Secretary of the Treasury's financial ability, Fessenden did, nevertheless, prove himself on most occasions a loyal and tireless champion of Chase's measures in the Senate. In fact, during the remainder of the long session, which ended on July 17, Fessenden was forced to expend almost unbelievable amounts of time and energy in behalf of Secretary Chase's somewhat amorphous financial program. Shortly after his return to Portland in late July he wrote to his friend Pike, apologizing for having been such a poor correspondent. "My work in the last eight months," he explained, "has been more in bulk and importance than in any preceding two years of my life." [22]

Among the more important measures to pass through Fessenden's committee during this session was the Internal Revenue Bill, which demanded much of the Senator's attention from early March until its passage by the Senate three months later. Sired by the Secretary of the Treasury, this first comprehensive tax measure of the war proposed to raise $85,000,000 in domestic taxes during the fiscal year of 1862–63 by increasing slightly the income tax rates provided for in the tariff act of the previous August, and by imposing moderate duties upon a large number of other items, rather than heavy duties upon a few. To the economist David A. Wells, later United States Commissioner of Revenue, the guiding principle of the bill appeared to be one of universality, best expressed by the dictum: "Whenever you find an article, a product, a trade, a profession, or a source of income, tax it." [23] Although many of Fessenden's colleagues looked upon any sort of tax legislation as political anathema, the Senator from Maine did not hesitate to give this measure his powerful backing. As he had declared in early March before the tax bill had reached the floor of the Senate, "It is high time for us to begin to think a little more about money. The event of this war depends upon whether we can support it or not, and at the rate we are going on we shall come to a conclusion before we are aware of it, I fear." [24] As matters turned out, this revenue measure, which was enacted into law on July 1, brought disappointing results by raising only $37,000,000 during the following fiscal year, an amount which was less than half that anticipated. However, by levying taxes of from three to five per cent on many manufactured goods and thereby exposing them to the ravages of foreign competition, the act of July 1 led almost immediately to a further boost in tariff rates, which in turn increased the Government's customs receipts by $20,000,000 for the 1862–63 fiscal year.[25]

During the spring and summer of 1862 Fessenden followed the course of Northern arms with keen interest, although he was convinced that nothing very brilliant in the way of military success could be achieved until the Union high command had undergone a drastic shake-up. To his son William, whom physical disability had kept out of the service, the Senator wrote in mid-March: "The army is on the move, but I have no confidence in McClellan. It is quite probable that the enemy has no power to resist our enormous force, but I look for nothing but blunders under such leaders as we have." [26] Five months later, after the long session of Congress had adjourned and Fessenden had returned to Portland, his opinions on the conduct of the war and especially on General McClellan remained much the same. To his friend Pike at The Hague he wrote in early August:

> Our affairs are not looking so well as I could wish, but much better than our ill-wishers in Europe represent. We have had great successes, and one great failure—viz. before Richmond. This last should have been a success, and, in my judgment, would have been but for the incapacity of the General. In the field he is a failure. This was more than feared before he went to Yorktown. The President, however, has been from the first McClellan-mad and to some degree remains so. Richmond could have been taken in three weeks from the time he landed. His caution, however, amounts to timidity, and has well nigh ruined one of the noblest armies in the world.

But despite the generally discouraging state of affairs, Fessenden was not given to despair. He felt that even in the dispiriting military situation with which the nation was then confronted, there was much cause for hope:

> Compared with our enemies we are stronger today than when we began the war. Their efforts are great but they are getting more

and more spasmodic every day, while ours are more and more determined and vigorous. The 300 thousand men recently called for by the President are literally springing out of the ground. The quota of Maine is about filled. Our cities and towns give bounties liberally. No draft is made. We will make one if need be. The South can raise men in no other way, and pay them nothing. They do not even draft, but force men into the service at the point of the bayonet. This I will say. They fight well, but not so well as we do. *Thus far,* they have had all the generalship. Our *man* has not yet appeared.[27]

To a greater extent than most of his Congressional colleagues Senator Fessenden could claim a personal stake in the war. With three of his sons in the army, he was in a constant state of anxiety, although "I do not allow myself to dwell upon coming events much. . . . Let us pray for better days, and wait patiently for the unfolding of time." [28] To his son, Captain Frank Fessenden, who had been assigned to prison guard in Northern Virginia, the Senator wrote in early March:

My Dear Frank,
  I have received your letter and am happy that you took so correct a view of your duties in relation to the prisoners under your charge. I am far from thinking that we should feel any animosity against the great mass of Southern people. . . . In addition, these poor prisoners are unfortunate, and though you would have little reason to expect kindness from them under similar circumstances, that consideration does not lessen the obligation which humanity and brotherhood impose upon you.[29]

Soon after, Frank was transferred to General D. C. Buell's command in the West, where he arrived in time for Shiloh and a Confederate bullet through his arm. A month later the Senator's eldest son, James, left the command of his company of Maine Sharpshooters for an assignment with General David Hunter's Department of the South at Port Royal, South Carolina. Here he was placed in charge of disciplining and drilling the abortive "First Regiment of South Carolina Volunteers," which, despite its early demise, bore the distinction of being the first regiment of freedmen to be mustered into the Union army.

On August 30, while Fessenden was at home in Portland, his youngest boy, Sam, an artillery lieutenant in General John Pope's Army of the Potomac, was mortally wounded at the second battle of Bull Run. "He lived about thirty-six hours, manifesting through all . . . the most heroic calmness and self-possession," the Senator wrote a few weeks later to his friend Grimes. "The loss has affected me most severely, and the fact that two others of my sons are exposed to the same fate renders me unquiet and unhappy; but I have nothing but patience and submission." [30] Upon learning of Sam's death, Fessenden had prepared to go himself behind enemy lines to retrieve the boy's body, but he was finally dissuaded from doing so by friends and family who reminded him that his capture or death would represent a far greater blow to Northern hopes than the battle in which his son had been killed. Eventually the body of the young lieutenant was exhumed under a flag of truce by a nephew of the Senator, and the remains of Samuel Fessenden, who had lived barely long enough to reach his majority, were then taken north to Portland for interment beside his mother and sister in Evergreen Cemetery.

XIII

Senator Fessenden
Speaks His Mind

IN LATE November of 1862 Senator Fessenden boarded the train at Portland's old Canal Street Station to begin his habitual autumn journey back to Washington. With him was his brother Tom, Congressman from Maine's second district. Not accompanying them, but also a member of the 37th Congress, was another brother, Samuel C. Fessenden, who represented the third district in the Lower House. Thus during the early years of the war could a single state claim the distinction of being represented by three brothers sitting in Congress at the same time, a situation unparalleled before or since in the history of the National Legislature.*

Since each of these legislators drew the handsome salary of $3000 a year, plus mileage allowances, it was inevitable perhaps that some resentment should be felt toward the Fessenden family, and that the Senator himself be suspected of using his influence to place the public till at the disposal of his kin. While there is no evidence to suggest that Senator Fessenden took unfair advantage of his high station by exerting unreasonable political pressure in behalf of his family, there can be no doubt that the charges of nepotism frequently levelled against him by his opponents during the early war years were not entirely without basis. The following facts seem worth noting: [1]

* In the previous (36th) Congress, three Washburn(e) brothers, all originally from Maine, sat in the Lower House. Unlike the Fessendens, however, they had been sent there by as many different states.

Name	Relation- ship to Senator Fessenden	Position	Employed by	Salary
W. P. Fessenden		U. S. Senator	Fed. Gov.	$3000
T. A. D. Fessenden	Brother	Congressman	Fed. Gov.	$3000
S. C. Fessenden	Brother	Congressman	Fed. Gov.	$3000
C. S. D. Fessenden	Brother	Surgeon at Port- land Marine Hos- pital	Fed. Gov.	$3000
J. F. Fessenden	Brother	Deputy Postmaster at Lewiston, Me.	Fed. Gov.	$2500
H. C. Fessenden	Brother	Port surgeon at Eastport, Me.	Fed. Gov.	$1000
D. W. Fessenden	Brother	Cumberland Cty. Clerk of Courts	Cumberland County	$2500
Ellen Fessenden	Sister	Matron at Port- land Marine Hos- pital	Fed. Gov.	undis- closed

In addition numerous attempts, some of them successful, were made by the Senator to find public positions for several of his nephews and more distant relatives. In late December of 1862, for example, Fessenden wrote to General George F. Shepley, then military governor of Louisiana, to ask that employment be given "a friend in New Orleans who is by marriage connected with my wife's family." [2] Nor should the fact be overlooked that three of the Senator's sons were on the military payroll as commissioned officers, and that two of them, James and Frank, who entered the service in 1861 with no prior military training, both emerged from their wartime experiences less than four years later as brevet generals. Regarding Fessenden's soldier sons, however, it is only fair to point out that all three served with rare distinction and courage, one contributing his life, and another a limb to the Union cause.

On their way back to Washington in late November of 1862, Pitt and his brother Tom were joined en route by the Senator's friends Foot and Collamer of Vermont, and later by Senator Orville Browning of Illinois whom they happened to run across at the Continental Hotel in Philadelphia. During the final leg of the journey the five legislators whiled away the time by exchanging views on the political and military situations then confronting the nation. It was generally agreed that the military picture had brightened somewhat as a result of Lee's recent failure at Antietam, but the prospects for Northern arms were still considered not very encouraging. Of principal interest to the group, however, were those events that had transpired in Washington since the adjournment of their last meeting more than four months before. The President's recent proclamation affecting the right of habeas corpus came in for much attention. Fessenden declared himself opposed to suspending the writ in the loyal states where no insurrection existed. He felt that action of this sort should be considered despotic and very dangerous for the country. Nevertheless, two weeks later on the floor of the Upper House Senator Fessenden, mainly for reasons of party harmony, delivered a long speech in defense of the President's policy of arbitrary arrests, causing the intensely pro-Union Washington *Chronicle* to remark: "Mr. Fessenden's arguments dispose at once and forever of all these noisy diatribes of the New York *Herald* and *World*, the Chicago *Times,* and all such semi-secession prints about the unconstitutionality of the arrests concerning which they have made such an uproar." [3]

During the course of their conversation, as the train neared Washington, it was only natural that the interest of Fessenden and his friends should come to focus itself upon the emancipation proclamation which had been issued by President Lincoln two months before, shortly after Lee's forces had been turned back at Antietam. Fessenden expressed surprise at the President's action. As Senator Browning remembered his colleague's remarks:

He [Fessenden] claimed that the President, as President, had nothing to do with the condition of the negro. That as Commander in Chief of the army he might do whatever was demanded by the exigencies of the service to the extent that he could enforce his purposes with the army, but that the proclamation itself did not and could not affect the status of a single negro. That if the President desired to say in advance what he intended to do he should simply have said that on the first of January he would direct his

Genls to seize all the negroes they could reach in the insurrectionary districts. That the proclamation was very unfortunately worded, and was, at best, but *brutem fulmen*.[4]

Upon reaching the Capital, Senator Fessenden found his party colleagues in an angry mood. The Congressional elections of the month before had gone against the Republicans, and for Fessenden the reasons were not hard to find. For nearly two years now the Administration had consistently failed to give any vigor to the war effort. While the people of the North contributed their blood and dollars, it appeared that President Lincoln and his band of incompetent advisors were, deliberately or otherwise, coddling the enemy. "Folly, stupidity, and wickedness rule the hour," the Senator wrote home a few days after his arrival in Washington. "The President gives no hope of improvement, and Seward still rules him." [5] Clearly the time for some sort of drastic cure was near at hand, and just as clearly, the seat of the nation's misfortunes rested within the higher echelons of the Executive Department. "This is not the time when legislation can do much good," Fessenden noted. "Everything must depend upon those at the head of affairs as Executive officers, and things have gone so badly thus far that the country has lost confidence in their capacity if not in their integrity." [6]

On December 17, four days after the tragic slaughter of Union troops at Fredericksburg, a caucus of Republican Senators was held to decide upon means of getting at the cause of the great trouble. After much haranguing against most of the members of President Lincoln's cabinet, Stanton and Chase being generally spared, the caucus agreed that a special committee of Republican Senators should be selected to wait upon the President and urge upon him a change of certain men and measures. Above all, the committee should see to it that the President drop from his Cabinet Secretary of State Seward, who was known to exert a powerful influence upon Lincoln and who was thought to be mainly responsible for the administration's confused policy toward the prosecution of the war.

At seven o'clock on the following evening the caucus committee, composed of nine Republican Senators, including Fessenden and his friends Collamer, Grimes, and Trumbull, met with President Lincoln

at the White House.* After Chairman Collamer had read a paper
which embodied the views of the Republican caucus, the individual
members of the committee proceeded to express their own feelings on
the administration's conduct of the war. Wade complained that the
war was being entrusted to men who had little sympathy with the
Union cause. Grimes and Howard singled out Seward for attack, both
declaring their complete lack of confidence in the Secretary of State.
Sumner was of the same opinion. Senator Fessenden, somewhat more
tactful than his colleagues, began by expressing confidence in the
patriotism and integrity of the President and making it clear that the
Senate had no desire to dictate to him concerning his Cabinet. He did
feel, however, that it was up to the members of the Senate, in compli-
ance with their role as the President's constitutional advisors, to offer
him their friendly counsel, when, in their judgment, the situation
seemed to merit such action. Obviously echoing the complaints of
Stanton and Chase, Fessenden declared that there was a general feeling in the country that the President was relying too heavily upon the
advice of a certain few individuals within the Cabinet, while paying
only slight attention to the considered judgment of other members.
As an advisory board the Cabinet had simply not been permitted to
play a very useful role. It had met sporadically and infrequently, and
it was common knowledge that on many occasions decisions of major
importance had been reached by the President without reference to his
full Cabinet, and in some instances without its knowledge. It was
also felt, Fessenden continued, that Secretary of State Seward tended
to exert an unfortunate influence upon his Cabinet colleagues and
upon the conduct of the war. In other words, although not explicitly
stated, it was clear that Fessenden, along with the other members of
the committee, was taking the President to task for depending too
much upon the erratic notions of Seward and other "incompetents"
in the Cabinet, and too little upon the matured wisdom of Chase and
Stanton who represented the only true metal among the President's
advisors.

* This account of the proceedings of the Republican caucus and the subsequent
meetings between the caucus committee and President Lincoln is based primarily
upon Senator Fessenden's own detailed history of the Cabinet affair, written down
shortly after the events had taken place. Fessenden's version is published in its
entirety in Fessenden, *Life*, I, 231–51.

Shortly after ten o'clock the meeting came to an end. No plan of action had been arrived at or even discussed, but the committee had the President's assurance that he would give careful thought to the issues that had been raised. "While they seemed to believe in my honesty," Lincoln remarked not long after the visit, "they also appeared to think that when I had in me any good purpose or intention Seward contrived to suck it out of me unperceived." [7]

On the following evening, at the invitation of the President, Senator Fessenden and his committee colleagues again called at the White House. This time Fessenden was surprised to discover that all the members of the President's Cabinet, except Seward, were also on hand. President Lincoln opened the meeting by admitting that the Cabinet had not met very regularly, primarily because of lack of time. He thought, however, that most matters of importance had been given "reasonable consideration." As for Mr. Seward, the President felt that he had been sincere in his duties, and that he had not interfered improperly in the business of prosecuting the war. Lincoln then called upon his Cabinet officers to state whether or not they were conscious of any lack of harmony or want of sufficient consultation insofar as the Cabinet was concerned. What were Secretary Chase's opinions?

The Secretary of the Treasury was caught in an unpleasant situation. His voice had been among the loudest in condemning Lincoln's haphazard attitude toward the Cabinet and in denouncing his colleague Seward, and he was in a sense the star witness upon whom the disgruntled Republicans had built their case. But he was also a member of the President's official family and to speak out openly against his chief, in the presence of his chief, would be most assuredly both embarrassing and unwise. So it was that he chose the less hazardous path. No, he was not aware that there had been any lack of unity in the Cabinet. Yes, he thought that matters of importance had generally been submitted to the Cabinet for consideration, and that there had been a general "acquiescence" on public measures.

With Chase's endorsement of the President, the committee's case for all intents and purposes collapsed, and on the following day, after a series of intricate maneuvers and counter-maneuvers involving Lincoln, Seward, and Chase, matters finally came to rest where they had been before the clamor commenced—with the Cabinet intact and President Lincoln uppermost. "The attack of the extreme senators has

Fessenden in 1836, at the age of thirty.

Fessenden in 1854. A new United States Senator for Maine.

Portland, 1855. *New York Public Library Picture Collection.*

Augusta, 1853. *New York Public Library Picture Collection.*

Constitutional Convention, Kansas Territory.
New York Public Library Picture Collection.

OPPOSITE PAGE

Upper left: Charles Sumner. *New York Public Library Picture Collection.*

Upper right: Stephen A. Douglas. *New York Public Library Picture Collection.*

Lower left: A Mathew Brady photograph of Secretary Fessenden, 1864. *Historical Collection of Ansco.*

Lower right: Hannibal Hamlin of Maine. *New York Public Library Picture Collection.*

I have to-day said Hon. W. P.
Fessenden, on his assuming the Of
fice of Sec of the Treasury, that
I will keep no person in office in
his Department, against his express
will, so long as I choose to continue
him; and he has said to me,
that in filling vacancies he will
strive to give his willing consent
to my wishes in cases where I
may let him know that I have
such wishes. It is, and will
be my sincere desire, not only
to advance the public interest,
by giving him complete control
of the Department, but also
to make his position agreeable
to him.

RUNNING THE "MACHINE":

A Currier and Ives cartoon depicting Senator Fessenden as chairman of the Senate Finance Committee, grinding out greenbacks for the Lincoln administration.

OPPOSITE PAGE

"I have to-day said [to] Hon. W. P. Fessenden, on his assuming the Office of Sec. of the Treasury, that I will keep no person in office in his Department, against his express will, so long as I choose to continue him; and he has said to me, that in filling vacancies he will strive to give his willing consent to my wishes in cases where I may let him know that I have such wishes. It is, and will be my sincere desire, not only to advance the public interest, by giving him complete control of the Department, but also to make his position agreeable to him."

Memorandum written by Lincoln on July 4, 1864, at the time of Fessenden's appointment to the Treasury. Fessenden Family Collection. *Courtesy of the Historical Collection of Ansco.*

The High Court of Impeachment in Session in the Senate Chamber, Monday, March 23, 1868. From a drawing in *Leslie's Weekly*, April 11, 1868. *New York Public Library Picture Collection.*

Fessenden in 1868, at the time of President Johnson's impeachment trial.

failed," garrulous old Attorney-General Edward Bates noted in his diary. "The thing has dribbled out." * Needless to say, the Republican Senators were hardly pleased by the about-face of their friend Chase. How could he have said such a thing, wondered Orville Browning. To Judge Collamer the answer was obvious: "He lied." [8] Writing to Pike at a later time, Fessenden maintained that "the Senate movement would have delivered the nation, but for the weak squeamishness of our friend Chase. . . . He will never be forgiven by many for deliberately sacrificing his friends to the fear of offending his and their enemies." [9]

Although quieted somewhat by the caucus fiasco, Fessenden continued during the following months to hold low opinions of the Lincoln administration. "The simple truth is," he wrote to his Cousin Lizzy in early January of 1863, "there never was such a shambling, half and half set of incapables collected in one government before since the world began." [10] And a few weeks later he complained: "The army is *not* moving, nor do I believe that it ever will, to any purpose, until thoroughly reorganized. The truth is, everything looks badly in all quarters, and I am sometimes almost in despair, the more so because I see no remedy. The 'head is sick' and of course the whole body must suffer." [11] A pity that the nation had to be plagued not only by an incompetent President but by a "weak, divided, vacillating" Cabinet as well. "However, there it is," and of the whole shameful lot Secretary of State Seward was clearly still the leading miscreant— Seward, whose hold on Lincoln continued to be as strong as ever. "Unhappily the President began by thinking Seward and [Thurlow] Weed the great wise men of the nation, and the delusion still remains." [12]

But while busy casting stones, Fessenden himself was not without occasional sin in making his own contributions towards the promotion of confusion and hindrance in the conduct of the war. It appears, in fact, that the Senator from Maine was too frequently ready to interfere with the prosecution of the war if he felt that the interests of his constituents or his party would be benefited thereby. In the summer

* Howard K. Beale (ed.), *Diary of Edward Bates, 1859–1866* (Washington, 1930), p. 271. The assertion by Bates that the affair was the work of "extreme" Senators does not do justice to the truth. In the Republican caucus of December 17, the resolution which impelled the action was adopted with no dissenting votes. See Fessenden, *Life*, I, 238.

of 1863, for instance, Fessenden supported Vice President Hamlin in an effort to persuade the President to designate Portland as a prize port to receive captured vessels for adjudication. The affair was referred by Lincoln to Secretary of the Navy Gideon Welles, who explained to the gentlemen from Maine that matters affecting national interest could not be arranged on grounds of favoritism. Portland, Welles pointed out, was badly located and was not equipped for the job. To grant their request would be to involve the government in a great deal of expense and inconvenience. Fessenden understood and appeared to be satisfied with the Secretary's explanation, while Hamlin, according to Welles, remained "rapacious as a wolf, to abate his demand for government favors." [13] Nearly half a year later, however, the matter was resurrected, this time by Fessenden acting on his own. Again Secretary Welles refused the Senator's request, reminding him that although a few would profit, the true interests of the country would not be promoted by such a move. And there the affair ended.

An even more striking instance of Senator Fessenden's willingness to place the war effort second to other considerations stemmed from his anxiety over Maine's off-year elections in September of 1863. Fearing that Republican chances were being injured by the drain placed upon the state's manpower, Fessenden wrote to his friend Secretary of War Stanton in late July, asking that the Secretary delay taking any more drafted men out of Maine until after the election. In reply Secretary Stanton admitted the importance of a Republican victory in Maine, but like Welles he felt compelled to deny Fessenden's request, since to act in accordance with the Senator's wishes would be to impair the prosecution of the war.

Perhaps the most persistent instance of political interference in military affairs by Fessenden resulted from the Senator's special solicitude for Commander George H. Preble. Commander Preble, nephew of the famous Commodore and acquaintance of the Fessenden family, was a prominent citizen of Portland. He was also a naval officer of long experience, and in the year following the outbreak of the war, Preble found himself in command of the steam sloop *Oneida,* which had been assigned to the blockade of Mobile. On September 4, 1862, Preble, who was then in temporary command of the Mobile squadron, committed the blunder of allowing the Confederate cruiser *Oreto* (*Florida*) to break through the Union blockade. Since the incident took place in broad daylight, the Commander's explanation that he had mistaken the cruiser for a British ship was considered unacceptable by Admiral David G. Farragut and Secretary Welles, and as a result Preble was immediately and summarily dismissed from the service.

Early in the following month Senator Fessenden interceded in behalf of his Portland neighbor by endorsing a petition signed by "a number of highly respectable persons in Maine," memorializing President Lincoln to reinstate the hapless Commander. The matter was referred by the President to Secretary of the Navy Welles, who wrote to Fessenden, then in Portland, that it would be impossible to revoke Preble's dismissal without causing injury to the service. "The subject is a difficult one to handle," Welles noted in his diary. "His friends believe that he has great merit as an officer, when he has but little, whatever may be his learning, respectability, and worth as a gentleman. It will not do to tell his friends the truth, for they would denounce it as unjust; besides it is ungenerous to state unpleasant facts of a stricken man." [14]

Undaunted by the Secretary's refusal, Fessenden pursued the matter, and following his return to Washington in early December made several visits to the Navy Department, with the result that after many weeks of persuasion, cajolery, and argument, the Senator was eventually successful in having Commander Preble reinstated. To the credit of Fessenden, it should be mentioned that the original action of the Secretary has generally been considered to have been both hasty and harsh, and in time the Commander's name was cleared by a naval court of inquiry. Still, the fact remains that in the Preble incident as in too many others during the war, Senator Fessenden did not hesitate to give precedence to political and personal considerations. In this respect, however, it is only fair to point out that his transgressions were for the most part of a distinctly minor nature and were probably far fewer in number than those of most of his colleagues.

During the short session of the 37th Congress Fessenden participated actively in discussion of most of the more significant measures to come before the Senate, although he had surprisingly little to say on the all-important Conscription Bill, which passed the Upper House by a one-sided vote on the final day of February, 1863. On the matter of Government compensation for emancipation in the border states he was especially vocal. To Senator Fessenden there was some question as to whether or not Congress had the constitutional right to pay out federal funds to aid the states in freeing their slaves. Furthermore, he was not satisfied that the money, if given over to the states, would be used in the proper manner. It seemed to him that the bill lacked safeguards in this respect. "In these matters of legislation," Senator Fessenden declared, "and especially in these times, when we are obliged to count every dollar that we take out of the Treasury, if we are to take it out by millions it is worth our while to wait and see whether we are to do any good with it after we have made the appropriation." [15] On the President's birthday, February 12, the compensation bill passed the Senate, only to meet with subsequent nonacceptance by the House. Voting against passage in the Senate, and the only New England member to do so, was Fessenden of Maine.

In late January Senator James Lane of Kansas brought before the Upper House a bill which called for removal of the Indian tribes from within the boundaries of his state. The measure itself was of relatively minor importance in those days of leviathan legislation—"a little bill . . . ," Lane announced, "which will excite no discussion." Fessenden's reaction to the proposal seems worth noting, however, since it indicates something of the man's character and compassion. It does, in fact, point up what was probably the predominant property of the Senator's mind—a strong sense of justice and a concomitant determination to do the right thing, regardless of expediency. Concerning the actual removal of the Kansas tribes, Fessenden announced to his Senate colleagues that he considered himself insufficiently informed to argue the merits of the matter against Senator Lane, who was backed by the unanimous opinion of the Committee on Indian Affairs. He did, nevertheless, want to make known his objection to the philosophy behind the measure, the idea that "all the rights and all the justice . . . are to be reserved exclusively for the whites." He had seen this same attitude applied to the Indians before, and he had seen its unhappy results. And where would it all end? Would it not be far wiser and fairer policy to attempt to receive the Indians into the white man's civilization, to make room for them in American society, rather than to continue to push them aside? "Suppose you remove them to the Indian territory," Senator Fessenden asked prophetically, "how long will it be before the whites encroach on them there? How long will it be before the same argument is again adduced . . . , and the feeble little remnant must go still further into the wilderness?" As Fessenden was well aware, however, his arguments had little effect upon the thinking of his colleagues, and on the following day the Senate approved the removal of the Kansas tribes to another "forever" home.[16]

As in the two earlier sessions of the 37th Congress, most of Fessenden's attention was given during the short session to matters concerning finance. In December, 1862, he was busy in committee and on the floor with the task of amending the Internal Revenue Act of the previous July. Later, he became involved with various deficiency bills and appropriations measures, including a giant military allocation of nearly three-quarters of a billion dollars, and a time-consuming civil appropriations bill which authorized expenditures for virtually everything from the maintenance of the Government's lighthouse system to repairs on the Capitol dome.

To furnish Secretary Chase with the necessary wherewithal to meet the mounting demands upon the national treasury, the Senate passed on February 13 a third Loan Bill which was eventually enacted into law on March 3, 1863. By the terms of this act Secretary Chase was authorized to borrow on the public credit during the period ending June 30, 1864, nearly one and a half billion dollars. In return the Secretary was to issue up to $900,000,000 in six per cent bonds, payable in not less than ten or more than forty years (the "ten-forties"), together with approximately a half-billion dollars' worth of short-term treasury notes. Besides its major features, the Loan Act of 1863 provided for the emission of another $150,000,000 of legal tender notes, thereby increasing the amount of greenbacks authorized by Congress to $450,000,000.* On the matter of legal tender Senator Fessenden still had his doubts, however, and it was on the recommendation of the Senator's committee that the original request of Secretary Chase for $300,000,000 in additional greenbacks was reduced by half. But the fact that Fessenden's views on legal tender had softened somewhat since the original issue of the year before, is in-

---

* The original amount of legal-tender currency ($150,000,000) authorized by the Act of February 25, 1862, had been increased by a subsequent act of Congress (July 11, 1862) to $300,000,000.

dicated by the following excerpt from a letter written to Pike not long after adjournment of the session:

> I agree with you upon the legal tender. My opinion yet is that it did no good. Our paper would have been just as good without it. Experience has shown that, thus far, it has done very little harm. That, if ever, is to come bye and bye, when we are getting back, and it will need much financial wisdom to soften the blow. The country is elastic, however, and will stand more than that.[17]

Undoubtedly the most important measure to come before Senator Fessenden's committee during this session was the National Currency Bill, which passed the Senate on February 12 and received the President's signature on February 25. The purpose of this bill was "to provide for a national currency, secured by a pledge of United States stocks, and to provide for the circulation and redemption thereof," aims which could best be realized, according to Secretary Chase, by the establishment of a national banking association.[18]

Since the demise of the Second Bank of the United States in the 1830's, the country had been noticeably lacking in anything resembling a central agency of control over the nation's currency, and as a result hundreds of kinds of paper, much of it worthless, had come to pass as money. In time of peace such a situation, fraught as it was with confusion, inefficiency, and frequent fraud, was bad enough, but with the country now pressed by the exigencies of a great civil war, the lack of any standardized currency system could easily cause untold damage to the Government's financial program, and consequently to the prosecution of the war. So it was that Secretary Chase in his first report to Congress in December of 1861 had urged the formation of a national banking association. This association, he maintained, could prove instrumental in standardizing the nation's currency and could serve the further purpose of acting as a clearing agency for Government securities. Although at the time his suggestions found little support, the events of the following year helped point up the need for some type of currency reform. As the Washington *Chronicle* noted in early February of 1863: "We have had separate and conflicting systems of currency, and the crisis demands that we shall have only one." [19]

Briefly described, the National Currency Act of February 25, 1863, called for the establishment of a Government Bureau of Currency to be headed by a comptroller appointed by the President. The act further provided for the formation of local banking associations, which, operating under the authority of the federal government, could emit standardized "national banknotes" supplied them by the Comptroller of the Currency. These notes were to be backed by Government bonds, purchased by the individual member banks, and could in each case be issued in amounts not exceeding ninety per cent of the aggregate face value of the bonds.

When the National Currency Bill passed the Senate on Lincoln's birthday, it did so over the opposition of most of Fessenden's more conservative colleagues, including Collamer, Foot, Grimes, and Trumbull. The bill also found little favor with Senator Fessenden himself, who felt that the plan as envisaged by Secretary Chase would be productive of few advantages and would have the evil effect of destroying the state banks. Although, in deference to Chase, Fessenden refrained from attacking the bill and eventually cast a reluctant vote in its favor, there was no secret about his feelings against the Secretary's proposal. He did in fact refuse to take personal responsibility for reporting the bill from his committee and assigned the task of bringing out the measure to Senator John Sherman of Ohio. Since the Currency Bill ultimately passed the Senate by the narrow margin of two votes, it seems safe to assume that, had the Senator from Maine seen fit to throw his weight against the measure, he could easily have prevented its passage. As it was, however, he had felt obliged by circumstances to hold his tongue and to vote against his better judgment. Writing to his friend Pike a year later, not long before the Currency Act was superseded by the more comprehensive National Banking Act of 1864, Senator Fessenden explained: "Chase's Bank scheme has been no favorite with me from the beginning. I yielded to it because he demanded it as essential to his financial success, and without which he would be responsible for nothing, and the President seconded his demand." [20]

It was a weary Mr. Fessenden who returned to Portland in mid-March of 1863. "I am worn out," he wrote to Pike, "pretty much both in body and mind. The excessive and exhausting labors of the last two months have so enfeebled me that I feel the need for quiet."

But the Senator's fatigue was assuaged somewhat by a sense of satisfaction with the accomplishments of the 37th Congress. For not only had war measures "been characterized by a force and boldness that will make this Congress memorable," but also the nation had been benefited by such paternalistic legislation as the long-awaited Homestead Act and an act to encourage the establishment of agricultural colleges in the several states, both of which had received Mr. Fessenden's vote. Furthermore, during the short period of two years the 37th Congress had gone a long way toward putting into operation many of those old Whig principles that Fessenden had battled for as a freshman in Washington two decades before—including tariff protection, centralized banking, and government-sponsored internal improvements. True, in regard to this apparent resurgence of Whiggery, everything had not turned out exactly as Senator Fessenden had wished. The Pacific Railroad Bill, he believed, should have been framed differently and postponed until a later time, and Chase's ideas on a national banking system were certainly not to his liking, "but I cannot say that the wiser course was not to make the most of our time, for no one knows how soon this country may again fall into a democratic slough." [21]

X I V

The Emergence of a Moderate

DURING THE summer and autumn of 1863, while Fessenden relaxed in the old house on State Street and cultivated his garden of vegetables and flowers, his spirits were given a substantial boost by a happy turn in the fortunes of Northern arms. By the time of his departure for Washington in late November a series of important Union victories at Gettysburg, Vicksburg, and Chattanooga had succeeded in giving an entirely new face to the military situation, and despite many discordant notes, such as Meade's failure to follow up his Gettysburg success, it now seemed to a gratified Fessenden that the end could not be far removed. By way of making the long recess even more pleasant for Pitt, there arrived in Portland during mid-November his good friend Grimes of Iowa who visited for a few days at Fessenden's home before accompanying his colleague back to Washington. "I judge Portland to be one of the pleasantest cities in the United States," Grimes wrote to his wife. "Fessenden has a grand old place; house and everything in it appearing to be not less than fifty years old and upward." [1]

Upon his return to the Capital, Fessenden rented a house on F Street between 6th and 7th where he lived for the remainder of his Washington days. Although not so conveniently near the Senate Chamber as Mrs. Shipman's establishment, Fessenden's new residence offered greater space, and room enough out back to plant a small garden once the weather got warmer. As for its location, now that Jay Cooke's horse railway system had begun operation, there was no real hardship involved in living a few blocks farther from the Capitol. There were, in fact, definite advantages in being nearer the center of the city, particularly now that the Senator was taking many of his meals out. In the evening he could visit with Grimes who lived only a few blocks up F Street; or if in the mood for professional entertainment, which he seldom was, he could attend any one of a half-dozen such star-studded productions as "The Lakes of Killarney" and "Po-ca-hon-tas," presented during December at Ford's New Theatre, "both very attractive pieces"; or witness an exciting exhibition of the world's greatest troop of Bedouin Arabs at Grover's. Then too there were frequent educational offerings by the Lyceum and the Washington Literary Society, which at the time of Fessenden's arrival were featuring respectively P. T. Barnum's widely-acclaimed lecture on "The Art of Money-Getting" and Horace Greeley's considered views on "Questions of the Hour." But for Senator Fessenden there would be precious little time for such diversions during the ensuing years, and those few moments that could be spared from his Congressional duties he would prefer to devote to his twin passions of walking and caring for his garden.

By the time the 38th Congress opened its doors on December 7, 1863, the air of Washington had become heavy with politics. With the Union nominating convention scheduled to meet in Baltimore that coming June, speculation had already begun to run high as to whom the convention would or should choose as its presidential candidate.* All things equal, it might have been safely assumed that President Lincoln would be renominated, but widespread dissatisfaction within Republican ranks over Lincoln's apparently half-hearted policy toward the rebellion, a policy which would be pointed up by the issuance of his liberal amnesty proclamation soon after the convening of Congress, had brought forth talk of dropping the President in favor of a more spirited candidate. Thus by late autumn of 1863 much attention had come to be focused upon Secretary of the Treasury Salmon P. Chase, who was known from his past behavior to entertain vigorous and well-reasoned attitudes towards the prosecution of the war.

* For purposes of attracting the support of those elements of the Democratic party that favored vigorous prosecution of the war (the War Democrats), the Republican organization early in the war took on the name of the "Union Party." Although enticing a considerable number of War Democrats into its fold, the Union party was at all times under the control of its predominantly Republican membership.

As a favorite with many of Fessenden's colleagues, particularly those holding the more radical views on questions of how and why the war should be conducted, Secretary Chase appeared in the thinking of some party leaders to have a better than fair chance of capturing the June convention. But on this score Mr. Fessenden was not deceived. "Our great men are busy in trying to make themselves Prest.," he wrote home in mid-January. "Abe, however, has the inside track, and as things look now, his renomination and reelection are sure. My friend Chase is nowhere, but he doesn't see it." [2] Nor did Fessenden allow himself to become in any way a part of the "Chase boom" which reached its height with the appearance in early February of the "Pomeroy circular." To this petition, passed among members of Congress in behalf of Chase's candidacy by Senator S. C. Pomeroy of Kansas, Mr. Fessenden bluntly refused to give his support. He did, in fact, make no effort to conceal his contempt for the entire furtive affair, assuring "a certain politician" that "I had resolved to have nothing to do with the concern, and none of them need apply to me." [3]

By the beginning of March it was apparent that the Chase boom had failed to get off the ground. On the 12th of the month Fessenden, whose views on Lincoln had mellowed somewhat with the brightening military outlook, wrote to his son William in Portland: "Mr. Chase . . . has withdrawn, the wisest thing he ever did in his life, for he had not the first chance, and by withdrawing he cuts loose from entanglements, and stands erect in his Department. . . . If nothing happens Mr. Lincoln will walk over the course, and perhaps, all things considered, it is best he should do so." [4] Three days earlier the Senator from Maine had written to his father's old law partner, Thomas Deblois:

> It looks very much as if we were to have Lincoln for another term, if we can beat the copperheads. Perhaps this is quite as well as to try any new man. Whatever may be his failings, and he is not without them, the people have a strong faith in his honesty of purpose, and at a time when their endurance is so largely drawn upon, that is a great point. [5]

All this does not mean, however, that Fessenden had become completely reconciled to the Lincoln administration's prosecution of the

war. He reserved his right to criticize, a right which he exercised frequently during the long session. Shortly after Congress had assembled,
in fact, he saw fit to attack the Executive Department for its mis-
management of the draft. In a speech delivered on December 21 Fessenden declared that administration leaders had subverted the efficacy
of the Conscription Act of the preceding March by their too-liberal
policy of exemption and by the regrettable practice of continuing, and
even increasing bounties for volunteers. In so doing, the administration had, he maintained, disregarded the intention of Congress as expressed in its conscription legislation, with the result that recruiting
was now being handled in "a very clumsy manner." "I do not intend
to quarrel with them," Senator Fessenden asserted, "but I say that the
duty of the Government is in all cases to carry out the law as it is
made." [6] Writing to a relative a few days later, the Senator commented:

> My friend the Secretary of War was a good deal cut up about it,
> and complained to me of injustice. Perhaps my language was a little
> too strong, but the lesson was needed, and I trust it will do good.
> Mr S[tanton] said he wouldn't have minded it from any other man,
> but the country believed everything I said, and he should be re-
> garded as having wilfully violated the law.[7]

Along with other military legislation, a bill was introduced into the
Senate early in the session which called upon Congress to confer the
special rank of lieutenant-general upon U. S. Grant. At first Fessenden
was opposed to the measure and spoke out against it on the floor,
declaring that the provisions of the bill tended to encroach upon the
President's powers as commander-in-chief. But at the final reckoning
he and several of his colleagues acted against their better judgment
and voted in favor of the Grant bill, since they had been assured by
Secretary Stanton that only in this way could the Army of the Potomac
be vitalized.[8] Senator Fessenden was still not entirely convinced, however, that any great good would come out of this somewhat questionable procedure. "The best I can do is hope," he confessed to Pike, "for
my faith in the men who control and direct our affairs is less than I
could wish. Our weight will crush the rebellion and end the struggle
at some time—but when?" [9]

At about the same time, there came before the Senate a bill to raise the amount of pay given Negro soldiers to the level of that received by other Union troops. Within a month after the passage of the Second Confiscation Act in July, 1862, the Government had adopted the official policy of accepting the military enlistment of Negroes, and since that time a substantial number of them had joined the Union ranks. Despite the Negroes' new status as bona fide Union soldiers, however, certain discriminatory provisions were imposed upon them by the army and the federal government. Not the least of these was a rate of pay lower than that given their white comrades-in-arms, and it was to rectify this situation that the proposal was brought before Congress in early 1864 to establish a standard pay scale for all Union troops, regardless of color. To Fessenden this proposal seemed only fair. He had, in fact, for some time been in favor of such a move. When, however, it was suggested that the Negro pay raise be made retroactive, Senator Fessenden balked. As chairman of the finance committee he was only too familiar with the demands being placed upon the nation's economy, and he objected to adding to the strain by indulging in such unwarranted generosity. "I think we ought to be a little careful in our expenditures," he declared. "We must not consider that the Treasury can meet everything." [10] In Boston, William Lloyd Garrison, still crusading for his black friends, was noticeably displeased. To abolitionist Senator Henry Wilson of Massachusetts, who had sponsored the Negro pay measure, Garrison wrote: "I wish Senator Fessenden could understand that rectitude is good political economy; and to do the right thing always pays. He does not seem to have the blood of his venerable and liberty-loving father running in his veins. His petty calculation of the sum that will be necessary to pay back dues is worthy only of a trickster." [11]

Not long after the beginning of the session, a resolution was brought before the Upper House by Senator Wilson calling for the expulsion of a fellow member on the grounds that he had recently urged upon the Senate floor that "the people North ought to revolt against their war leaders and take matters into their own hands." [12] The offending Senator was Garrett Davis of Kentucky, probably the most interminable talker ever to sit in the United States Senate, and without doubt richly deserving of the "Garrulous Garrett" label that had been affixed to him by the Washington press. Despite many noble traits of character and an undeniable forensic talent, the diminutive Senator from Kentucky was, with his tireless tongue, an almost constant source of *ennui* and annoyance to his colleagues, and there was little disagreement among them that the Cincinnati *Commercial* had erred not at all in attributing to Davis the doubtful distinction of being "the greatest bore that ever lived."

As representative of a border state Davis had continually denied the Government's right to interfere with slavery, and his endless denunciations of what he considered to be a disregard of the Constitution on the part of the Republican party had long proved vexatious to many of his colleagues. Consequently, Davis' recent resolution urging the people to rise up against their leaders was seized upon by some of the Republican members as just cause for expelling the talkative trouble-maker from his Senate seat. To such action Fessenden was squarely opposed, however. In a speech that indicates something of his statesmanlike nature, Fessenden began by declaring that he saw no justification for the expulsion of Davis. He certainly didn't agree with Davis' views, but one man could not judge another's sentiments by his own, and on the floor of the Senate there should be room for all types of opinion, no matter how unpleasantly or interminably expressed. The Senate Chamber was in a sense a Liberty Hall in which each member could follow his own inclinations and taste. Of course, all this might at times prove rather severe upon the Senate, but the Senate was nonetheless obliged to submit. The last thing that he would want to have used as grounds for punishment, Fessenden asserted, was free and unlimited commentary upon the acts of the Government. A great deal depended upon the right of every member to express his disapproval of the conduct of affairs. It was a barrier against corruption. It should not be limited in any manner or degree. He considered Senator Davis to have been unjust in many of his remarks, but Senators who supported the administration should attempt to answer his charges rather than stifle them. "I support the Administration," declared Fessenden. "I uphold it . . . , and I expect to stand by it hereafter. But sir, if I cannot defend it against any attacks which the Senator from Kentucky or any other Senator on this floor may choose to make, then he must have the advantage of me and he should be allowed to go out to the country and obtain all the advantage he can on that account."

As for the Davis resolution itself, Fessenden could find nothing in it to merit even censure. He could, in fact, imagine a state of affairs which at some future time might compel him in his duty as a Senator to rise and say: "I, from this place, call on the people of the United States to resist this outrageous exercise of power," and he wished to retain the privilege of being able to do so. If there were to be censure in this case, let it be administered by public opinion, and not by the Senate. For if the practice were once commenced in Congress of submitting dissenting views to the approval of a heavy-handed majority, then the nation would soon find itself travelling a downward road.[13] On the day following Fessenden's speech Senator Wilson was permitted by the unanimous consent of his colleagues to withdraw his expulsion resolution, and "Garrulous Garrett" was left to continue his noisy membership in the United States Senate.

During the first session of the 38th Congress the problem of reconstruction became for the first time a subject of major legislative concern, and with the emergence of this new and complex problem the lines between the radical and conservative elements of the Republican party began to harden. Congressional attention to the matter was given special incentive by President Lincoln's amnesty proclamation on December 8, 1863. This decree extended what amounted to a standing offer of complete pardon to all those members of the Confederacy, save for a few exceptions, who would swear allegiance to the Constitution of the United States "and the Union of States thereunder." Growled a disgusted Fessenden: "Think of telling the rebels that they may fight as long as they can, and take a pardon when they have had enough of it." [14]

The proclamation further enunciated what has generally been referred to as "the Presidential plan of Reconstruction." According to the provisions of this plan, as soon as ten per cent of the voters of any insurrectionary state should submit to the amnesty oath and organize a state government which was republican in form and which prohibited the existence of slavery, the state would be considered eligible for recognition by the National Executive. The President was careful to add, however, that "whether members sent to Congress from any state shall be admitted to seats rests exclusively with the respective houses, and not to any extent with the Executive."

Fessenden's reaction to the President's proclamation was clearly revealed a few months later when he voted with the majority of his col-

leagues against admitting to Senate seats W. M. Fishback and Elisha
Baxter, who had been sent to Washington by what purported to be
the new state government of Arkansas. Since Arkansas was the first
state to have been "reconstructed" under the Presidential plan,* the
application of its representatives for admission to Congress set off a
long debate during which most of the major attitudes and points of
controversy in regard to the question of reconstruction were pre-
viewed. According to Fessenden's views, a state should give solidly
convincing evidence of its readiness to resume a loyal and otherwise
normal relationship with the Union. "It is not enough," he argued,
"that a small portion or even a considerable portion of that people
sustained by our military authority in the State declare themselves to
be a State." Furthermore, he felt that the entire matter should be
handled by Congress, rather than by the President. "I am of the
opinion, and have been for some time," he declared, "that the
question of reconstruction as it is called, the question of what is and
what is not a State entitled to be represented here, should properly be
settled by Congress, and cannot be settled by any other power but
Congress in any possible way." [15]

Senator Fessenden, then, was dedicated to the idea of Congressional
reconstruction, and favored more substantial evidence of remissness
on the part of the rebels than had been called for by Lincoln's ten
per cent plan. He was also in favor of abolishing slavery, provided it
could be done legally, and on April 8, 1864, he voted in favor of a
Constitutional amendment to that effect. He could not agree, though,
with the more radical of his colleagues who felt that Congress possessed at that time the Constitutional power to include the general
welfare of the Negro among the prerequisites for restoration of the
Southern states. Consequently, as the session wore on he found himself and many of his moderate friends drawing further away in sentiment from the opinions expressed by such members as Wade, Sumner,
and Chandler.

When on the next to the last day of the session (July 2), the Wade-
Davis bill, a Radical-sponsored plan for reconstruction, reached a
vote in the Senate, the fact became clear that a major division of

---

* Actually Louisiana had earlier fulfilled the President's requirements for recognition. Election difficulties in that state had, however, postponed its sending of
representatives to Congress.

opinion had arisen in Republican ranks. This bill, which in contrast
to Lincoln's lenient ten per cent plan prescribed severe conditions
for restoring the Southern states, provided in essence that reconstruction would not be undertaken in any insurrectionary state until
fifty per cent of its white male citizens had subscribed to the amnesty
oath. Governments would then be set up by the "loyal" people of the
state, that is, those who could swear that they had not voluntarily
borne arms against the United States. In addition the bill declared an
end to slavery in the seceded areas and in so doing alienated Fessenden
and many of his more moderate colleagues in the Senate. To these
men the thought of abolition was an attractive one, but they could not
overlook the fact that until such time as the proposed Constitutional
amendment then before Congress went into effect, Congress had no
power to interfere with the domestic institutions of the states. Although reluctant because of party considerations to oppose the Wade-
Davis measure outright, Senator Fessenden made little attempt to
conceal his hostility towards what he felt to be a dangerously radical
abuse of power, and on the day of the Senate vote on the bill he
absented himself from the roll call. In this he was joined by sixteen of
his moderate colleagues. A few days later, during a meeting with
President Lincoln, Fessenden commended the President for his pocket-
veto of the Wade-Davis bill, agreeing with Lincoln that the emancipation feature of the bill had given it an unconstitutional character. "I
even had my doubts," he told the President, "of the constitutional
efficacy of your decree of emancipation, in such cases where it has not
been carried into effect by the actual advance of the Army." [16]

During the spring and early summer of 1864, Senator Fessenden was
severely oppressed with the work required of him by the exigencies of
the nation's finances. On March 3 and June 30 two more loan bills,
authorizing Secretary Chase to borrow an additional $600,000,000,
were enacted into law; and to provide for the increase of revenue
needed to keep pace with the growing interest demands of the national debt, Congress was once again forced to revise the federal tax
program.

In mid-May Fessenden reported from his finance committee a
drastically amended version of the Internal Revenue Act of two years
before. This new tax bill, the most comprehensive that had yet been
devised by an American Congress, filled nearly two hundred and fifty

pages of fine print and embraced virtually everything from incomes and pianofortes to insurance agents and rivets. To its preparation and passage Fessenden was obliged to devote much of his attention during the long session, and letters written home by the Senator at this time tell of seemingly endless hours of fatigue and aggravation spent in behalf of the measure. Worked out in constant communication with Secretary Chase, the bill adhered rather closely to the framework of the earlier revenue act, but provided for a general, and in some instances an extreme, increase of rates. On the floor of the Senate the tax bill evoked long and spirited debate, and many attempts at amendment were made, some of them proving successful. Finally, however, in the late evening of June 6 the measure passed the Upper House in essentially the same form as it had been reported from committee. To a gratified Fessenden the new revenue bill represented something of a triumph, both for himself and for the nation—"a complete revision of the subject, largely increasing taxes in all directions." [17] His only regret was that a move of this sort had not been made long before, but "you must remember," he had reminded his friend Pike a few months earlier, "that it takes time to find out how much a people can bear, and in what way best to impose the burden." [18] Accompanying the passage of the Internal Revenue Bill was a substantial raise in customs duties, an act designed ostensibly to prevent European competition from profiting as a result of the increased taxes levied on American manufacturing. And it was largely due to these new twin measures of taxation, which as matters turned out bore most heavily upon the poorer classes, that the nation could by late July claim the unheard-of figure of one million dollars a day in Federal revenue.

In early June while Senator Fessenden was deeply immersed in Congressional affairs, not many miles away at the Union nominating convention in Baltimore events were unfolding which would have a profound effect upon his future career. With the renomination of Lincoln assured, the attention of the Baltimore delegates, and particularly of Fessenden back in Washington, focused upon the coming choice of the Union Party's Vice Presidential nominee. It was supposed by many that Hannibal Hamlin of Maine would again be nominated, a selection earnestly desired by Fessenden for the obvious reason that as Vice President, the popular Hamlin would remain out of political circulation for another four years. There were, however, powerful movements afoot which were destined to succeed in casting Hamlin adrift. The traditional account of the Vice Presidential nomination at Baltimore has it that President Lincoln, intent upon the choice of a War Democrat as his running-mate, personally intervened to secure the selection of Andrew Johnson of Tennessee; and it is of course true that the politically shrewd Lincoln, who had used his patronage powers to good advantage, was able to exert a powerful influence over the convention in behalf of Johnson. The fact is clear, however, that there were other forces at Baltimore which were working toward the same end, although for far different reasons.

During the late 1850's Charles Sumner and Pitt Fessenden had been friends, but all that was a long time ago, and in recent years the relationship between the two men had withered into an unattractive one. As early as the spring of 1862 Fessenden had confessed: "If I could cut the throats of about half a dozen Republican Senators . . . , Sumner would be the first victim, as by far the greatest fool in the lot." [19] The truth was that Fessenden had long since come to look upon Sumner as a nuisance and a sanctimonious bore whose hypocrisy and insolence were exceeded only by his astounding egotism. No one, in fact, in the entire Senate was more provoked by Sumner's endless and often pointless oratory, usually delivered with a "holier than thou" intonation, than was the Senator from Maine; and now that the handsome Boston charmer had identified himself with Radical views for which Fessenden could find little sympathy, clashes between the two men became frequent and apparently inevitable. Perhaps the bitterest of these occurred in the Senate Chamber during debate on the revised bank bill, only a few weeks before the opening of the Union Convention at Baltimore. On this occasion Fessenden, who was in charge of the 1864 bank bill then before the Senate, became exasperated with Sumner's irrelevant and abusive oratory and attacked his colleague savagely. When Sumner complained that he had been unfairly treated, the Senator from Maine continued his assault by accusing his antagonist of deliberately provoking arguments and then "whining" his way out of them. Well, Mr. Fessenden had stood enough. He did not intend to sit quietly by and allow himself to be "scalped" by this insufferable bore. "I must tomahawk him in self defense," he wrote home a few days later. "I would gladly let the dirty dog alone if I could, but to bear his insolence, and suffer his malignity to have full swing would only be to destroy myself." [20]

But the antipathy between the two Senators was far from a one-sided affair. For his part, the Radical Sumner had become increasingly exasperated with Fessenden over what he considered Fessenden's half-hearted attitude toward certain procedures affecting the conduct of the war, such as confiscation of enemy property, and especially toward the burgeoning problems of reconstruction. But above and beyond all that was the fact that Sumner had come to regard Senator Fessenden as his chief persecutor, and against his former friend he was known now to harbor the most unkindly of feelings. When, therefore, in early June of 1864 the Union nominating convention at Baltimore presented a situation which Sumner realized might be exploited in such a way as to rid himself once and for all of his great antagonist, the Massachusetts Senator lost little time in putting his influence to work.

With Fessenden's term due to expire in March of the following year, how pleasantly convenient it would prove for Sumner if Hannibal Hamlin should suddenly find himself politically unemployed. Obviously Hamlin would declare himself a candidate for the Senate seat then held by Fessenden, and in view of his great popularity in Augusta, Hamlin would, in Sumner's estimation, stand a strong chance of defeating Fessenden in the Maine Legislature. It behooved Sumner, then, to see to it that the Vice President would be dropped from the Lincoln ticket, and to accomplish this end he betook himself to Baltimore to exert his personal influence over the members of the Massachusetts delegation. That the prophet was not without honor among his own people is indicated by the following account related to Hamlin's son by a member of the Massachusetts delegation a few days after the convention had adjourned:

Charles Sumner and the Massachusetts delegation desired another candidate. They were not opposed to Mr. Hamlin for personal reasons. Mr. Sumner desired to prevent William Pitt Fessenden from returning to the Senate. He thought that the best way to accomplish this would be to nominate a new man for Vice-President, because he thought that Mr. Hamlin would be returned by the people of Maine to the Senate, and Mr. Fessenden would be retired to private life. . . . The Massachusetts men had no objection to Mr. Hamlin on any personal score, but acted in accordance with Mr. Sumner's desires and wishes.[21]

According to Fessenden's fellow Senator from Maine, Lot M. Morrill, who was on the scene in Baltimore to support Vice President Hamlin, once the fact became known that Massachusetts would not stand behind the New England candidate, state after state broke away from the Hamlin ranks. "It was their [Massachusetts'] efforts and representations that New England was not for you that broke up New York . . . ," Morrill explained to Hamlin, "so . . . New Jersey, Maryland, and others." [22] Writing to Fessenden a week later, Simon Cameron, who had headed the Pennsylvania delegation at Baltimore, told much the same story: "I strove hard to renominate Hamlin," he declared, "as well for his own sake as for yours, but failed only because New England, especially Massachusetts, did not adhere to him." [23]

So it was that Fessenden's feud with Charles Sumner of Massachusetts had its repercussions at the Union nominating convention in Baltimore, and doubtless had much to do with the selection of Andrew Johnson as Lincoln's running-mate. And for the devotees of that fascinating school of historical "might have beens," the questions are always posed: Might matters have worked out differently at Baltimore, had the relationship between the two New England Senators been more cordial? And if so, how differently would have gone the trend of affairs, had Hannibal Hamlin rather than Johnson been given the second spot in 1864 and ultimately ascended to the presidency on the death of Lincoln?

X V

Secretary of the Treasury

As THE long session of the 38th Congress drew to a close, Fessenden looked forward with great impatience to his return to Portland. The past few months had been especially trying for him. His health had taken a turn for the worse in early March, and since that time the burden of his Congressional duties had become increasingly difficult to bear. Furthermore, he had grown despondent over the condition of his son Frank, who had in late April of that year lost a leg in the disastrous Red River campaign and was reported to be making a slow recovery. And then there was the intolerable heat of the Capital which wore heavily upon him. Senator Fessenden felt desperately the need of relief. "I hope to get home in all events next week," he wrote to his son William on the first of July. "Indeed I can't hold out much longer, for I was never so near utter exhaustion." [1]

For Fessenden, however, there was to be little rest during the succeeding months. On the morning of June 30th, Secretary Chase had gone to the Capitol to confer with Senator Fessenden, and as the two men discussed the need for increased taxation, a messenger appeared at the door of the Senator's office. Fessenden spoke privately with the messenger for a moment and then returned to his desk. "Have you resigned?" he asked Chase. "I am called to the Senate and told that the President has sent in the nomination of your successor." [2] Thus did Secretary Chase learn that his resignation, so often tendered during the past two years, had finally been accepted by the President. "He is either determined to annoy me," Lincoln had concluded, "or that I shall pat him on the shoulder and coax him to stay. I don't think I ought to do it. I will not do it. I will take him at his word." [3]

Immediately after accepting Chase's resignation, the President appointed to the Treasury post the Youngstown capitalist David Tod, prominent War Democrat and ex-governor of Ohio. Fortunately for the nation, however, Tod, totally inexperienced in matters of government finance, refused the position on grounds of ill health. At this point Senator Fessenden paid a personal visit to Lincoln to urge the appointment of his friend Hugh McCulloch, then Comptroller of the Currency, but the President declared he had already decided upon the man for the job, and that man was Fessenden himself. At that very moment, in fact, the Senator's name was on its way to the Senate for confirmation.

Mr. Fessenden sprang to his feet. "You must withdraw it," he exclaimed. "I cannot accept."

"If you decline it," answered the President, "you must do it in open day, for I shall not recall the nomination." [4]

The decision now confronting Senator Fessenden was a momentous one both for himself and for the nation. Upon leaving the White House he returned to the Senate Chamber where he learned that his appointment had been unanimously confirmed by his colleagues. He then went directly to his house on F Street and wrote out a letter to the President declining to accept the position. "My reasons were," he explained later to a friend, "that I did not wish to leave the Senate, had no fancy for an executive office, and considered myself physically unable to discharge its duties. I was utterly exhausted by hard work and rest was absolutely essential. In fact, I had no idea I could continue in office for a month if I accepted it." [5] Before he had completed the letter, Fessenden was visited by delegations from the House, urging him to accept, and within the course of the evening "almost every member of the Senate" came to express the same wish. To find temporary escape from his colleagues, Fessenden left his house for a time shortly before supper and called upon his friend Chase who lived only a block away on E Street. There too he met with pleas that he take over the Treasury post. According to Chase, the job wouldn't be nearly so demanding as Fessenden supposed. The machinery was already set up, and all that would be required was a skillful and experienced hand to keep it running.

Could he count on Chase for help and advice, Senator Fessenden asked. Chase assured him that he could, and the two men then rode in Chase's carriage to the Capitol where Fessenden got out and entered the Senate wing to ponder the matter for a time in the quiet of his office before returning home.

By ten o'clock that evening Senator Fessenden had determined not to take the Treasury position, and he once again set out for the White House, this time carrying with him his letter of refusal which he planned to present to the President. "I have reached a point," the letter stated, "where my physical powers, already much impaired, can only be restored and sustained by a period of absolute rest, [and] I feel that to undertake, at this time, the duties and responsibilities of an office involving labor and interests so vast, would be an act of folly on my part, and certain to result in speedy failure." [6] Since President Lincoln had retired, however, the Senator was forced to return on the following morning (July 2). "I told him that I had a letter for him which I deemed it most respectful to present in person," Fessenden later wrote to a friend in telling of his early morning visit with Lincoln. "He said that if it was a letter declining to accept the Treasury, he would not receive it." [7]

Not long after this interview with the President, an urged, cajoled, and flattered Mr. Fessenden, severely set upon by fears that to do otherwise would be to expose his country to grave danger, finally and most reluctantly decided to accept the Treasury portfolio. "It may result in the destruction of all the reputation I have gained," he remarked to his friend Grimes. "Be it so, I owe that to my country as well as my life." If only he weren't so constantly bothered by that confounded aching in his head, "but I do not feel like complaining when I think of Frank's amputated limb. . . ." [8]

The news of Fessenden's acceptance met with almost universal approval. In national interest it rivalled even the report of the sinking of the Confederate cruiser *Alabama,* which reached the country early the following week. "This is a bright day," wrote Hamilton Fish to the new Secretary, "at the same time your acceptance of the Treasury department, and the destruction of the 'Alabama,' both causes of thankfulness. . . . My good friend, you have an arduous duty before you, but if any man can, you can accomplish what the nation so much needs." [9] In the Northern press praise for Fessenden ran high. "A Senator who never left his post," remarked the Washington *Chronicle,* "never made a speech without a purpose, and always sharp, clear, brief in debate . . . a positive, daring statesman . . . of purity and whiteness." [10] "Unquestionably the fittest man in his party for that high trust," echoed Manton Marble's Democratic and somewhat suspect New York *World*.[11] And on Wall Street over the weekend following Fessenden's Friday appointment, long-term Government bonds, which had been hovering near par, jumped as much as two and a half points.

The situation facing the Treasury when Fessenden took office on July 5 was anything but an encouraging one. The national debt then stood at one and three-quarters billions of dollars, much of it in green-backs, certificates of indebtedness, and other types of short-term Government paper which passed more or less freely as currency and kept values in an unsettled state. Gold in terms of paper was selling at 270, which meant that $4000 in gold would purchase more than $10,000 of United States Government bonds. Since most of these bonds bore six per cent interest in specie, it figured that the Treasury was actually paying out in real value approximately sixteen per cent interest annually on money borrowed on its long-term securities, a practice which had a dangerously inflating effect upon the nation's paper. "The business of the country is all but fatally deranged," complained Greeley's *Tribune* in early July. "All nominal values are so inflated and unsettled that no one knows what to ask nor how to trade; the Laboring Class are stinted in spite of ample work and large wages; and there is danger of Social Convulsion. . . ." [12]

The major question confronting Fessenden was how to raise an estimated $800,000,000 for the coming fiscal year, nearly $100,000,000 of which was needed immediately to accommodate delayed accounts and requisitions. Since little more than $300,000,000 was expected through revenue channels, and since Fessenden opposed the further issuance of legal tender, the problem became, then, one of borrowing an additional half-billion dollars on Government securities and short-term notes. Because of his feeling that further emissions of short-term notes would greatly accelerate the inflationary trend, Fessenden had previously tended to favor the sale of long-term securities as the lesser of two evils, but by the time of his accession to the Cabinet he had concluded that at the current market price the Government could no longer afford to sell its gold-bearing bonds in return for inflated paper. The point was rapidly being reached, in fact, at which the aggregate interest on these bonds would exceed the national intake of specie. Therefore, during his brief administration Fessenden would rely principally upon the sale of the three-year "seven-thirties," which bore seven and three-tenths per cent interest payable in paper and which had already given proof of their popularity during the administration of his predecessor.

On July 9, while Confederate General Jubal Early was staging his daring raid against Washington, Secretary Fessenden travelled to New York to attempt to borrow from the bankers of that city at least $50,-000,000 with which to meet the most urgent of those immediate demands then facing the Treasury. "The New York people have pressed me so hard to place myself in this unhappy condition," he wrote to his assistant, George Harrington, "that they must now show their willingness to sustain me, or rather help me carry the load." [13] But from the banks Secretary Fessenden was able to extract nothing better than a promise of future credit, and a few days later he returned empty-handed to Washington where, in order to meet the present demands upon the Treasury, he was forced to authorize a limited release of "ten-forty" gold-bearing bonds left over from Chase's administration.*

Immediately after his unsuccessful trip to New York, Fessenden began preparations for a large-scale seven-thirty loan. To advise him in this venture he sent for Jay Cooke, Philadelphia financier who had previously acted with great success in marketing notes and securities for Chase, until Congressional protests against Cooke's intimate relationship with the United States Treasury had caused him to be dropped by the former Secretary. Arriving from Philadelphia on July 21, the young banker visited with Fessenden at the Treasury building and volunteered his views upon how the coming loan should be conducted. According to Cooke, the secret of a successful loan, provided the terms were attractive, was to channel the loan through agents, to whom the Government should "offer a commission large enough to induce active exertions. . . ." The various branches of the national banking system might serve as suitable agents for handling distribution of the seven-thirties, or, Cooke assured Fessenden, the far-reaching firm of Jay Cooke and Company could in rapid order

* To give greater appeal to the ten-forties, Fessenden restored their interest rate to six per cent. Only a few months before, Chase had caused a near cessation of sales on these bonds by reducing their interest to five per cent.

dispose of the loan at small cost to the Government. This last suggestion was for Secretary Fessenden a tempting one. Cooke's system of outlets was certainly extensive, one of the largest in the country. His methods were known to be daring, and yet sound. His flair for publicity was almost unique, and his devotion to the Government was unquestioned by those who knew him. There was little doubt that he could make good his claims. Still, Fessenden was reluctant to bring down upon himself and his department the same sort of criticism that had been levelled at Chase, charges that the Treasury had dealt in favoritism in regard to its relationship with Cooke. He therefore decided, much to Cooke's disgust, to avoid any direct connection with the Philadelphia financier and to adopt the alternative policy of distributing the seven-thirties through the national banking system. To Chase's way of thinking Fessenden was making a grave error. "I tried all the modes and the single responsible general agency plan was the best," the former Secretary declared. "I hoped to find Department supervision with national bank agencies as good but it was not, and I had made up my mind to return to the plan which had proved so successful. . . . Mr. Fessenden would also I believe, if he were willing to encounter the misrepresentations of malevolence." [14]

Secretary Fessenden's seven-thirty loan had its official opening on August 15, shortly before the Secretary's return to Washington from a three-week vacation in Maine, where he had gone for a desperately needed rest. Advanced sales had begun earlier in the month, however, amidst much publicity by the Department and promotional cooperation on the part of the Northern press. "We call earnestly for immediate and energetic response to Mr. Fessenden's noble appeal," exclaimed the *New York Tribune:*

> We ask every loyal man and woman to answer promptly this question: How much can I lend the Government without injustice to my creditors or my family . . . ? Patriots! your bleeding country calls loudly for your aid . . . ! Do not stop with half. Lend your country every dollar you can spare, and sell or collect freely in order that you may spare the more.[15]

The initial response to the loan was encouraging. "All goes smoothly," Assistant Secretary George Harrington wrote on August

6 to the vacationing Fessenden. "The subscriptions yesterday were
$1,457,600, and today they were $926,850." [16] A week later, however,
it was apparent to Fessenden that the loan drive had lost much of
its momentum and was showing alarming signs of stalling. "We are
not meeting with the hoped for success with regard to the loan," he
wrote to Harrington, "and I am afraid we shall find ourselves in
trouble unless General Grant can help us." [17] By August 17 total sales
of the seven-thirties amounted to nearly $17,000,000, but daily receipts
were growing progressively smaller. "I am at my wits' end, as well as
at the bottom of my purse," Fessenden wrote home in late August.
"Gen. Grant does not seem to get ahead much, but if the people
hold out we are safe. . . . All will depend very much on the results
of the elections. If we carry them the war is substantially over. If not,
all is over with us." [18] By the final week of September, after nearly
two months of actual sales, only slightly more than one-fifth of the
$200,000,000 seven-thirty loan authorized by the Act of June 30, 1864,
had been subscribed to. And during October Secretary Fessenden was
frequently forced to report sales of no more than $300,000 a day.

Confronted by the unpleasant fact that the seven-thirties were not
moving, Fessenden looked about him during the late summer and
early autumn of 1864 for some other method of raising urgently
needed funds. For a time he thought seriously of sending Chase abroad
to sound out European financiers in regard to the possibilities of a
foreign loan. This project failed to progress beyond the planning
stage, however, largely because of widespread popular opposition to
the idea. As the *New York Tribune* had remarked somewhat earlier,
it was hardly good business for Americans to encourage European capi-
talists to buy "the bonds of your Government—your obligations to
pay so much gold—for about forty cents on the dollar, though they
will be worth par directly after peace." [19]

Secretary Fessenden then turned reluctantly to what appeared to
be his only other resource—the further emission of gold-bearing bonds.
Under the terms of the Act of June 30, 1864, the same which had provided for Fessenden's seven-thirty loan, the Secretary was permitted
to issue up to $200,000,000 in Government long-term securities, and on
October 1 he availed himself of this authority by releasing $40,000,000
of the once-popular "five-twenty" bonds. Here too, however, the results soon proved disappointing. The market had become glutted with

Government securities of one sort or another, so much so, according to Cooke, that bankers could barely keep track of them and the people at large were constantly bewildered. Then too, there was throughout the North a noticeable anxiety over the coming presidential election, coupled with a reluctance on the part of the banks and people alike to invest more heavily in the war until the results of the November voting could be known.

For Fessenden these days immediately preceding the election were the darkest. Government securities, which had stood as high as 104 at the time of his accession to the Treasury, had dropped to 100½, while gold, which had sold for 193 only six weeks before, had risen to 249½. The national debt had increased to over two billion dollars, nearly $300,000,000 more than when Fessenden had taken office four months earlier, and on the Secretary's desk in the Treasury Department lay suspended requisitions totaling to approximately $130,000,000. But just as Secretary Fessenden had about concluded that the financial situation was a hopeless one, the affairs of his department took a sudden and happy turn, with the result that by the time Congress reconvened on December 5, the entire $40,000,000 issue of five-twenties had been disposed of by the Treasury at an average of approximately one per cent above par.[20]

This welcome shift can be explained to a large degree by the reelection of President Lincoln during the second week of November, and the consequent assuaging of political doubts. But the appearance of Jay Cooke on Mr. Fessenden's Treasury team must also be reckoned as a factor. Only a few days before the election the Philadelphia banker was invited to visit the Treasury Department for consultation with the Secretary. There he found Fessenden in a much harassed frame of mind. Requisitions were mounting, the Secretary explained, and he had no funds with which to meet them. He had recently travelled to New York in an attempt to sell a $10,000,000 lot of five-twenties, but he had failed to get an acceptable offer from the banks.

"What do you want for them?" Cooke asked.

"I want par, and your commission will be the accrued interest," Fessenden answered.

"I will take them myself," the banker replied. "I will take three millions at once, and you can give me an option on the rest of the ten millions, which I will close after a visit to New York."[21]

This bold move by the head of the famed House of Cooke, followed closely by the news of Lincoln's re-election, furnished the needed impetus for the Secretary's bond drive, and from that moment on there would be little question as to the success of Fessenden's five-twenties. Thus did Secretary Fessenden survive the darkest hour of his administration, and with money once more entering the Treasury, and victory over the Confederacy now all but assured, the prospects for national finances became infinitely brighter.

The seven-thirty notes continued to move slowly, however, and by mid-November Fessenden had begun to think somewhat of following Chase's advice and employing Cooke as general distributing agent for the loan. But the Secretary still hesitated to adopt the single agency system which had met with so much prior disapproval from Congress, and in early December he decided to give the national banks one final opportunity to take up the seven-thirty loan. In a Treasury Department Circular sent out on December 13 to the various member branches of the national banking system, the Secretary declared:

> Sir: Desiring to avoid any further issue of bonds, the interest of which is payable in coin, or any further increase of paper circulation, I ask your attention to the seven three-tenths notes now offered to the public. It is believed that these notes present advantages which should recommend them to all who have money to invest. . . . It is only necessary that people should understand the advantages offered by this class of securities to insure sales in sufficient daily amounts to meet the current demands of the Treasury.

Fessenden then expressed his disappointment over the fact that the member banks had thus far responded very poorly to the seven-thirty loan. He confessed that he had expected the banks to jump at the offer, since they were connected with the Government, and since liberal commissions had been allowed. This had not been the case, however, and the Secretary declared that he was now thinking in terms of some other means of outlet. But before turning elsewhere he wished to give the national banks one more chance, "in the hope that they will undertake this most necessary work with a spirit and energy which will demonstrate that the recognized fiscal agents of the government may at all times be relied on for adequate exertions to procure the means necessary to its daily wants." [22]

Despite Secretary Fessenden's appeal, the progress of the loan during the ensuing month continued to be disappointing. By January 9, 1865, after more than five months of sales, total receipts from the seven-thirties had reached only $115,000,000, and of this amount $20,000,000 had gone directly to soldiers who had agreed to accept the notes as pay in place of cash. Consequently on January 28 Fessenden, whose own political future had been assured two weeks earlier by his re-election to the United States Senate, put aside his fears of criticism and appointed Jay Cooke general agent of the Treasury Department for disposing of Government loans. "My bargain with Cooke and Co.," Fessenden later explained to his successor Hugh McCulloch, "was ¾ of 1 per cent [commission] on the first fifty millions, ⅝ on the second, and the rest was to be at such rate as I might fix. It was my intention to reduce after the first hundred millions, unless there were good reasons to the contrary." [23] On the same day Secretary Fessenden's Department was given authority by Congress to issue an additional $100,000,000 in seven-thirty notes.

Cooke immediately made the sales ring. On February 4, only four days after the banker had begun his operations, Fessenden declared himself highly gratified. "We begin to feel the new agency already," he remarked happily.[24] Two weeks later the Secretary was, according to Cooke's partner-brother Henry, "delighted, but couldn't believe the subscriptions were so large. . . . He said he wasn't afraid now that there would be any lack of money to pay off the army." [25] In the final week of February the far-flung House of Cooke, with its many outlets and enterprising methods of advertising, reported sales of over $35,000,000—nearly one-third as much as Fessenden had managed to sell through the national banking system during the first five months of the loan. And for Secretary Fessenden the principal problem had suddenly become one of keeping Cooke supplied with this all-important paper merchandise. Meanwhile not far away in the hard-pressed Confederate capital, the Richmond *Examiner* expressed its sullen amazement at the progress of the seven-thirty loan under the direction of "an eccentric financier named Jaye [sic] Cooke." "The efforts of the Yankees to sustain this explosive and inflated paper system, have so far been marked by great ingenuity, resolution and success," commented the *Examiner*. "Whether they will succeed in conquering the South, depends in a great degree upon their continued success in upholding this paper system." [26]

On March 3, 1865, Secretary Fessenden provided further grist for Jay Cooke's mill by obtaining from Congress authorization to issue an additional $600,000,000 in seven-thirty notes. Later that same day Fessenden stepped down from the Treasury post in favor of his Comptroller of the Currency Hugh McCulloch. When the position had first been thrust upon him, Fessenden had agreed to remain in the Treasury only so long as he deemed his leadership essential to the welfare of the Department and the country, and now he felt that the time had arrived when his services could safely be dispensed with. Furthermore, on the following day his new term in the United States Senate would officially begin, and in view of his often-expressed feelings against plural office-holding he could not permit himself to continue in the Treasury beyond the midnight deadline of March 3. Thus, during the final hours of President Lincoln's first administration Secretary Fessenden called together his various bureau chiefs to bid them his official farewell. To them he declared:

> With regard to my daily intercourse with you, gentlemen, I can only say, in my opinion, however we may be placed, relatively, either in the Department or elsewhere, no man in this country is above the rank of gentleman, and every man who honorably and conscientiously performs his duty is entitled to be treated as such. I have regarded the humblest clerk in this office, so long as he discharged his duty honestly and faithfully, as my equal, and entitled not only to my protection, but to equal rights with myself.[27]

When Fessenden left the Treasury on March 3, 1865, after only eight months in office, he could look back with some gratification upon the quality of leadership he had provided during his brief tenure. True, his program and his accomplishments had been in no way spectacular. He had in fact for the most part adhered closely to the pattern set by his solemn predecessor. But he had served diligently and well, not only in pursuing his principal task of raising and disbursing funds for the Union war machine, but also in meeting the perplexing and time-consuming responsibilities involved in such matters as overseeing captured Confederate property and providing for the purchase of precious cotton brought out of the South. He had, moreover, done much to clean up the corruption and inefficiency that had plagued the Treasury during the regime of Secretary Chase, and when he stepped down from his post he was able to turn over to McCulloch a noticeably improved Department, insofar as both personnel and procedure were concerned.* From Greeley's *Tribune,* which considered Fessenden's administration "not brilliant, [but] eminently faithful and upright," the retiring Secretary received no end of praise:

A picture of the man—unassuming, conscientious, just, wise, democratic. There is not a bit of nonsense in him, official or personal, and no assimilation of humbug or folly in any form. It is these qualities of simplicity and integrity that have saved his administration of the Treasury in the most critical epoch of our Finances, and saved the country from new systems and untried experiments. A vain or a weak man would not have been content to run the machine as he found it. He would inevitably have sought financial instead of administrative reputation out of his place, and inevitably have afflicted the nation. . . . Mr. Fessenden can well afford to let his fame as Secretary of the Treasury rest upon his wise and successful raising of money to carry the war through. . . . A just History of the war or the Union will give him a place beside the great Generals who have won the Union victories.[28]

Less exuberant but not dissatisfied with his performance as Secretary of the Treasury was Fessenden himself. Thinking back on it all a year later, he wrote to George Harrington who had served so loyally and well as his Assistant: "I shouldn't be surprised if it is found out some day that we did not manage very badly, considering the difficulties we had to encounter." [29]

* Remarked Charles Dana of the Treasury situation at the time of Fessenden's accession: "Of all the eminent men of my acquaintance, no one has ever been so unlucky in appointments as Mr. Chase. Himself a man of strict honesty, he has succeeded in putting into places of importance, some of the biggest scamps and most desperate fools that the country has ever produced. It will be a long while, and will require a great deal of hard work and courage before Fessenden gets them all cleaned out." Dana to Pike, July 10, 1864, in Pike Papers (Calais). For examples of Fessenden's reforms see: Treasury Department Circular, November 15, 1864, in *Circulars to Collectors and Others, 1861–69* (bound collection), in Treasury Department Records (National Archives); and, Fessenden to Lucien Draper, September 27, 1864, in Fessenden Letterbook (Library of Congress).

Chairman of the Joint Committee

WHILE HE was busy caring for the affairs of the United States Treasury, Fessenden watched with some misgivings the trend of politics in his home state. As Sumner had so clearly foreseen a few months before, Hannibal Hamlin had determined, soon after his convention defeat by Johnson, to seek reelection to the United States Senate at the first opportunity. Such an opportunity was scheduled to present itself in early January of 1865 when the Republican-controlled Maine Legislature would decide upon a successor to Nathan A. Farwell of Rockland, a pro-Hamlin nonentity who was then filling out the final few weeks of Fessenden's unexpired term. Since it was generally known that Fessenden himself desired to leave the Treasury and return to his seat in the Senate, the coming intra-party contest promised to be one of intense interest and speculation, in which for the first time the two most powerful figures in Maine politics would square off against one another. "He [Fessenden] has a strong competitor in Mr. Hamlin," wrote Charles Dana to Pike in mid-December of 1864:

> . . . and the politicians of Maine seem to think that it is more for the advantage of the state, to have one prominent citizen at the head of the Treasury Department and two others in the Senate, than to have one of the three at home doing nothing. Still, Pitt, as you know, is a shrewd politician who has always kept a sharp look for his own interest, and I should not be surprised if he were to beat Hamlin after all.[1]

Led by young Congressman James Blaine, who thought he saw a winner in the swarthy Hannibal, the Hamlin forces at first hoped to avoid a head-on clash with a man of Fessenden's following. They therefore endeavored to dissuade the Secretary of the Treasury from returning to the Senate by dangling other temptations before him. Since it was apparent that Fessenden had no desire to continue at his Treasury post, a movement was begun to have him elevated to the Chief-Justiceship, recently left vacant by the death of the aged Roger Taney. In October Blaine wrote to Hamlin:

> I had anticipated the "confidential" part of your note in regard to the Chief Justice-ship so far as to write Fessenden himself, pricking his ambition for the place and suggesting it as by far the most desirable capstone in his political edifice. I will see [Senator] Morrill and unite with him in a letter to the President. I shall have Cong.'s concurrence in the communication. . . . If Fessenden *desires* the place, he can get it. The point is to induce him to seek it. Regard all this as private.[2]

Fessenden would have none of it, however. As a lawyer he was naturally attracted to the position, but, as he remarked to Senator Browning at the time, the President had earlier mentioned to him that Chase was being considered as Taney's successor. "Mr. Fessenden added that he had communicated this conversation to Mr. Chase as his friend," noted Browning in his diary, "that he was satisfied Mr. Chase would accept, and that he could not now, honorably consent that any movement should be made in his behalf." [3]

During the following weeks similar attempts were made to side-track Fessenden, but all with the same negative result. As the Secretary explained to his Maine friend Israel Washburn in late December, only a few days before the convening of the Maine Legislature:

> My very able successor, Mr. Farwell, is so devoted to my interests that he would undoubtedly desire me to remain Secretary of the Treasury. Failing that, he would like to have me go to France, and has offered me his aid and influence for that eminent position. Failing both these, he would undoubtedly be willing that I should go to the Devil, and give me a seat in the Cabinet there, *provided* I will get out of Hamlin's way for the Senate. . . . At any rate, the question is one which requires my concurrence. My wishes are for my old place, and none other, as my friends very well know.[4]

Despite all indications of a close contest and possible defeat at the hands of the popular Hamlin, Secretary Fessenden refused to seek political support by dealing in promises or bargains of any sort. "As to the future," he pointed out to the politically powerful C. L. Gilman of Brunswick, "I shall endeavor to act as becomes a Senator, judging every case upon its merits, and trying to render justice to all men. If Mr. Jewett, or any body else, expects me to say more, or to pledge myself beforehand to any particular course of action, he will be disappointed." [5] Nor would Secretary Fessenden agree to leave his Treasury post to campaign for re-election. "I am not coming home until after March 20th," he wrote to Washburn in November:

My presence here is necessary. I have not a moment to spare, and must remain. I *will not* go home to beg for a new term. My friends must see to that, if they will, and I have no doubt they will do all they honorably can. More I could not ask or wish. If the Legislature think Mr. Hamlin *must* have any place he asks for, in consideration of his . . . ability and the poor reward he has had, so be it. I must be resigned. If the Whigs of old think the old Democrats must have everything, let it be so. If the younger men of the state think Hamlin and his crew must rule, it is their business. For my own part I think him a very ordinary affair, at best, and that he should not have the place anyhow. But that is not my business.[6]

Early in the following month he replied in a similar vein to another of his political backers who had urged him to return home for at least a brief period before the Legislature convened. "Every moment," Fessenden wrote, "is occupied with the cares and duties of my present office. They cannot be neglected for the sake of looking after an election to the Senate. This is not, perhaps, the surest road to success, but it meets, at any rate, my own approval." [7]

On January 5, 1865, William Pitt Fessenden of Portland was renominated by an overwhelming vote of his party in the Augusta Legislature. Six days later his election followed as a matter of form. According to Fessenden's Maine friend Nelson Dingley, who had labored diligently for Senator Fessenden's re-election, the Hamlin forces had managed to present a deceptive show of strength, principally because of shrewd political maneuvering on the part of Blaine and others. But the Legislature was more impressed by the almost solid support given Fessenden by the people, and when the time for voting arrived, the Hamlin movement suddenly collapsed under its own ill-supported weight. Perhaps it was true, as a long-time political colleague of Senator Fessenden remarked at the time of the election, that the people of Maine had "a great measure of pride in their senior senator." [8] Understandably Fessenden was well-pleased. To the members of the Maine Legislature he wrote:

I am gratified, Gentlemen, for the honor conferred, and more for the evidence it affords that the State I have been proud to represent in the legislative councils of the nation is well satisfied with my endeavors, in executing the trust committed to my care, to protect its interests, and uphold its dignity. . . .

I will venture to express the hope that hereafter, as heretofore, no act of mine will tarnish the lustre which their patriotism and devotion to the Union, and to freedom, have won for the people we are so proud to serve.[9]

Following his resignation from the Treasury in March of 1865, Fessenden went almost immediately to his home in Portland where he remained with few interruptions until his return to Washington in early December. During that time events of great significance were transpiring on the national scene. With the assassination of President Lincoln only a few days after Lee's surrender to Grant at Appomattox, Andrew Johnson of Tennessee ascended to the nation's first office. Determined to carry out his predecessor's policy of a generous and rapid restoration of the Southern states, Johnson issued on May 29 an amnesty edict which with some modification reiterated Lincoln's liberal pardon terms of a year and a half before. At the same time the new President revealed his intended program of reconstruction in a proclamation appointing W. W. Holden provisional governor of North Carolina. According to the President, the "North Carolina plan" was to serve as a model for subsequent restoration through all other areas of the South. In essence it provided that under the guiding hand of the provisional governor the "loyal" people of each state (i.e., those who had taken the amnesty oath) should elect a Convention for the purpose of altering the state's constitution in such a way as to render it conformable to the fact of Northern victory. It was expected, in a word, that ordinances of secession be annulled, that slavery be abolished, and that the Confederate war debt be repudiated. This much satisfactorily accomplished, state governments could then be set up, the provisional governors withdrawn in favor of elected successors, and representatives chosen to apply for admission to the national Legislature in Washington. No insistence was made in the President's proclamation that the new constitutions extend voting rights to the Negro. Suffrage was in fact, declared Johnson, a matter traditionally and constitutionally belonging within the realm of state jurisdiction—all of which meant that once the new machinery of government had been erected, the recently insurrectionary states were to be left more or less free to decide upon their own qualifications for voting and office-holding.

From afar Senator Fessenden and many of his Republican colleagues watched the progress of the President's plan with misgivings. Already upset by Johnson's failure to call Congress into special session at this very critical time, Fessenden was further disturbed by the leniency of the President's program. "It strikes me," he wrote to his friend Grimes in mid-July, "that the rebels are having it all their own way." [10] Fessenden had hopes, however, that once Congress had assembled, Johnson could be brought around to a more reasonable policy by "time and firmness and prudence on our part. . . ." [11] Characteristically more outspoken in opposition to "this wretched experiment which the President is making" were the Radicals, who were particularly perturbed by Johnson's disregard of Negro suffrage, and were already making ominously angry noises. To his friend Ben Wade the Radical Charles Sumner wrote in early August:

> The course of the Presdt is so absurd that he cannot force it upon Congress. It must fail. . . . I think we shall be able through Congress to accomplish our purposes and save the country, but at what cost? Meanwhile the rebels are springing into their old life, and the copperheads also. This is the President's work. I do not understand the Presdt. . . . We must let him know frankly that we will not follow his fatal lead. [12]

By the time the 39th Congress convened in early December of 1865, the Southern states had completed the restoration of their civil governments in accordance with the terms of Johnson's reconstruction plan, and had sent their representatives to Washington to seek admission to the National Legislature. Thus, to Congressmen returning to their duties after an absence of nine months, a strange spectacle was presented. As one writer of obviously Northern sympathies noted:

> When Congress had adjourned in March, the war was still in progress, the Confederate armies were in the field, and battles were still to be fought. When in December members returned for the first session of the next Congress, they found there many of the most prominent leaders of the Rebellion coolly demanding the seats in the Senate and House of Representatives to which their various "sovereign peoples" had elected them. . . . In March they were attempting to overthrow the Constitution; in December they were prepared to construe it to its defenders. The power of the government which they had failed to overthrow they now claimed to share.[13]

It immediately became apparent, however, that Congress had its own ideas on reconstruction, and the more outspoken of its members made no secret of the fact that they resented Johnson's attempts to restore the Southern states without referring the matter to the legislative branch.

Soon after the beginning of the session the Republican majority in Congress turned its back on the President's work by refusing to admit the Southern representatives, and by announcing its intentions to devise its own program for restoring the Confederate states. "The way in which you have opened Congress and thrown down the gauntlet to the President's policy," exclaimed *Independent* editor Theodore Tilton to his friend Thaddeus Stevens, "has pleased our Radical friends hereabouts so thoroughly that we are all hearty, merry, and tumultuous with gratitude."[14] Less merry and tumultuous, however, was Senator Fessenden, who was fearful lest the "yelping of the dogs" lead to an open break between Congress and the President and drive Johnson irretrievably into the waiting arms of the Democrats.

With the Republican majority in Congress insisting that the formulation of reconstruction policy was a legislative function, and with

President Johnson and his supporters, most of them Democrats, holding fast to the North Carolina plan, relations between the two groups grew increasingly strained during the ensuing months. Convinced that a genuine effort at understanding by both sides could reconcile the differences, Fessenden at first acted the role of peacemaker. On a Sunday afternoon, not long after Congress had assembled, the Senator visited Johnson at the White House, where for several hours the two men discussed points of policy. At this time Fessenden emphasized the fact that Congress felt the need for more substantial guarantees than those offered by the President's plan. There was, for example, no provision in the President's program for the protection and welfare of the freedman, nor had any safeguards been erected against a return to power by those Southern leaders who had been largely responsible for bringing on the war. Fessenden maintained that Buchanan's conduct in permitting the rebellion to gain momentum had been infamous, but it would be even greater infamy to allow the insurrectionary states to return to the Union without first securing proper guarantees for their future behavior. How the President reacted to Fessenden's views is not known, but when the Senator left the White House late that afternoon, he was apparently satisfied that cooperation between Johnson and Congress was by no means out of the question.[15]

Throughout the winter months Fessenden continued his attempts to avoid an open break between the President and Congress. To his friend and former assistant in the Treasury, George Harrington, he wrote in early February:

> One of my duties (unwritten) is to keep the peace, if possible, between the President and Congress—a matter of some difficulty as you can well understand, when there are many desirous of making a break, and others who have not sense enough to hold their tongues, when talking will only do harm. The President's views differ with those of Congress somewhat as to the early admission of the States to their old relations. . . . We think it wise to move slowly and cautiously. This difference does not necessarily involve a quarrel, but Copperheads, ultra abolitionists and rowdies are very anxious to make it one. . . . From all I have seen, the President

desires, and means, to stand by those who elected him, and I am resolved to keep him there, if it can be done consistently with the best interests of the country, as I think it can.[16]

At the same time he wrote to a relative: "I have [been] busy in making our friends go to the President's levees, so as to have somebody about him besides Democrats and Secessionists, and I must go to one now myself, tho' I hate all those things mortally." [17] His efforts in the direction of conciliation were seriously hampered, however, by the intemperate behavior of many of his more Radical Congressional colleagues, particularly Stevens and Sumner, who had become especially vocal on the matter of Negro suffrage. Of the latter Senator Fessenden commented in mid-February: "Mr. Sumner, with his impracticable notions, his vanity, his hatred of the President, coupled with his powers over public opinion, is doing infinite harm. So are some others." [18]

As winter gave way to spring, the trend of affairs in Washington became such that even Fessenden and his moderate friends began to despair of maintaining any semblance of harmony between the President and the Republican majority in Congress. On February 19 Johnson vetoed a bill designed to provide more effective care for the Negro by extending the powers of the Freedmen's Bureau, a measure which had received the hearty support of Fessenden. In his veto message the President contended somewhat brashly that the 39th Congress was not a legal body since the eleven reconstructed states of the South were not represented. Three days later in an impromptu public address, the President delivered an ill-reasoned and unfortunate harangue in which he denounced Congressional opposition to restoration of the Southern states, and in which he labelled the Congressional joint committee on reconstruction "an irresponsible central directory."

On the following day Fessenden took the floor to reply at great length to the President's attack. The Senator's speech, which was mainly a defense of Congressional authority and views, drew loud applause from Johnson's foes. It was, according to Forney's Washington *Chronicle*, "admirable, marked with that close reasoning for which he is so justly distinguished." [19] But although forceful, in its over-all tone the speech was a dignified and moderate one in which Fessenden was careful to deal respectfully with the President, and to imply that his colleagues would be sensible to do likewise:

> He is the Chief Magistrate of this nation [Fessenden declared], and I treat him on all occasions as such. . . . I do not know how gentlemen around me may feel. They may be in a state of excitement and wrath which prevents their speaking and acting calmly. For me, I am too old a man not to be able to get over excitement of that sort, at any rate with one night's sleep, and we have all of us had that.[20]

President Johnson seemed bent upon contrariness, however, and when a month later the President again exercised his veto power, this time against Senator Lyman Trumbull's popular Civil Rights Bill, which purported to guarantee the rights of citizenship to the freedmen, Fessenden was forced to admit that his kind words and efforts at conciliation had amounted to little. "I have tried hard to save Johnson," he wrote to Pike, "but I am afraid he is beyond hope. His 'policy' has driven all sense and direction out of him. . . . As things are, we must hold on, and make an issue upon which we can go to the country. I do not intend to yield the fruits of the war, unless the people overrule me—and I don't think they will." [21] On the same day that Johnson's veto message on the Civil Rights Bill was read to the Senate, the Republican majority struck back by seizing upon a technicality to oust Democratic John P. Stockton of New Jersey from his Senate seat, an outrageously partisan and dishonorable business to which Fessenden lent his support. "It is all important now," he wrote to his son William in attempting to justify his resort to Machiavellianism, "that we shall have two-thirds in each branch." [22]

The first session of the 39th Congress was the busiest period of Senator Fessenden's public career. Reappointed to the chairmanship of the Finance Committee, he was called upon to devote considerable time and energy to the loan bill which passed the Senate on April 9, a measure designed to provide Secretary McCulloch with the wherewithal for paying off the seven-thirty issue coming due in 1867. Even more attention had to be given to the job of preparing the national finances for a return to peacetime conditions. To do this it was necessary for Fessenden to retrace his steps and reduce the volume of internal revenue which he had so laboriously built up during the war years. In one area of revenue, however, there was little or no serious thought of reduction among respectable Republicans: clearly the customs houses must be spared, for by this time most Republicans had come to look kindly upon the principle and practice of tariff protection. In fact during June and early July, Senator Fessenden was hard at work on a new tariff bill which proposed a general increase in the existing rates. "I am now at full tilt on the Tax [tariff] bill, which embraces only about 230 pages," he wrote to a relative during the second week of June. "I hope to finish it up and report it . . . next week, having had a few hours leisure today." [23] On the projected tariff revisions, however, Senator Fessenden's labor went for naught, for by early July it was apparent that the measure could not pass the House. "I shall not be sorry," remarked Fessenden, "for it is a bad bill, and I cannot agree to it without much alteration and revision." [24]

But for Fessenden, by far the most important and demanding duties of the session were those arising from the question of reconstruction. Shortly after Congress had convened he was named to head the fifteen-man joint committee which had been set up by Congress to study the problems involved in restoring the Southern states, and to determine a suitable course of action. Although gratified by the tribute paid him by his colleagues, Fessenden was at first reluctant to accept this great new responsibility because of the condition of his health and the burdens already placed upon him by his work on the Finance Committee. Accept he did, however, partly out of fear that his refusal would result in the ascendancy of those holding less moderate opinions. "I could not decline it any more than I could decline the Treasury," he wrote to his cousin a few days after his appointment:

Mr. Sumner was very anxious for the place, but, standing as he does before the country, and committed to the most ultra views, even his friends declined to support him, and almost to a man fixed upon me. Luckily I had marked out my line, and everybody understands where I am. I think I can see my way through, and if Sumner and Stevens, and a few other such men do not embroil us with the President, matters can be satisfactorily arranged—satisfactorily, I mean, to the great bulk of Union men throughout the states.[25]

The Joint Committee on Reconstruction stemmed from a resolution presented by Thaddeus Stevens, who as unchallenged leader of the Republican caucus exerted almost dictatorial control over the Lower House. Pushed through the House by Stevens on the first day of the session and adopted shortly thereafter by the Senate, the resolution provided for a committee of fifteen members, nine of them from the Lower House and the remaining six from the Senate. Of this number only three were Democrats. At the head of the House contingent was Stevens himself, a man of advanced years and failing health but dauntless in spirit. "His great genius, indomitable will, and his great passions, inflamed into an intensity of hate . . . ," remarked a political adversary many years after Stevens' death "[and] made him burn and flame like an electric light, so intense and fierce that lesser lights were dim; and the Blaines and Logans were boys under him." [26] Long devoted to equalitarian principles, Stevens was intent upon securing suffrage rights for the Negro, but he was politician enough to realize that popular sentiment in the North was not yet prepared to accept outright and immediate enfranchisement of the freedmen. Thus, despite his Radical reputation, Stevens' stand during the first session of the 39th Congress in regard to the suffrage question was actually one of moderation, and unlike many of his Radical brethren he made a virtue of necessity by agreeing to foresake the unobtainable.

From the first, Senator Fessenden favored the idea of a Congressional committee as a vehicle by which a carefully studied solution of reconstruction problems could be arrived at. "The Reconstruction Committee was a fortunate invention," he wrote to Pike in early April, "and we do not mean to be driven, or coaxed into surrender. The future of this nation is of too much importance to be sacrificed to any impatience in the public mind, and that is what we have most to fear." [27] As head of the joint committee, Fessenden was in a position to make his views felt, and it is safe to say that despite frequent periods of absence due to illness, his was a most powerful influence on the committee during the first session of Congress. In regard to the restoration of the Southern states, Mr. Fessenden held no vindictive thoughts. His main concern was that the job be done safely and well, in such a way that the nation would be provided with suitable guarantees against a recurrence of the conditions and leadership in the South which had brought on the war. "I never will consent to take in a man from one of the Confederate states," he wrote to his son in late March, "until we have some security for the future." [28] As to the freedmen, he considered the government morally obligated to provide for their protection, and by this time Fessenden had come to agree with his more Radical colleagues that there could be no real protection for the freedmen without enfranchisement. He did not, however, wish to force the South to accept without mitigation black ignorance and irresponsibility at the polls. He had no objections to restrictions imposed by literacy tests and similar qualifying devices, but he was strong in his insistence that the Negroes be given equal treatment with the Whites.

During the first session of the 39th Congress the Joint Committee on Reconstruction met twenty-two times, the last of these occurring on June 6. In addition to the regular meetings, subcommittees assembled frequently to consider special phases of the problem. For five months facts, figures, and opinions were diligently gathered and discussed. Testimony was received from generals, politicians, and humble colored folks. The information after being pruned by the committee was then officially passed on to Congress in the form of reports, the first of which was submitted on March 5. All matters pertaining to the restoration of the Southern states were channeled through this body, carefully watched over by Chairman Fessenden of Maine, with the result that by mid-June Congress had apparently settled upon a final policy, under which Tennessee was soon after admitted to the Union as a model of Congressional reconstruction.

The crux of the Congressional program, as drawn up by Fessenden's committee and later amended somewhat on the floor, was a constitutional amendment designed primarily to restrict the political activities of certain former Confederate luminaries and to provide for the enfranchisement (eventual if not immediate) of the freedmen. However, the preparation of this amendment in such a way as to render it acceptable to two-thirds of the membership of both Houses proved to be no easy task. On January 20 two propositions for an amendment were brought before the Joint Committee. The first, which was Fessenden's, declared:

Representatives and direct taxes shall be apportioned among the several States within this Union, according to the respective numbers of citizens of the United States in each State; and all provisions in the Constitution or laws of any State, whereby any distinction is made in political or civil rights or privileges, on account of race, creed or color, shall be inoperative and void.

The second proposition had the support of Thaddeus Stevens and provided that:

> Representatives and direct taxes shall be apportioned among the several States which may be included within this Union, according to their respective numbers, counting the whole number of citizens of the United States in each State; provided that, whenever the elective franchise shall be denied or abridged in any State on account of race, creed or color, all persons of such race, creed or color, shall be excluded from the basis of representation.

By a vote of 11–3 the committee accepted the second proposal, and it was shortly thereafter reported by Stevens to the Lower House.[29]

Senator Fessenden was less than completely satisfied with the committee's decision to offer the South a "way out" on the suffrage question. To Fessenden's thinking the Stevens measure was indirect and lacking in courage. It failed to meet the situation squarely. Far better, thought Fessenden, to make a clear and simple avowal of principle. Far better to declare outright that the ballot must not be denied a person because of his color. Perhaps, however, Stevens was right in insisting that neither Congress nor the people were yet ready to support so unequivocal a position. At any rate Senator Fessenden was convinced that his own proposition had been rejected on grounds of expediency rather than conviction. In a speech at his home in Portland two years later, Fessenden declared: "The first proposition was voted down in committee because it was thought that Congress and the people of the Western States would not accept it." [30]

The proposed amendment was pushed through the Lower House by the intrepid Stevens on January 31, 1866, by the one-sided vote of 120–46, and was then passed on to the Senate where Fessenden introduced and championed the measure despite his feelings that it was somewhat less than perfect. In the Upper Chamber, however, the amendment met with less success. Sumner was particularly rabid in his opposition, and spoke endlessly against the measure, maintaining that it was eminently unfair to the Negro. Plagued by fatigue and a recurrence of severe headaches, Senator Fessenden soon found his patience exhausted, and, exasperated by Sumner's long oratory, he lashed out at the Massachusetts Senator in early February. "My constituents did not send me here to philosophize," Fessenden exclaimed angrily. "They sent me here to act, and to find out, if I could, what is best for the good of the whole, and to do it, and they are not so short-sighted as to resolve that if they cannot do what they would, therefore they will do nothing." [31] Writing to his cousin a few weeks later, the Senator explained: "Everyone is yelping at the Reconstruction Committee, and I can't get along without kicking some of them." [32]

On March 9 Chairman Fessenden delivered his closing argument in support of the proposed amendment. The amendment was not perfect, he agreed, but it was practical and in the long run would have the desired results. It did not provide for open, immediate, and impartial suffrage, but he contended that its intelligent application would make such an end inevitable, "and that at no distant day." Later that same day, however, the proposal failed to receive the necessary two-thirds approval of the Senate, and, thus, despite Fessenden's determined efforts, the Joint Committee was forced to begin anew its labors in fashioning what would ultimately become the fourteenth amendment.

In late March of 1866, while the Committee of Reconstruction was showing little progress in shaping a new amendment, Robert Dale Owen, long-time reformer and ex-congressman, arrived in Washington. Fearful lest the committee become stalled and accomplish nothing, the equalitarian Owen had devised a scheme of his own which he felt would provide a solution to the amendment problem. He at once proceeded to look up his old friend Thaddeus Stevens, to whom he explained his plan in detail. The amendment proposition which had been drawn up by Owen was as ingenious as it was simple. In essence it declared that henceforth no state should deny or restrict the civil rights of any person because of race, color, or previous condition of servitude. Furthermore, after July 4, 1876, no discrimination on these grounds should be exercised regarding the right of suffrage. Until that date, all persons excluded by a state from the franchise for reason of race, color, etc., should not be counted in determining the number of representatives sent by that state to Congress.

Stevens was immediately impressed with Owen's plan. Under the terms of the Owen amendment the South could be protected for a time against black ignorance and irresponsibility at the polls. In ten years, however, the Negroes would vote, and realizing that fact the Southern White would presumably understand that it behooved him to use that precious decade for educating the freedmen and otherwise preparing them for political participation. In the meantime, of course, the civil rights of the Negroes would be protected.

"The freedmen ought to be regarded as the wards of the Federal government," Owen declared.

"Yes," Stevens replied, "our very first duty is to them. Let the cursed rebels lie on the bed they have made."

"But," warned Owen, "we cannot separate the interests and the fate of the Negro from those of the planter. If we chafe and sour the whites of the South, the blacks must necessarily suffer thereby."

"Is that your reason for proposing prospective suffrage?"

"Not the chief reason. The fact that the Negro is, for the present unprepared wisely to use the right of suffrage, and, still more, incapable of legislating with prudence, is not less a fact because it has occurred through no fault of his. We must think and act for him as he is, and not as, but for life-long servitude, he would have been. . . ."

"I hate to delay justice so long."

"Consider if it be not for the freedman's welfare and good name that he should be kept away from the duties and responsibilities of political life until he shall have been, in a measure, prepared to fulfill these with credit to himself and advantage to the public service."

Stevens pondered the matter for a time, and then: "I'll be plain with you Owen. We've had nothing before us that comes anywhere near being as good as this, or as complete. It would be likely to pass too; that's the best of it. We haven't a majority, either in our committee or in Congress, for immediate suffrage; and I don't believe the States have yet advanced so far that they would be willing to ratify it. I'll lay that amendment before our committee tomorrow, if you say so, and I'll do my best to put it through."

Owen was understandably gratified, but before having the plan considered by the committee he wanted first to sound out the chairman. Therefore, not long after his visit with Stevens, Owen found the opportunity to present his amendment to Fessenden. The Senator listened patiently while the plan was explained in detail. Owen thought him cold and dispassionate and was disturbed by the fact that he uttered hardly a word of comment. But as the reformer was about to leave, Fessenden asked that a copy of the amendment be left with him in order that he might study it at his leisure. "When, two days later, I called upon him," Owen related many years afterward, "he told me in guarded and general terms, that he thought well of my proposal, as the best that had yet been presented. . . ." [33]

Shortly thereafter, on April 21, the Owen amendment was brought before the Joint Committee on Reconstruction where section by section it was approved by the majority—but not before Congressman John Bingham of Ohio had successfully inserted the famous "due process" clause which at a later time would take on great meaning. Meanwhile, Senator Fessenden had contracted a mild case of varioloid and was forced to remain aloof from his colleagues and his duties. "I rode out yesterday and have taken a walk this morning," he wrote to his son the day Owen's amendment was adopted by the committee, "but shall not be able to go to the Senate, or mix with people for some days yet. . . . The worst is that I am obliged to seclude myself from friends, and as I can neither write nor read much, time passes rather stupidly." [34]

Since, however, Senator Fessenden was known to favor the Owen plan, the committee proceeded to order the amendment reported to the floor; but at the last moment it was suggested that as a matter of courtesy the measure should be kept in committee until Fessenden returned. After all, this would presumably result in something of a legislative landmark, and it was only fitting that Chairman Fessenden be allowed to claim a hand in it. What could be lost? Only a few days at most. Stevens was reluctant to wait, though, and was on the verge of saying so. "But I let it pass, thinking that a few days would make no difference. God forgive me for my folly. Damn the varioloid." [35] By the time of Fessenden's return, reaction had set in. From sizable groups in both Houses of Congress had come protests that the suffrage provision, despite its prospective nature, was too extreme, and the fact soon became clear to Stevens and his committee colleagues that the measure could not hope to receive the necessary two-thirds support.

Consequently, the Owen amendment which had given such early promise was reconsidered, tabled, and, after being stripped of its usable parts, assigned to oblivion.

During the remainder of the session Fessenden was frequently ill, and was consequently less active than he might otherwise have been. By mid-May the Reconstruction Committee had fashioned another amendment, largely out of parts taken from the unsuccessful Stevens and Owen proposals, and had watched it pass the House with some revision. Soon after, it appeared before the Senate where it was supposed the measure would be championed by Fessenden. But as the Senator explained at this time in a letter to his son, "I am very weak and shall, I fear, continue so until I get a chance to rest. I shall pass over the reconstruction debate to somebody else, as I am utterly unable to undergo the fatigue." [36] A week later he complained to his friend Harrington: "My health is not good, and I shall be lucky if I can hold out to the end of the session. I am thinking seriously of retiring altogether." [37]

Thus, Fessenden's role in the proceedings leading up to the passage of the fourteenth amendment by the Senate on June 8 was a restricted one. Despite the poor condition of his health, however, he was able to prepare for presentation to Congress in early June the final majority report of the Joint Committee on Reconstruction. In this report the Senator carefully reviewed at great length the general subject of reconstruction and set forth the majority opinions of the committee. Reconstruction was declared to be a Congressional function. The Southern states were described as disorganized communities not yet ready to return to the Union. Contrasts were made between the President's plan and that of Congress, with emphasis given to the need for further guarantees, lest rebellion "become a pastime which any State may play at." Although because of Fessenden's illness the report was submitted too late to influence debate on the fourteenth amendment, its usefulness as a Congressional "bible" and, incidentally, as a campaign document in the 1866 elections, was undeniably great. Written in the terse, forceful style that Fessenden had so consciously striven to perfect through the years, the committee report was generally recognized as a masterpiece of concise logic. "In my opinion it is the ablest paper submitted to Congress since I have been in the Senate," remarked Grimes.[38] And from the

Washington *Chronicle,* which would one day soon find few kind words for Fessenden, came high praise for "the clear, incisive, unpretentious style, and the pure unimpeachable logic of Senator Fessenden . . . :

> The report is severe and exact in its style, but sometimes rises to warmth and eloquence. It is, though long, a model of conciseness. It abounds with minor arguments and antitheses, anyone of which would furnish the text for an article. A brief of it could not be made in less than one-half of the space it occupies. There are no waste words and no impertinent arguments.[39]

Whatever else he himself may have thought of the report, Fessenden's first feelings were those of relief. "Writing a report has been very troublesome," he confessed to his cousin, "as it was extra work, to be done as I could pick up an hour, and I was sick all the time." [40]

The first session of the 39th Congress dragged on until mid-summer. During that time relations between Congress and the President grew progressively worse. On July 16 both Houses passed the Freedmen's Bureau Bill over Johnson's veto, as they had earlier done with Trumbull's Civil Rights Bill. Less successful, however, were attempts made in the face of Presidential protest to admit as states into the Union the strongly Republican territories of Colorado and Nebraska and thereby add to the already substantial Republican majority in Congress. Similarly, Congressional efforts to extend the suffrage to Negroes in the District of Columbia were thwarted by the opposition of the President. From his seat of power in the Lower House, Thaddeus Stevens, angrily dissatisfied with the trend of affairs, was determined to keep Congress in session indefinitely, lest the field be deserted to the enemy. Eventually, however, heat, *ennui,* and Congressional desires to campaign for the coming fall elections, defeated Stevens' scheme; and on July 28, as America thrilled to the news that Cyrus Field aboard the *Heart's Content* had successfully completed laying the Atlantic cable, the long session of the 39th Congress adjourned.

For Senator Fessenden adjournment came none too soon that year. The past few months had been especially trying for him, not only because of his ill health and burdensome duties, but for other cogent reasons as well. On a day in late March, not long after the November death of his good friend Jacob Collamer, Fessenden had stood across

from Charles Sumner in bearing pall for his long-time companion
Solomon Foot. Thus, at this crucial juncture in national affairs, when
statesmanship was at a premium, the Senate was suddenly deprived
of the solid, conservative influence of two of its foremost members;
and of Fessenden's close circle of friends in the Upper Chamber there
remained now only Grimes of Iowa. Further sadness for the Senator
came with the report in early July that a giant fire had swept through
Portland, leaving the city "an appalling waste":

> More than six miles of streets, but yesterday closely lined on both
> sides with buildings, and thronged by a busy and happy people,
> now scarcely afford foot paths through the universal ruin. We at-
> tempt to find where the homes of our friends were standing three
> days ago, and we lose ourselves in a wilderness, without one familiar
> object for a guide.[41]

Fortunately, the Senator's house on State Street had escaped the
blaze, but in the center of the city much of the property that Fessenden had inherited from his father-in-law had been completely
destroyed. Gone too was the old family home on India Street, where
his father had resided for so many years, and where the aged, blind
General Sam had hoped to live out his few remaining days.

With the session over and Washington sweltering in mid-summer
heat, a sick and exhausted Fessenden prepared for his return to Maine.
The events of the past months had been momentous ones, and he
could take satisfaction from the realization that he had played no
inconsequential role in shaping them. And yet had it all been worth
the price? Senator Fessenden sometimes thought not. As he had commented earlier in the session:

> The longer I live the better I am convinced that a man loses his
> time, and makes himself unhappy by attempting to serve the public.
> If I were to live my life over again, my time and comfort should
> not be sacrificed to any such vain pursuit. I would take care of my-
> self first, and my care of others should be only a vacation. This
> may not sound well, but after all, it is the soundest philosophy.[42]

XVII

"Captain of the Obstructives"

IN THE colorful and all-important mid-term elections of that autumn, 1866, the Republicans scored a thumping victory. During the summer months the Southern Whites had behaved badly. Encouraged by President Johnson, the former states of the Confederacy, with the exception of Tennessee, had given unmistakable signs that they would not willingly ratify the fourteenth amendment, and from New Orleans and a dozen other Southern communities had come reports that Negroes were being badly abused by vicious white elements. Consequently, in the elections of that autumn Northern voters, angered and distressed by these latest indications of Southern recalcitrance, declared themselves decisively opposed to the President's policy of leniency toward the defeated South. First to repudiate the President was Maine, where in its early-bird September elections the state placed itself solidly within the Radical ranks. "Maine's decision is before the world that the loyal men of this government shall not be ruled by the disloyal . . . ," commented the *Kennebec Journal*, "and that the government shall be just and faithful in the discharge of its obligations to those who bravely perilled their lives that the government might be saved." [1]

Despite his lingering illness, Senator Fessenden campaigned actively in behalf of the Republican cause in the late summer contest in Maine. Disturbed by the President's stubborn behavior and by his increasingly vituperative assaults against the Republican-controlled Congress, Fessenden wrote in mid-September to Hugh McCulloch, his successor in the Treasury:

I have been compelled to take some part in our election, and to defend myself and Congress against the attacks of the President. . . . I do not intend, however, to go out of the state, unless driven to it, and I will not be led into personal abuse of any body, having regard to my own character as a Senator. I think the President will find abundant occasion to regret that he has not followed my example. Personally, he has always treated me kindly, and I shall *try* not to forget it, however much we may differ, or however grieved I may feel.[2]

Much has been written of economic influences at work in the election of 1866, especially in reference to the consummation of the long burgeoning romance between big business and the Republican party. Less attention has been given, however, to the subject of patronage, a matter dear to the hearts of all Congressmen and of salient importance in hardening the opposition against Johnson. As one writer, himself a member of Congress, remarked several years later: "When Johnson struck at the offices, he dealt a blow at . . . a sore spot in the make-up of the average Congressman. . . . When his district or state is invaded and his friends are ruthlessly turned out of post offices and clerkships and custom houses, and his enemies put in their places, freedom is very apt to shriek." [3] Beginning in the early spring of 1866 the President, spurred on by his supporters, had embarked upon the understandable policy of turning out of office those whom he suspected of harboring Radical sympathies and replacing them with persons favoring his own views. "Of what account is it to have Heads of Departments composed of friends, *real* or *pretended*," complained newly-appointed Minister to Mexico Lewis Campbell, in an April letter to Senator Doolittle, "if these tens of thousands of subalterns all over the land are permitted to remain in official position actively operating as his real enemies . . . ? The Commander in Chief of a great army can never win a battle if he permits his enemy to seize his batteries, his arms and his ammunition." [4]

But in attempting to bolster his own political position by manipulating the patronage, President Johnson only added further fuel to the fire of opposition already raging about him. Particularly distressed by Johnson's behavior in this respect were Senator Fessenden and many of his moderate friends who felt themselves deserving of kinder treatment at the hands of the President. "I can only regret," commented Fessenden in late August, "that the President finds himself compelled by his unfortunate complications with bad men to remove faithful and competent officers, and to fill their places with copperheads and flunkies. He must take the consequences." [5] Two weeks later he wrote to his friend McCulloch urging the Secretary to advise his chief against further removals in Maine:

> The election is now over [in Maine]. No further changes can produce the least effect, except to exchange good officers in whom the people confide for bad ones, whose appointment will disgust thinking men of all parties. My advice to the President is to turn a deaf ear to these fellows when they come about him, talking of support. All they mean by it is the necessity of supporting them[selves] out of the Treasury, not caring how odious they make the President. . . .[6]

It appears, however, that despite a determined shaking of the patronage tree by Johnson in the summer and autumn of 1866, the greater part of Senator Fessenden's appointments were left unmolested. This was particularly true of the Senator's personal friends, who were almost without exception spared removal. Undoubtedly this deference paid Fessenden was attributable in part at least to Johnson's reluctance to alienate the powerful moderating influence of the Maine Senator, whose relations with the President up to this time had remained, if not cordial, at least civil. It seems clear, though, that the presence of Fessenden's friend McCulloch in the President's Cabinet was also a factor operating in Fessenden's favor. Even after the autumn elections, in fact, Mr. Fessenden customarily showed little hesitancy in approaching the Secretary of the Treasury with patronage requests, which, it appears, were more often than not granted.[7]

By the time the second session of the 39th Congress assembled, the complexion of national affairs had changed noticeably. The refusal of the Southern states to ratify the fourteenth amendment, coupled with a substantial gain of Radical strength in the November elections, had marked a turning point in reconstruction policy. Interpreted by politicians as a public demand for a "get tough" policy toward the South, the elections had in a very emphatic manner signalled an end to moderate reconstruction attempts and had cleared the way for the ascendancy of Radical views. So it was that moderate members of the Republican Congress, like Trumbull and Fessenden, who had figured so prominently in steering the Congressional reconstruction program during the first session, now found their power and prestige seriously diminished. As a result they were to play a surprisingly subordinate role in shaping policy during the months following the reconvening of Congress in early December of 1866. To what extent this was true may be indicated by the fact that the Joint Committee on Reconstruction, over which Chairman Fessenden exerted a powerful influence, was during the second session reduced by Stevens and his Radical friends to little more than a legislative cipher.*

All this does not mean, however, that Fessenden was now docilely content to follow the lead of his Radical Republican colleagues. True —and surprisingly so in view of his legalistic nature—he tended during this and subsequent sessions to favor many of those measures of questionable constitutionality fashioned by the Radicals to increase the powers of Congress, largely at the expense of the Executive and the Supreme Court. He did, for example, lend his support in February of 1867 to amending the Army Appropriations Bill in such a way as to lessen the President's authority as commander-in-chief; † and not long after the session had begun he voted in favor of an admittedly high-handed measure which purported to move up the meeting date of subsequent Congresses to March 4 in order to prevent the President from having any "breathing spells" between Congresses. But of those persistent attempts inspired by the Radicals to admit Colorado and Nebraska prematurely into the Union for the sake of increasing Republican strength in Congress, Senator Fessenden registered his disapproval. Similarly, he felt compelled to argue against passage of the Tenure of Office Bill, a measure designed to restrict the President's power to remove federal officers. "I do not think we are treating the office of President with very great respect," he declared on the floor

* Although the Joint Committee on Reconstruction was reappointed on December 5, 1866, it met only twice during the second session. During the previous session twenty-two meetings of the Committee had been held. See Kendrick, *Journal of the Joint Committee on Reconstruction*, pp. 121–29.

† Actually Fessenden voted against the amendment because of a technicality. He had during the debate, however, declared himself in sympathy with the purpose of the amendment. *Cong. Globe*, 39th Cong., 2 sess., p. 1894.

of the Senate in early January, "when we say that he shall not, in the recess of Congress, remove a Cabinet officer if he deems it necessary." [8]

On the more important matter of Southern reconstruction Fessenden could not bring himself to abandon his moderate position in order to support the ascending views of the Radical element, and as the second session of the 39th Congress wore on, he found himself more and more out of step with the majority opinion of his Republican colleagues. To Fessenden's way of thinking, the terms of reconstruction had already been arrived at by Congress and had been duly presented to the Southern states. The fact that these terms had not met with immediate acceptance was no reason to abandon the program that had previously been agreed upon. The fourteenth amendment, he maintained, was a fair and practicable basis for restoration. Under its terms the civil rights of the freedmen were protected; reasonable provisions had been made regarding Negro suffrage; and political restrictions had been placed on former Confederate leaders as a guarantee against their future misbehavior. It was necessary now only to wait, for eventually the Southern states would be bound to come around naturally and voluntarily to ratifying the amendment. Until then let them remain outside the Union and ponder their misfortunes under continued liabilities and discomfiture. To attempt to coerce the recalcitrant states by the erection of forced governments, Senator Fessenden felt, might prove a grievous error. He had always been, he assured his colleagues shortly before the passage of the Reconstruction Bill in late February, one of those people who felt that in situations such as these patience tended to pay the greatest dividends. "We proposed to these rebel States guarantees that were demanded of them before we would listen to the subject of reconstruction," Fessenden declared in looking back upon the work of the first session. "I am willing to stand upon that and wait, because I think we can afford to wait." [9]

Less patient, however, were the Radical members of Congress, who were doubtless swayed by the realization that Fessenden's policy of entrusting reconstruction to time and Southern acquiescence would almost certainly result in the return of the Southern states to their erstwhile Democratic allegiance. Thus, during January and early February of 1867 the Radicals of the Lower House busily engaged themselves in pushing through that Chamber a substitute plan for reconstruction which had been introduced by their intrepid leader Thaddeus Stevens. The Stevens bill, out of which grew the Military Government Act, or more familiarly the Reconstruction Act, proposed to set aside the "pretended" governments of the Southern states and in their stead provide for a division of the unrestored areas into five military districts in which final governmental and judicial authority would be exercised by the respective military commanders.

When the measure reached the Senate, loud objection was made to the fact that no actual means had been prescribed by the Stevens bill whereby military control could be ended. The bill could, in fact, scarcely be considered a reconstruction measure at all since it gave no attention to the question of preparing the states for restoration. Consequently, the Senate almost immediately set about the task of amending the Stevens bill by incorporating into the measure the prescribed conditions for reconstruction of the South. As to exactly what these conditions should be, there was great division of opinion, and with time rapidly running out for the 39th Congress, it was decided that the luxury of long debate could not be allowed. Therefore on Saturday morning, February 16, the Republican caucus of the Senate met and appointed a committee composed of seven of its members to thrash out some sort of compromise arrangement which would be acceptable to the caucus. Among the seven Senators chosen for this task were Fessenden of Maine and his heart's abhorrence, Charles Sumner.

As had been anticipated, the principal point of difference encountered by the committee concerned the matter of Negro suffrage. All members agreed that constitutional conventions should be chosen on the basis of universal manhood suffrage to begin the work of reconstruction in the several Southern states. It was also generally conceded that the fourteenth amendment should be specified as one of the conditions of restoration. But the question of requiring that Negro suffrage be written into state constitutions caused dissension. Sumner insisted that only in this way could the freedmen be assured of the elective franchise, but Fessenden, still shying away from unqualified Negro suffrage, opposed such a provision and was upheld in his views by a 5–2 vote of the committee. Shortly thereafter, however, when the committee recommendations came before the caucus, Sumner was able to persuade his colleagues to reverse the committee's decision. And thus by a vote of 17–15, with Senator Fessenden very much in opposition, Negro suffrage became a condition of Southern reconstruction. "Then and there, in that small room, in that caucus," remarked Radical Senator Henry Wilson some time later, "was decided the greatest pending question on the North American continent." [10]

On March 2, 1867, after considerable disagreement and interplay between the two Chambers, the Reconstruction Bill became law—notwithstanding the objections of the President, whose veto was easily and quickly overriden by both Houses. To this measure and its later supplements Senator Fessenden gave his reluctant vote, but he made no secret of the fact that he had little sympathy for the new plan. To his friend Freeman Morse, still consul in London, Mr. Fessenden wrote many months later:

> I got my name of conservative by advising against the reconstruction acts. It seemed to me, that when we had proposed the Fourteenth Amendment, the rebel States had rejected it, and we had provided military protection for our friends, enough was done by Congress towards reconstruction, and we had better leave the matter where it was until the people of those States asked for admission in proper form. Our furious radical friends, however, thought they could secure the votes of all those States through the aid of the negroes.[11]

Still, what was done was done, and it was incumbent upon all concerned to make the best of the new situation. Writing to a Southern acquaintance not long after the Reconstruction Bill had become law, Fessenden stated:

> You ask me if, in my opinion, the Southern States may rely that, upon compliance with the terms of the Military Bill, they will be recognized and admitted as states in the Union.
>
> In reply I can only say that there seems now to be a very general disposition, both in Congress and out of it, to see all the Southern states occupying their old places in the Union. Of course, there are some who do not entertain this desire, and some who would like to impose other conditions. Still, I have no doubt the general sentiment is to recognize those states, upon compliance with the terms

stated in the Bill. Much will depend, probably, upon the business of the proceedings, and the conviction that the suffrage has been full and free, and upon the provisions of the Constitution adopted, as manifesting a disposition to conform to the new order of things. I do not believe, however, that you will be met by an over captious spirit.

I think your great difficulty in the way of readmission has arisen from the belief, fostered by Southern newspapers, that the prevalent feeling among you is one of intense hostility to the Union, and that you would be dangerous members of it, if restored. It is much to be desired that the process of reconstruction now pointed out may develop an improvement in this particular, and promote a greater degree of cordiality between the Sections.[12]

A few weeks later in a letter to Delaware's Democratic Thomas Bayard, future Secretary of State for President Cleveland, Fessenden declared:

I wish to . . . see a termination of existing evils. Probably, all the animosities consequent upon it [the war], will not be extinguished in our day. But in my heart there is no desire for vengeance upon individuals, and I am confident that no such feeling agitates the great mass of our people. . . . I hope the Southern people will by their speedy adoption of the terms of reconstruction demonstrate their intention to conform, in a right spirit, to the necessities of the situation erected by themselves.[13]

When the 39th Congress adjourned in March of 1867, Mr. Fessenden stepped down from his position as chairman of the Senate Finance Committee. With the exception of his brief tenure in the Treasury he had headed this all-important committee for six years, and had perhaps done as much as any other man to guide the nation's imperiled economy safely through four years of war. During the session just past he had been forced to give much of his time in committee-room and on the floor to preparation and passage of the inevitable deficiency and appropriations measures which customarily made up a large part of the committee's work. In addition he had labored long and late on various tax proposals, the most important of which was the comprehensive, time-consuming Wells Tariff Bill which called for a general lowering of wartime rates, particularly on raw materials. After great, albeit unsympathetic, exertion on Fessenden's part, this measure finally passed the Senate in the early morning hours of February 1, only to lose its way later in the Lower House. The Republican majority was clearly in no mood for tariff reduction, nor would it be for several decades to come.

But now Senator Fessenden felt the time had arrived for him to relinquish his long-time control of the committee. No longer a young man, nor a robust one, he found that the demands of the Finance position were taking too great a toll of his energy and health, and each new year seemed to bring more burdensome responsibilities. Thus, at the beginning of the 40th Congress he turned over his chairmanship to John Sherman of Ohio in whom he had ample, although somewhat qualified, confidence. Simultaneously with his resignation, and by way of something in the nature of a tribute to Senator Fessenden's industry and ability, the Finance Committee was relieved of its appropriations responsibilities, and a separate committee was set up under Fessenden's Maine colleague, Lot Morrill, to handle all such measures. As for Fessenden himself, immediately after resigning his Finance chair he was appointed to a place on Charles Sumner's Foreign Relations Committee, where a few weeks later he found occasion to express his disapproval of Secretary Seward's Alaska treaty, a stupid and nefarious business clearly designed to squander public funds for no worthwhile purpose.

At noon on March 4 the 39th Congress adjourned, and almost at once the 40th was convened, in accordance with the Meeting of Congress resolution of a few weeks before. As the anti-Radical Washington *National Intelligencer* commented: "In the Capitol of the United States yesterday was enacted a scene utterly without precedent in the annals of the nation. For the first time in American history an incoming Congress was organized ere the retiring members of the one just expired had vacated their seats. . . ." [14] For Fessenden and his fellow legislators this first session of the 40th Congress turned out to be an especially long and tedious one; for, fearful lest President Johnson commit some mischief during their absence, the Radicals contrived successfully to keep Congress officially on the Washington scene until the opening date of the second session in the following

December. This they managed to accomplish by a series of "recessed" sittings, held for short periods of time in March, July, and November.

To Senator Fessenden, who prized his leisure in the cool ocean atmosphere of Portland, the whole idea of recessed sittings was pointless and ridiculous, and he was not reluctant to say so. In late March before the session had taken its first recess, Fessenden had argued for outright adjournment. After all, the session had accomplished its principal purpose by setting up machinery to carry out the Reconstruction Act. In regard to the removal of Federal officers, the President's hands were now pretty much tied by the Tenure Act, and there should be little danger on that score. As for the Alaska treaty, there would be ample opportunity for considering that during the special session of the Upper House already slated for early April. Beyond all this, what else was there? What good reason could be found for not closing Congressional doors and keeping them closed until the beginning of the second session in December?

But the Radicals, not content to abandon the field to the enemy, defeated all adjournment attempts, and managed to persuade Congress to recess only until the first Wednesday of July. It was generally understood, however, that if at the time of the July meeting the political horizon seemed clear of storm clouds, no serious attempt would be made to secure a quorum and the session would be adjourned "without day." Since, barring the unforeseen, the chance seemed remote that the July meeting would amount to anything more than a formality, Fessenden saw no cause to object to this arrangement, and in late April following a brief special session of the Senate, he betook himself to Portland, where in the big house on State Street he settled down for a welcome respite from the Washington scene. Within two months, however, the Senator was called upon to return to the Capital, where in mid-June a quorum for the July session was assured by Attorney-General Henry Stanbery's alarming opinion on the reconstruction acts. In effect Stanbery's opinion declared that until new governments could be set up in the Southern states, the Johnson state governments, rather than the military, should be considered the natural seat of authority—an interpretation which, according to Radical General Philip Sheridan, "opens a broad macadamized road for perjury and fraud to travel on." [15] Convinced that the President and his Attorney-General were intent upon subverting the entire

Congressional program of reconstruction, the Washington *Chronicle* sent out frantic appeals for all loyal members of Congress to return to their posts in time for the July session. And from his sick room in Lancaster, Pennsylvania, old Thaddeus Stevens responded by sounding his unforgiving trumpet for the faithful to converge upon Washington. Scarcely pleased by this unexpected turn of events was Senator Fessenden, who had little relish for another summer in Washington. "Shall you go?" he inquired of his friend Grimes. "It is all nonsense in my judgment, and Stevens and others are jumping at a pretense. I am disgusted with Johnson for giving them such a pretense. God only knows what mischief will be done if we get together." [16]

During the July meeting, while Congress was busily preparing a third reconstruction act, designed to express "the true intent and meaning" of the previous two, the Radicals launched their long-expected attack against Senator Fessenden. For more than a year Fessenden's behavior had been looked upon with increasing suspicion by his extreme colleagues. His apparent "coddling" of Johnson during the winter and early spring of 1866 had caused much irritation among the Radical element, and there were many indications that Fessenden was still too prone to take the President's part. Only a few weeks before, in fact, during the special session of the Senate, he had dared defend Johnson openly on the floor by declaring that the President had a perfect right to appoint to office whomever he wished. After all, the Executive was just as much a part of the government as the Senate, and the one was under no obligations to conform to the desires of the other insofar as appointments were concerned. To Fessenden's way of thinking, the President was just as entitled to say that the Senate stood in his way, as the Senate was that Johnson stood in theirs. President Johnson was certainly committing no offense in nominating his political friends to office. If the Senators didn't wish to confirm them, it was their privilege not to do so, but in such matters they had no right to accuse the President of wrongdoing.[17]

More upsetting, though, to many of Fessenden's colleagues than his occasionally kind words for Johnson, was the Senator's lukewarm attitude towards the Radical program, as indicated by his reluctance to support the Tenure Act and the reconstruction acts, and by his recent attempts to adjourn Congress and thereby entrust the direction of Southern reconstruction to the hands of Andrew Johnson. Further-

more, it was known that Senator Fessenden had consistently refused
to declare his views on impeaching the President, a matter then being
pondered by the Lower House. As Fessenden wrote to his ailing friend
Grimes during the July session, it would be in his opinion "improper
for one, who was to act as a judge in the case, to commit himself in
advance upon the guilt of the accused." [18]

For Senator Fessenden the 40th Congress had opened on an
ominous note when the Republican caucus passed him by in favor of
Radical Ben Wade for the office of president pro-tempore of the
Senate. The feeling that had long been building up against him was
not unleashed, however, until shortly after Congress reassembled for
its July meeting. Then it was that his Radical antagonists embarked
upon a campaign designed to discredit him and if possible drive him
from the ranks of the Republican party into the arms of the President.
Writing home in early July, the Senator complained of the fact that
the Radicals seemed very angry with him. He was particularly perturbed by the nettlesome conduct of Sumner, who persisted in
labelling him a "reactionist." "If he doesn't behave better, I am afraid
we shall quarrel again," Fessenden commented. "He is getting to be
absolutely intolerable." [19]

But it was on the last day of the July session, after Fessenden had
again argued unsuccessfully for final adjournment, that the storm of
criticism broke forth against him in its full fury. In a long and exceedingly bitter harangue, Senator Zachariah Chandler of Michigan
denounced "the conservative Senator from Maine" and all his kind
as "hybrids" and political "perverts." These men, these conservative
Republicans, Chandler asserted, made up a mean, despicable lot,
which grew smaller and beautifully less by degrees. They were a
vanishing tribe. They had no power of reproduction. "The race dies
out with the first generation. . . . Sir, the path of conservative republicanism is as clearly marked by tombstones as is the great high-
way to California by the carcasses and bones of dead mules;" and on
each of these tombstones could be found the inscription: "Here lies
the body of a recusant: a man who could not be trusted by the
people. . . . Sir, the people have not yet got done erecting tombstones. The people are in earnest." Turning then to Fessenden, the
Senator from Michigan exclaimed: "Sir, it is known, not only to this
body but to the country, that [this] Senator has stood here month

after month, the defender of Andrew Johnson and his Cabinet. . . ."

Immediately Fessenden was on his feet to reply to Chandler. He had listened to the Senator's carefully prepared tirade, Mr. Fessenden stated, with no great feeling of astonishment:

> I have been aware for some time that the Senator and some other Senators on the floor designed deliberately, if they could, to injure my standing and position, such as it may be, in the party to which I have the honor to belong. This is not the first open attack which has been made upon me by that Senator; and he stands not alone. I am aware, also, that that Senator—and he is not the only one— has taken pains privately to represent me as unfaithful because I do not agree with him in his notions with reference to the conduct of some public affairs.

Well, let him and his friends say what they wished. "I shall leave my public record to take care of itself," Fessenden declared. He wanted it understood, however, that, contrary to the belief of some, his position on the great issues before them was in no way influenced by any feeling of confidence in Andrew Johnson. "No, sir; it is a want of confidence that actuates me and some others in those who would assume to direct what they have not the capacity to direct. . . ." And as for Chandler and his charges, Senator Fessenden had for a long time been undecided as to whether he should even bother to notice them. "If I had the slightest idea that anything the Senator from Michigan can say would affect . . . [my record] before the people of the country," Fessenden exclaimed, "I should look upon myself with a contempt which I do not feel at present." [20]

Throughout the late summer and early autumn of 1867, after Fessenden had returned from the July session to enjoy the comforts of his garden and grandchildren in Portland, the Radical attacks upon him continued. In late August, Thaddeus Stevens proclaimed to the press, with unaccustomed mildness, that "a few senators of great ability, undoubted patriotism and purity, have become so saturated with what they are pleased to call conservatism . . . that I fear they will forget the monster that was slain in 1776 and again in 1861, and will thus do great damage to the creation of a government now so capable of being converted into a political paradise." [21] Less than a week later, Charles Sumner at a press interview denounced Fessenden as the "captain of the obstructives." Since the beginning of Congressional attempts to reconstruct the South, the Senator from Maine had been a drag, Sumner declared, and more than any other Republican in Congress had been all too ready to side with the President. "All the slave-masters in the Senate never wounded me as did this colleague from New England," lamented the Boston charmer. Clearly Fessenden should be reckoned "an evil influence in the Senate." [22]

At his home in Maine, Fessenden was concerned but not noticeably disturbed. "The truth is," he wrote to Grimes in late September, "that for some reason or other, this particular clique have resolved to write and talk me down, to persuade the people that I am untrue to the principles of the party, a friend and defender of Andrew Johnson." But Senator Fessenden had been on the public scene too long to be bothered by the rantings of men like Stevens and Sumner, whose "malice is only equalled by their meanness and cowardice." [23] The late summer weeks in Maine had, in fact, proved so thoroughly enjoyable for the Senator that he had refused to allow his pleasures to be marred by political antagonisms. In early August he had spent the better part of a week in Brunswick at a meeting of the Bowdoin College trustees—"resulting from my deep interest in what Sumner calls 'knowledge.' " [24] A few days later he had taken an excursion with "the ladies" to Mt. Desert Island, and in early September had gone with Pike, now back from The Hague, and New York's junior Senator Roscoe Conkling on a fishing expedition up the St. John River. It was soon after his return to Portland from this trip that he first learned of Sumner's attack. But no matter. As he explained in a letter to Grimes:

I have just finished my evening cigar, and, as it happens to be a good one, I am in a most desirable condition. Beside the cigar, I am just now in excellent health, eat well (in spite of chronic dyspepsia which my friends assign in excuse of my bad temper), sleep well, my garden flourishes, and Frank with his charming little wife and pretty boy make a part of my family. Should not all these happy circumstances and surroundings enable me to bear even Mr. Sumner's philippics with a reasonable degree of equanimity? [25]

XVIII

Senator Fessenden
Takes His Stand

SINCE BEFORE the autumn elections of 1866, there had been heard among many of the Radical members of Congress strong mention of impeaching the President. As the Portland *Eastern Argus* noted at the time: "The extreme radicals talk about the impeachment of President Johnson as glibly as though it were to be a sort of holiday sport with which the short days of next winter are to be enlivened." [1] Senator Henry Wilson of Massachusetts had, in fact, openly expressed the opinion in mid-September that if the Radicals were successful in the coming elections, impeachment proceedings would be attempted against Johnson during the next session of the 39th Congress. Nor did Wilson err in his prediction, for on January 7 of the following year the Lower House adopted, by the one-sided vote of 108–38, a resolution instructing its Judiciary Committee to "inquire into . . . the conduct of Andrew Johnson."

During the spring and summer of 1867 the House Judiciary Committee, headed by James Wilson of Iowa, pondered its great problem. On June 1 a majority of the committee decided that there were not sufficient grounds for impeachment, but upon the insistence of Massachusetts Radical George Boutwell, it was agreed that hearings would be continued until the end of the session. Then, in August while Congress was in "temporary recess," the complexion of matters appeared suddenly changed by the impulsive behavior of President Johnson, who in a series of brash strokes removed the Radical Generals Sheridan and Sickles from their Southern commands, and, far worse, suspended from office Secretary of War Edwin Stanton. From

Johnson's point of view the removal of the Radical Stanton was under-standable enough. Obviously the Secretary of War was not in sym-pathy with the President's views on reconstruction, and just as ob-viously he had long been doing everything in his power to embarrass the President and to give aid and comfort to Johnson's Congressional enemies. Nevertheless, the suspension of Stanton, a Lincoln appointee closely associated with Northern victory in the War, by a President who was already under serious suspicion for his alleged disloyalty, and at a time when public sentiment was running strongly against the President, was perhaps more courageous than wise. "I think the Presi-dent has now put himself plainly in the wrong by removing Stanton," remarked lukewarm Radical Horace White, editor of the Chicago *Tribune*. "[I think] that he can be impeached, and I am for im-peaching him." [2] And from his home in Portland, Senator Fessenden wrote to his friend McCulloch in early September: "The sentiment of New England was decidedly, almost unanimously, adverse to the operations of Wade, Butler, and Co., when we last adjourned [July 20]. Now, I meet no man who is not in favor of impeachment if any decent pretense for it can be found. It does seem as if Johnson was resolved upon destruction." [3]

By late November, with Congress once again upon the Washington scene, Chairman Wilson's Judiciary Committee was ready to report its findings to the House, and it was generally felt that in view of the President's recent conduct, impeachment proceedings would be begun against Johnson. "I am very much afraid that the Judiciary Com. will report in favor of impeachment, and that it will pass the House," Fes-senden wrote home at this time. "This I shall regard as ruin to our party, and it will be just punishment for our cowardice and folly." [4] But for the impeachers the hour had not yet arrived, for despite the committee's recommendation to the contrary, the House decided by a nearly two-thirds majority on December 7 that there existed no suffi-cient justification for opening proceedings against the President. Senator Fessenden was much relieved. "The impeachment is a fizzle . . . ," he wrote to a relative on the day following the House vote. "The country will now breathe more freely, and if we *can* act like sensible men I shall have some hopes of the future. Yet we have many most troublesome and important problems to solve, while the folly and madness of such men as Stevens and Sumner keep us in constant peril." [5]

Fessenden's relief was short-lived, however, for on January 13, over his opposition, the Senate availed itself of the recently created Tenure of Office Act by refusing to concur in the President's attempted removal of Stanton. Soon after this, the Secretary of War returned uninvited and unwanted to his Cabinet post, and thus the stage was set for a reenactment with ominous variations of the same drama. Scarcely more than a month later, President Johnson, who seldom gave in without a struggle, rose to the occasion and dismissed his Radical Secretary outright in a bold attempt to bring the Tenure Act before the courts. On the same day, February 21, the Senate, meeting in executive session, resolved: "that under the Constitution and laws the President has no power to remove the Secretary of War and to designate any other officer to perform the duties of that office." Opposed to the adoption of this resolution was Senator Fessenden, not only because he felt that the President had the legal right to dismiss Stanton, but also because he feared that the resolution would serve as a signal for the Lower House to begin impeachment. As he explained to his son a few months later: "After that vote the House could hardly be expected to do otherwise than impeach him, and the Senate is therefore responsible both as accuser and judge." [6] On February 24, 1868, three days after Johnson's removal of Secretary of War Stanton, the Lower House by a vote of 126-47 declared itself in favor of impeaching the President of the United States.

The trial of Andrew Johnson consumed the better part of three months in its preparation and execution, and during that time little else was accomplished by Congress. Since, under the provisions of the Constitution, impeachment proceedings are conducted by the Lower House before the Senate sitting as a court of judges, Fessenden's role in the trial was a passive one. Nevertheless, the ordeal of this additional burden wore heavily upon him, and he soon felt his health and energy failing once again under the strain. "This trial has almost killed me," he wrote to his cousin in mid-April, "and will probably quite do so by the time it is finished." [7] Indeed, during the marathon proceedings younger and stronger men than he succumbed to the relentless exigencies and tensions. His recent fishing companion

Roscoe Conkling, for instance, and Senator Jacob Howard, moderate turned Radical from Michigan—both in the course of the trial were temporarily laid low by the pressures upon them. And then, only a few days before the trial's end, Fessenden was saddened to learn that his devoted friend James Grimes had suffered a stroke which had left him partially paralyzed. And who could say for certain that the noble Grimes would outlive the session?

Finally the long trial of the President, and incidentally the public career of Senator Fessenden, reached a climax on May 16, 1868, when Fessenden and his Senate colleagues assembled shortly before noon to vote upon the guilt or innocence of Andrew Johnson. Senator Fessenden was in his seat early that day. During his years of public service punctuality had always been customary with him. He prided himself on having been avoidably late no more than two or three times during his nearly two decades of public office-holding. But on this occasion his punctuality doubtless stemmed as much from impatience as from habit. To his way of thinking this impeachment business had taken entirely too long. He was anxious to have it over and done with. There were a great many important legislative matters in the Congressional hopper, and in Senator Fessenden's opinion the nation's welfare demanded that some of these be given immediate attention. Furthermore, the Senator had his own personal reasons for wanting to get back to business at the earliest possible moment. He was tired and ill and not at all sure that he could hang on much longer. He wished desperately to return to Portland before the beginning of the hot season, which would soon descend upon the Capital. He doubted, in fact, that there was strength enough left in him to sustain him through another Washington summer. He needed the tonic of long, unbroken rest in his invigorating city by the sea, and he felt that he needed it soon. And yet obviously there could be little progress made toward adjournment as long as this "confounded impeachment nonsense" continued. High time it was finished, once and for all.[8]

To Senator Fessenden this May 16, 1868, was to be one of the most deadly serious days of his political career. How strange, it seemed to him, that a matter of such consequence should have been allowed to assume the proportions of a circus side-show. The galleries were crowded with chattering onlookers, many of them women, fitted out in dazzling finery and brushing the heavy air with their fancy fans.

To them it was enough that an affair of great importance was going on, and that their presence represented something of a social triumph. Outside in the corridors were surging multitudes, pressing against the Capitol police who guarded the giant doors and straining to catch occasional glimpses into the Senate Chamber as the chosen few were admitted. Tickets, including four for each Senator, had been at a precious premium and had long before this time fallen into the hands of the very influential and the very enterprising. "I want one," a prominent Massachusetts man had written a month before to his friend Charles Sumner, "and I don't know where else to apply. Of course, you are over-run with applications and have given away all your own to persistent petticoats, but you may know of some person who could oblige so illustrious a citizen as myself." [9]

By a few minutes before noon most of the Senators had already entered the hall. Some were at their desks, sitting silently, conscious of the occasion and a thousand pairs of eyes staring down at them from the gallery. Others visited the desks of colleagues or gathered in little groups in the rear of the Chamber and whispered things to one another. Occasionally a smartly-dressed page would flit along the center aisle bearing a note to one of the clusters of men in the rear, or carrying a pitcher of water to the managers' table in the front of the Chamber. But despite the churning about of some, there was an over-all static quality about the floor of the Senate that day. Those Senators sitting at their desks appeared to sit more erectly than was their custom, and the steps of their circulating colleagues seemed more measured and deliberate. After all, a United States President was on trial for his political life, and the verdict was about to be rendered. Even the air was possessed of a calculated heaviness—or so at least it seemed to Senator Fessenden as he waited for the polling of his vote.

What a pity! What a huge error this impeachment business had been from the very beginning! More than an error, really. A tragedy for the Republican party and the country as well. From the outset Senator Fessenden had been convinced that nothing but harm could come from the proceedings. "The trial will be very dull and stupid work," he had remarked several weeks earlier, "and the country will probably be tired and disgusted with it. The result will, in my judgment, be politically disastrous, whatever else may come of it." [10] But how disastrous the trial would prove, the Senator had no way of knowing until the proceedings had progressed to a point that left no doubt as to the extremes his party colleagues were willing to go to in order to slough off the President. What had begun as an apparently sincere, albeit ill-considered, attempt by the majority to prove the President legally guilty of misconduct, had degenerated into a wholly partisan affair in which party fealty rather than regard for justice dominated men's minds. Even many of Fessenden's most respected friends in the Senate had yielded to this party frenzy, and had used their influence with him to persuade the Senator to join them in voting for Johnson's conviction. "The whole thing . . . has made me sick at heart," Fessenden declared a few days after the May 16 vote. "I have seen in the Senate so much of meanness, such utter want of conscientiousness, such base cowardice, even among men calling themselves Christians, that I almost despair of the future. . . ." [11]

From the beginning it had been understood that Fessenden held little sympathy with the impeachment proceedings, and although as a judge the Senator had insisted upon maintaining throughout the trial a discreet silence on his opinions, it had been generally felt that in the final reckoning he would stand in favor of acquittal unless he could in some way be persuaded by the right application of the right pressures to follow the path of political rectitude. He therefore had been a pet proselyting project for the Radicals, particularly so since the fact was recognized that as one of the leading and most highly respected members of the Senate, he would by his example be bound to influence the course of others. But Senator Fessenden was not a man to be pushed. Upon a person of his standing and temperament it behooved the Radicals to use the gentlest and subtlest of methods, lest they drive him irretrievably beyond reach. Thus, until late in the trial he had escaped the harsher treatment meted out to some of his less intrepid "doubtful" Republican colleagues, and with a few exceptions had been subjected to nothing more severe than the repeated exhortations of his friends.

As the trial had entered its final phase, however, the Radicals had grown less coy in their treatment of him. This was especially true after May 11 when in a supposedly secret session of the Senate, Fessenden, along with Republican Senators Grimes, Trumbull, and Henderson, had made known that, party or no party, he would vote for acquittal. "Mr. Fessenden was the last speaker of the day," the Portland *Eastern Argus* noted in reporting the affair two days later:

> He spoke at more length than any other Senator, treating the whole question . . . with much fulness of examination and enforcing his views in the calm and clear manner common to him. He will vote against every one of the articles [of impeachment], and it may be added that his influence is such in the Senate that the outsiders believe his speech has turned the scale against impeachment.[12]

It appears moreover that not a few of the impeachers were of much the same opinion as the Democratic *Argus* in assessing the likely effects of Fessenden's statement. Although his decision had long been expected, the announcement of it in such an emphatic and unequivocal manner had come as a sickening blow to Radical hopes. As General Grant confided to a friend soon after hearing the results of the May 11 session, the "defection" of Fessenden constituted a most serious setback for the impeachers. The General wondered, in fact, if real hope could any longer be entertained for conviction of the President. Senator Fessenden would, after all, be likely to carry others with him.[13]

Immediately after Fessenden's statement, the storm against the Senator from Maine had broken out in all its fury. Among the Radical members angry words were audible. "Denunciation for those who have betrayed the country is the only path to safety," exclaimed an enraged Ben Butler, leader of the House impeachers. "The reasons why we are betrayed should be shown—that other true men may avoid the *pitt* into which others have fallen." [14] Particularly aggressive was the Radical press, with Greeley's *Tribune* and the Washington *Chronicle* leading the pack in hurling choice invectives against that nefarious group of "over-sensitive, double-refined, old-woman politicians, whose feet are covered all over with political corns." [15] As the New York *Nation*, itself in favor of conviction, had noted at the time:

> Senators of the highest character who, in being simply honest and in having a mind of their own, render more service to the country than fifty thousand of the windy blatherskites who assail them, have been abused like pickpockets, simply because they chose to think.

We have, during the last week, heard language applied to Mr. Fessenden and Mr. Trumbull, for instance, which was fit only for a compound of Benedict Arnold and John Morrissey. . . .[16]

Nor had the general public been slow to denounce Fessenden as soon as his stand had become known. Clearly the sentiment of the North was overwhelmingly in favor of conviction, and in most areas this sentiment was an unusually vocal one. Not since the Kansas-Nebraska controversy of several years before, in fact, had the people of the North been so ready to express their opinions on a political issue, and to make these opinions known to their representatives in Washington. To these people the declaration by Fessenden and his recusant colleagues on May 11 had come as a maddening disappointment. "It is sadder than the darkest defeat of the war," wrote a Massachusetts man to Sumner. "If there was heart-break then, there was also hope, but this tells us that all those sacrifices were made in vain. . . ." [17] And from another writing at the same time: "What are we coming to? Where are we drifting? I hope God will not forsake us in this our darkest hour." [18] As a Pennsylvania friend of Radical Senator Simon Cameron commented: "The course of certain Republican Senators, who, recreant to their high trust, intimate their intentions to vote for the acquittal of that bad and base Executive, Andrew Johnson, has created an excitement more intense if possible, than did ever the attack upon Fort Sumter, or the disaster of first Bull Run." [19]

From friends and strangers alike an ever-mounting volume of mail had descended upon Senator Fessenden, advising, begging, demanding that he change his mind. Mass meetings, inspired by Radical party managers, had been held in Bangor and Lewiston, and in the Senator's own hometown of Portland, to denounce the President and demand that Fessenden do Maine proud with his vote. Even from Bangor's Rufus Dwinell, Fessenden's close friend for nearly thirty-five years, had come anxious letters and telegrams virtually demanding that he vote for conviction. Earlier the Senator had received similar messages from Neal Dow and from his old political crony James Pike of Washington County. And from others had come threats. But to them all Senator Fessenden had turned a deaf ear. Despite the pressures brought to bear upon him by his colleagues and constituents, by the press and personal friends and a disgruntled public, he had remained determined to act as an impartial judge, regardless of the cost to himself. "I cannot and will not violate my oath," he had declared. "I would rather be confined to planting cabbages for the remainder of my days." [20] And there was nothing in that oath about pleasing either his constituents or himself. It was clearly a matter of honor and justice, and Fessenden would vote with his conviction. "If they [the people of Maine]," he had replied to Dwinell, "wish for a Senator a man who will commit perjury at their bidding, either from party necessity or a love of popular favor, I am not that man." [21]

It had not been easy for Fessenden to arrive at this decision. Certainly he would have preferred to stand with his party and friends. But from the beginning he had felt that Andrew Johnson had committed no impeachable offense, and there had been no evidence presented during the course of the trial to change his opinion. The managers of the trial had offered up a rag-bag assortment of charges which had seemed to him far short of convincing. Of the eleven articles composing the prosecution's case, nine depended directly or indirectly upon a strained interpretation of the Tenure of Office Act as it applied to the President's removal of Secretary Stanton. The other two articles, charging Johnson respectively with "condemning and vilifying Congress," and with attempting to subvert the Army Appropriations Act, were both so weak that even the Radicals appeared to be ashamed of them. Success for the impeachers, then, rested essentially upon their ability to persuade two-thirds of the Senate that President Johnson had willfully violated the Tenure Act by removing his Secretary of War.

From the time of its inception the Tenure Act had held little appeal for Fessenden. He had, indeed, openly advised against its passage when it had come before the Senate more than a year before. The fact remained, however, that the measure had met with the approval of most of his colleagues, and had been enacted into law despite the veto of the President. Thus it had become incumbent upon Fessenden to see to it that the law was obeyed, regardless of his own personal feelings toward it. In this instance, though, he could recognize no violation, since it seemed eminently apparent to him that the President's dismissal of Stanton did not come within the meaning of that act. The Tenure of Office Act did, after all, provide in this respect that: "the Secretaries . . shall hold their offices respectively for and during the term of the

President by whom they may have been appointed." Clearly, the act could not be made to apply to Secretary Stanton, who had been appointed by Johnson's predecessor. So, at least, thought Senator Fessenden, and he had found unconvincing the persistent contention of the impeachment managers that Andrew Johnson was not a president in his own right, but simply a place-filler for Lincoln's unexpired term. To the penetrating mind of Mr. Fessenden such an argument seemed far-fetched.

As the trial had progressed, Senator Fessenden had grown increasingly disgusted with the course of events. All things considered, the trial had proved unworthy of its name. It had been a travesty of justice, bludgeoned over by the six managers from the House. Of these, the most violently abusive was Benjamin F. Butler, who preferred to be called "General" and who, by his own admission, had conducted the trial as if he were arraigning a horse thief. A man of fierce emotions and questionable standards, Butler's entire life had been marked with a personal aggressiveness, caused in part perhaps by a pronounced cast in one eye which proved a physical and social cross for him to bear. Himself frequently hurt and ridiculed because of this tragi-comic deformity, he had apparently steeled his sensitivities and had learned to place small value on the feelings of others. Throughout the trial it was Butler who "carried" the prosecution on his squat frame. He was, indeed, as he later described himself, "the leading figure of the impeachment for better or worse."

Short and stocky, with a slow waddle to his walk, the fifty-year-old Butler in his swallow-tail coat "looked like a bass walking on his tail" as he moved about officiously in the front of the chamber. But his role in the proceedings had been in striking contrast to his unimposing figure. During the trial his triumphs at bullying witnesses and indulging in that juristic trickery he had practiced so successfully in Massachusetts courts, had proved painful for the defense. And his tireless industry in behalf of impeachment had seemed worthy of a better cause. As a speaker, however, Butler lacked effectiveness, a fact explained in part by his ocular deficiency which forced him to bury his face in his papers, and to a greater degree by the exceedingly offensive quality of his voice, which according to Greeley's *Tribune* was "ground out between his teeth like the screeching of a hundred saws, comingled with the rumbling of an artillery piece carried across a rugged pavement." [22] Of such endowments was General Ben Butler, the "hero of Ft. Fisher," who held strong views on the matter of Andrew Johnson, and who, it was said, had already been promised the position of Secretary of State in the event Johnson were successfully ousted. Not long before the end of the trial, before the May 16 vote was taken, this honorable advocate had sent paid spies to rummage through the President's wastebasket in search of new evidence.

Twelve o'clock noon, May 16, 1868. Andrew Johnson's hour had arrived. Chief Justice Salmon P. Chase entered the chamber and took his seat, and with his appearance the mingled noises of the floor and galleries rapidly dimmed and then disappeared. A strange foreboding silence hung over the place as from the front of the Senate the Sergeant-at-Arms began droning out his customary proclamation. Meanwhile, the managers and the counsels for the respondent entered and took their places, the former at a large table in the front of the Chamber.

At the managers' table with Butler sat old Thad Stevens whom illness had robbed of top billing in the proceedings and reduced to a secondary role. Broken in health, he now had little time left, and had been compelled during the trial to dole out his energy in meagre amounts. "My sands are nearly run," he would declare prophetically to his colleagues in the House a short time after the trial, "and I can see only with the eye of faith. I am fast descending the down-hill of life, at the foot of which stands an open grave." [23] Intensely partisan, brilliant, and unforgiving, this leonine old Radical had long led where others had followed, and in the matter of impeachment he could claim a special proprietary interest. For it was Stevens who had seized upon the opportunity afforded by Stanton's removal to launch the proceedings against Andrew Johnson. "What good did your moderation do?" he had shouted. "If you don't kill the beast, it will kill you." * But if the impeachment trial had been in truth, as some insisted, Thad Stevens' show, it was fated to be his last production. Three months later the old irreconcilable would lie dead in his equalitarian grave.

Seated with Butler and Stevens were the lesser lights of the prosecu-

---

* Georges Clemenceau, *American Reconstruction, 1865–1870* (New York, 1928), p. 153. Although the impeachment resolution carried the name of Representative John Covode of Pennsylvania, it was largely the work of Stevens. An early draft of the resolution may be found among the Stevens papers in the Library of Congress. For Stevens' argument before the House in its behalf see: *Cong. Globe*, 40th Cong., 2 sess., p. 1336.

tion. Of these, John A. Logan of Illinois and George Boutwell of Massachusetts had played the most prominent roles in the proceedings. General John A. Logan, former Union volunteer and eminent performer at Ft. Donelson and Vicksburg, father of Memorial Day, and unbending Radical, was a man of intense eyes and drooping moustache who had rivalled even Ben Butler during the trial in his vituperation against the President. Sumner had thought his main speech: "Capital! Capital! —one of the best arguments I have read for many a day." [24] Less favorably impressed, the Richmond *Dispatch* had dubbed Logan's attempt "a mere fanfaronade of malignant nonsense." [25] George Boutwell, old-line Free-Soiler and former member of Fessenden's Reconstruction Committee, had liberally donated his handsome face and figure to the Radical crusade. His efforts on behalf of conviction had fallen short of effectiveness, however, and on occasion his bungling rhetoric must have proved painful to his colleagues. Still, to the cause of impeachment he had lent the support of a strong persuasion which was probably sincerely based. Years later as a prolific writer for well-paying magazines, Boutwell would still claim that "the proceedings against Mr. Johnson were free from any element or quality of injustice." [26] Such loyalty as Boutwell's could not go unrewarded. A place would later be found for him in President Grant's cabinet.

Generally conceded to be of higher ability and distinction than the board of managers were the members of the President's defense counsel. Of this all-star group, Henry Stanbery had been considered at the beginning of the trial to be the natural leader. Acting on "an impulse of chivalric devotion," Stanbery had resigned his post as Johnson's Attorney-General in order that he might help defend his chief; but like Stevens he had been forced by ill health to assume a secondary role in the proceedings. The mantle of leadership had fallen then to William M. Evarts, who had undertaken to defend Johnson at the urging of his friend and political preceptor, Secretary of State William H. Seward. A product of the Weed-Seward machine of New York State, Evarts was no stranger to the national arena. Retained by the Government as counsel in the famous Prize Cases of the Civil War, he had later served abroad as legal agent for the State Department, returning after a short time to resume his lucrative law practice in New York. Intelligent, polished, and witty, he was unquestionably a man of many parts and faces. Only four months before, he had stood under a banner emblazoned with "Andrew Johnson, Traitor, Renegade, Outcast" and roundly denounced the President at a Cooper Union Republican rally.

In view of this and other evidence of Radical leanings in Evarts' past behavior, it seems probable that his reasons for taking on the unpopular chore of defending Johnson had not been of the purest mold. He was, however, something more than the "hireling counsel" denounced by the Radical press for "pawn[ing] his honor for a lawyer's fee." Upon a man of Evarts' profitable clientele, the $2025 fee he would receive for pleading the President's case could have had little influence. It is more likely that he had been lured by the vision of prestige and political opportunity, a vision which would be made real soon after the trial by his appointment to the Attorney-General's chair left vacant by Stanbery. That he was a man of great adaptability may be further indicated by the fact that he was later to be offered the first portfolio in President Hayes' Republican cabinet.

Evarts' performance at the trial had given indisputable testimony to his high talents and industry. In his main speech, which had lasted for fourteen hours over a period of four days, he had seriously jarred the frail fabric of the prosecution's case, and with his keen wit had reduced many of the managers' arguments to obvious absurdities. "He is an orator," proclaimed James G. Blaine, "affluent in diction, graceful in manner, with all the rare and rich gifts which attract and enchain an audience. He possesses a remarkable combination of wit and humor, and has the happy faculty of using both effectively without inflicting deadly wounds, without incurring hurtful enmities." [27] Manager John Bingham of the prosecution thought somewhat less of Evarts' long oratory, however. "The gentleman sought to render his speech immortal," Bingham commented, "by making it eternal." [28]

Along with Stanbery and Evarts, the defense had relied upon the dignity and prestige of one of the nation's most venerable jurists, Benjamin R. Curtis, one-time member of the Supreme Court and dissenter in the thunderous Dred Scott decision. Having retired from the high court in protest against Taney's handling of the Scott case, Curtis had emerged from private practice more than a decade later to lend his talents to the defense of the President. As opening speaker for the defense he had presented a brilliant argument which, even Butler was forced to admit, had left little more to be said. But in the strength of his dignity and juristic bearing lay Curtis' main weakness. In hand-to-hand fighting he had proved himself hardly a match for the slashing tactics of Butler and Logan. This lack had been partly compensated for by his defense colleague, Thomas A. R. Nelson of Tennessee, who, although no lawyer in the Curtis sense of the word, had brought into the trial an intense personal loyalty to his old friend, Andrew Johnson, and a readiness to meet the honorable managers on their own ground.

Rounding out the defense team was William S. Groesbeck, studious, unobtrusive Cincinnati lawyer. Virtually unknown at the time, he had been brought into the trial to replace the eccentric old politico, Jeremiah S. Black, whom a sudden pique against Johnson had driven from the defense fold. Although originally intended for a silent partner, Groesbeck had been forced by circumstances to take an active part in the proceedings. In his final argument he had delivered a forensic masterpiece which had come as one of the real surprises of the trial. "No one who heard it can forget the wonderful impression which the brief argument of Mr. Groesbeck made upon the Senate . . . ," remarked Sumner's secretary Moorfield Storey. "No senator wrote on his desk, no page was summoned, no conversation could be heard in gallery or cloakroom, and a silence prevailed almost unknown in the Senate while everyone listened with rapt attention to each word that the speaker uttered. It was an oratorical feat which had no parallel at the trial, and few in the experience of the Senate." [29] Upon men of such talents rested the defense of Andrew Johnson.

At his desk in the Senate Chamber, Fessenden heard the secretary read the journal of the previous sitting. Looking down upon the Senators from the president's chair, Chief Justice Chase waited. It was doubtless with a great sense of relief that Chase had opened what he supposed would be the last session of the trial. For him the impeachment proceedings had been a cross to bear. "To me the whole business seems wrong," he had declared earlier, "and if I had my option I would not take part in it." [30] Striving for impartiality, he had become suspect by his behavior and been denounced by the Radicals as a Johnson hireling and an exerter of evil influence. Almost at the beginning of the trial his judicial wings had been clipped by a ruling which permitted his bench decisions to be overridden by a majority vote of the Senate. By such a ruling his position had been virtually reduced to that of moderator. "Under the rules of the Senate," declared Sumner who had helped "neutralize" Chase, "he can become its organ, but nothing more." [31]

Even on such purely judicial matters as the admission of evidence, the Chief Justice had been stripped of final authority. "It is melancholy and ridiculous," noted testy old Gideon Welles, Johnson's Secretary of the Navy, "to see such men as Morgan, Chandler, and other small lights sit in their seats and overrule the Chief Justice on law points and questions essential to develop truth." [32] Aggravating Chase's unpleasant predicament was the fact that his son-in-law, William Sprague, sat in the Chamber as a Republican Senator from Rhode Island. And Sprague was thought by some to be "doubtful."

After the secretary had completed his reading of the journal, Senator George Edmunds, Radical from Vermont, arose and asked that the House be notified of the resumption of impeachment proceedings. Led by Elihu Washburne, friend of General Grant and chairman of the House Committee of the Whole, the members of the Lower House soon poured through the Senate doors and distributed themselves into make-shift seats scattered throughout the Chamber. The crowd inside the hall was now immense. From his seat in the press gallery, young Georges Clemenceau, who would attend the humiliation of another American president a half-century later, judged that upwards of five hundred people were standing throughout the hall. Scarcely an unclaimed space remained in any part of the Chamber—save for the empty seat of Senator Grimes.

A few minutes past twelve now, May 16, 1868. Soon the world would know how easily a future America would be able to cast adrift its unwanted presidents. Predictions of the outcome had ranged rampant in both camps. "Those who are well advised think success of the impeachment certain," Secretary Stanton had confided only three days before to J. Russell Young of the *New York Tribune*. "I have no reason for a different opinion as matters now stand." [33] Similar views were held by Pennsylvania's Simon Cameron, a politicians' politician who made a point of always knowing what was going on among his colleagues. And on the Democratic side of the Senate, Thomas A. Hendricks had expressed the same feeling. "I suppose the vote will be very close," he had declared, "but I think by one or two votes they will convict the President." [34] More certain of conviction was the violently partisan Parson Brownlow, now Governor Brownlow of Tennessee. Three days earlier he had proclaimed gleefully in the Knoxville *Whig:* "Wade will be President ad interim, whilst Johnson will be President ad out-

erim. . . ." [35] Conservative old Orville Browning, now a member of
Johnson's cabinet, had kept up a bold front, but secretly he had de-
spaired of acquittal. "Mr. Evarts . . . is very confidant [sic] of it," he
had noted in his diary a week before the May 16 vote, "still I cannot
think so. The Senators are cowards; they fear the party lash, and will
convict the President to escape it." [36]

There were those who felt otherwise, however. Both Evarts and
Groesbeck had for the past week appeared completely convinced that
the President would be acquitted, and their confidence was of a sort
that suggested something more than mere professional bravado. Secretary Seward had also seemed certain of the results, and had shown a
readiness to bet a basket of champagne on the President's acquittal.
Having found no takers, he had upped the odds to two-to-one not long
before the end of the trial. As for Senator Fessenden, he had refrained
from all prophecies. He knew how he himself would vote and that was
enough. Throughout the entire trial he had conscientiously refrained
from uttering any prediction on either the course or the outcome of
the proceedings against Johnson. In fact, with certain rare exceptions he
had refused consistently and categorically to discuss the impeachment
trial with even his most intimate associates. To have done otherwise
would have been unseemly for one acting as a judge in the case. It is
not surprising, therefore, that Fessenden had not permitted himself to
take any active part in the occasional and somewhat surreptitious meetings of the miniature band of Republican anti-impeachment Senators
held during the week preceding the May 16 vote. Only to his family in
Portland had he ventured to declare his personal views on the outcome,
and even then he had cautiously avoided outright prediction. "The result is, in my judgment, quite uncertain," he had written to his son in
early May. "It takes but seven Republicans to acquit. Three have informed me of their intention to vote for acquittal on all the articles,
and there are seven or eight more who say they find great difficulties in
their way." [37]

But in spite of all bets and oracles, it had been apparent to the better
informed that the vote would be a near thing. The lines were too evenly
drawn, it was felt, to allow for much confidence one way or the other.
True, the Radicals could count for certain on thirty-three of the Senate's fifty-four votes, or so they claimed, but this number was three short
of the two-thirds needed for conviction. As for the anti-impeachers, the

twelve Democratic Senators seemed safe enough, but seven more votes were needed, and these must come from among the Republican ranks. Four of these seven, including Fessenden's, had been pledged earlier that week. But what of the remainder? Entering the final stages, then, both sides had found themselves three votes short of victory, and each camp had grasped covetously at the five "loose" Solons.*

The last-minute pressure brought to bear upon the five reluctant Republican Senators had surpassed even that which had been expended earlier on the now generally despaired-of Fessenden. The story of these proselyting attempts and the various reactions of the recusants is a study in itself. It is enough to say here that during the final hours few tricks had been left untried by the Radical whips. Organized for the unveiled purpose of coercing the five doubtful Senators, the "Union Congressional Committee" had served as a filter station for applying party pressures. Under the aegis of this august group, friends and colleagues of the "loose" five had been sent forward to try their special pleadings one more time. To the states of the five Senators (and as a final futile gesture to those of Fessenden, Grimes, Henderson, and Trumbull as well), the following circular telegram had been sent out on May 12 by Committee Chairman Robert Schenck in a twelfth-hour move to hit each reluctant Senator in his most tender spot—his constituency:

> Great danger to the peace of the country and the Republican cause if impeachment fails. Send to your senators public opinion by resolutions, letters, and delegations.[38]

Bearing the brunt of the Radical attack had been Senators Fowler and Ross, the former an ex-college professor from Nashville and unnatural product of the Brownlow machine, the latter a small-town Kansas editor filling in the unexpired term of his suicidal predecessor, James Lane. Both were political youngsters and on uncertain enough ground to be considered especially impressionable by the Radical bosses.

Of the captured Radical votes, Fessenden's old friend of pre-war days, Senator Ben Wade, represented one. As president pro-tempore of the Senate, Wade stood to succeed to the Presidency in the event of John-

* These five doubtful Senators were Joseph Fowler (Tenn.); Edmund Ross (Kansas); William Sprague (Rhode Island); and Peter Van Winkle and W. T. Willey (West Virginia).

son's conviction. But despite his delicate position of heir apparent, Wade had made it eminently clear that he would entertain no qualms about casting his vote for conviction. If allowed, he had proclaimed, he would cast twenty votes against Andrew Johnson. "He may vote or not, as he pleases," Charles Sumner had contended successfully, "and there is no authority in the Constitution 'or any of its contemporary expounders, to criticize him." [39] But in "Honest Old Wade" the Radicals had a champion whose ardor for the cause was more than counterbalanced by a practiced mediocrity which is suggested here by Wade's exalted view of Presidential functions: "When I am asked what my policy will be in case I have to discharge the Presidential duties," he had declared early in the trial, "I generally answer that I won't have any policy." [40] Unsavory to the taste of his more level-headed colleagues, Wade might well have contributed more to the acquittal of Andrew Johnson than all the fancy phrases of Evarts, Curtis, and company. As General William T. Sherman had written to his Senator brother shortly after the beginnings of impeachment: "No sooner than you have got rid of Johnson, the same process must occur with Wade, who is exactly the same sort of man, who will quarrel with Congress in six weeks. . . . A change from Johnson to Wade will be paying dear 'for the candle.' " [41] Even while the managers had still been busily engaged in preparing their case in early March, Whitelaw Reid, reporter for the Cincinnati *Gazette*, had declared his belief that conviction would appear much more attractive to Fessenden and his friends if some person other than Wade were in line to succeed to the Presidency.[42]

Recognizing the fact that they were dragging an anchor, certain Radicals, led by Senator Henry Wilson of Massachusetts, had thought in terms of a political deal whereby upon his accession to the Presidency, Wade would agree to resign the office in favor of Schuyler Colfax, popular, teetotaling Speaker of the House. In return Wade would be promised second spot on the Republican ticket for the Presidential election coming up that autumn. The deal had never passed beyond the talking stage, however, and it was Colfax who eventually went on to seize for himself second laurels at the Chicago Convention and eventually the Vice-Presidency, whereas Wade ended up in the long run, as he later explained, "sucking hind tit." [43]

At quarter after twelve in the front of the Chamber next to Grimes' empty seat, Senator G. H. Williams of Oregon, caucus mouthpiece for the Radicals, rose to move that the Senate vote first upon the eleventh article of impeachment, the catch-all article that had been personally prepared by Butler and Stevens and was generally considered the strongest of the lot. Since this stratagem had been previously decided upon in caucus, Senator Williams' resolution passed with no difficulty, although the 34–19 vote must have seemed ominous to many of the faithful. Senator Edmunds of Vermont then moved that the body proceed to judgment. Immediately Fessenden was on his feet. "Before that motion is made," he exclaimed, "I wish to make a motion that voting be postponed for half an hour. . . . I saw Mr. Grimes last evening, and he told me he should certainly be here this morning. It was his intention——" [44] Mr. Fessenden was interrupted at this point by Democratic Senator Reverdy Johnson of Maryland, who informed him that Senator Grimes was at that moment entering the hall. And sure enough, there was Grimes being carried down the aisle by four men. Fessenden rushed over to his stricken friend and grasped his hand. "I would not exchange the recollection of that grasp of the hand," Grimes wrote afterward to a friend in Iowa, "and that glorified smile given me by that purest and ablest of men I have ever known, Mr. Fessenden, when I was borne into the Senate chamber in the arms of four men to cast my vote, for the highest distinction of my life." [45] Senator Grimes was taken by his bearers to the front of the Chamber and deposited into his seat between the Radicals, Edmunds and Williams. A moment later Chief Justice Chase ordered the clerk to poll the vote of the Senators on the eleventh article.

Senator Fessenden, "his thin face framed in spare gray hair and side-whiskers," sat erect at his desk and waited for his name to be reached. There in seat #26 of the United States Senate, shortly after noon on May 16, 1868, he prepared to take his stand—William Pitt Fessenden, the veteran warrior from Portland, Maine, nearly sixty-two years old, broken in health, and near the end of his road. He could look back upon a long and distinguished career in national politics, to days when old John Quincy Adams had harangued against the gag rule in the Lower House; to harsh pre-war words with Douglas and Davis; to long and fatiguing toil on behalf of the nation's precarious finances during the darkest hours of the Civil War; to high position, respect, and the friendship and confidence of his colleagues. Now, because he happened to believe that Andrew Johnson was innocent, he would soon be forced

by his sense of justice to snap the ties that had been so large a part of
his life; and by an alphabetic irony he would be the first of the Republican recusants to be called upon to do so. Friends, colleagues, and his
constituents back in Maine—Fessenden suspected they would not be
quick to forgive him for his apostasy, but for him there was no honorable alternative. In his written opinion submitted earlier that week he
had stated:

> I should consider myself undeserving the confidence of that just
> and intelligent people who imposed upon me this great responsi-
> bility, if for any fear of public reprobation, and for the sake of se-
> curing popular favor, I should disregard the conviction of my judg-
> ment and my conscience.[46]

The alphabet unrolled and finally the oppressive wait was ended.
"Mr. Senator Fessenden, how say you?" asked the Chief Justice. "Is the
respondent, Andrew Johnson, President of the United States, guilty or
not guilty of a high misdemeanor, as charged in this article?"

Senator Fessenden rose beside his desk. In a high, clear voice that
could be heard plainly throughout the Chamber he called out: "Not
guilty."

The dramatic account of the May 16 poll is a familiar one. Of the five
doubtful Senators, three refused to respond to party pressure and vote
for conviction. The final results revealed a count of 35–19, only one
short of the two-thirds necessary to convict. And so by this narrowest
of margins the schemes of the impeachers were foiled—or so the story
goes. Several years after the death of many of the main actors, however,
a disconcerting postscript was added to the story of the trial by Senator
Henderson. According to the Missouri Senator, Johnson's danger was
not so great as has been generally supposed. At an anti-impeachers'
meeting a short time before the polling, Senators Sprague and Willey
had pledged themselves to vote against conviction—but only if their
votes were needed. To their way of thinking there was no reason to
commit political suicide unless it were absolutely necessary for securing the President's acquittal. Consequently, the Johnson forces
might be said to have had hidden reserves, strategically placed near the
end of the alphabet and ready to jump into the fray if the battle appeared to be going badly. As matters turned out, however, by the time

the roll call had reached Sprague, the anti-impeachers were lacking only two Republican votes. With the safe Trumbull standing behind him, and Willey on guard at the end of the alphabet, no need for Sprague to do anything rash. When his name was called, he voted "Guilty." In a like manner Willey was saved from apostasy, and was enabled to go with the crowd by his West Virginia colleague, Peter Van Winkle, who cast the last of the votes needed to assure acquittal.*

Henderson's story has never been satisfactorily substantiated. If it is true, and there is no reason to doubt it, then in retrospect much of the drama of the May 16 polling disappears. True or otherwise, however, one fact seems clear. In the acquittal of Andrew Johnson no man played a more significant and decisive role than the senior Senator from Maine, and hidden reserves and persuasive oratory to the contrary, it is exceedingly doubtful that Johnson would have escaped conviction without the benefit of Fessenden's powerful example. To others, particularly Fowler and Ross, has the salvation of President Johnson traditionally been credited, but it seems safe to assume that had it not been for the position taken by Fessenden, the anti-impeachment movement within Republican ranks would have amounted to little. "The rumors come on swiftly of Fessenden's disaffection . . . ," wrote Young of the *Tribune* to Stanton in early May. "I am more in doubt about impeachment than at any time. Fessenden's defection will take others and there is no knowing where it may stop." [47] And a few days later Maine Congressman John Lynch lamented to Fessenden's erstwhile crony, Israel Washburn, that impeachment appeared to be foundering: "The responsibility of the whole is credited to Mr. Fessenden, with how much justice I know not, although I believe, if he had been known to be for impeachment, there would not have been a Republican vote against it." [48]

* This information was given by Henderson to William A. Dunning during an interview held in 1901. The same account was given somewhat later by Henderson to Horace White, Trumbull's biographer. See: W. A. Dunning, *Reconstruction, Political and Economic, 1865–1877* (New York, 1907), p. 107; and, White, *Trumbull*, p. 321. Comments made soon after the May 16 vote by supposedly well-informed political figures on the Washington scene would seem to indicate that there was some basis in fact for Senator Henderson's assertions. Typical of these comments was the unqualified assurance given a friend by Samuel J. Randall, a leading Democratic member of the Lower House and shortly thereafter its Speaker, that other Senators would have voted for acquittal if their votes had been needed. See: W. S. Howley to Samuel J. Tilden, May 22, 1868, in Tilden Papers (New York Public Library).

The Radicals, visibly shaken by the defeat of their strongest article, immediately forced a recess in the proceedings until May 26. There would be further voting on Andrew Johnson's impeachment at that time. But for all intents and purposes the scheme to oust the President had been smashed, and after May 16 all but the most fanatical of the impeachers appeared to realize that they were flogging a dead horse.

After the crowds in the galleries had dispersed and the members of the House had filed out of the Chamber, the Senate held a short meeting to discuss matters of appropriations. Following its adjournment at four o'clock, Mr. Fessenden, ashen-faced but erect, left the Senate Hall and walked alone through the Capitol. Here and there in the corridors and on the grounds outside he passed by small clusters of curious lingerers, and from some of them jeers and insults were audible. No matter, though. He had voted to acquit Andrew Johnson, and that was that. "I have no explanations to make and no apologies to offer to anybody. . . . I stand upon my character, and I suppose that will take care of itself." [49]

The Final Reckoning

DURING THE months following the trial of the President, Senator Fessenden and his recusant colleagues were subjected to a merciless torrent of abuse. "When the news came last Saturday that the Senate had failed to convict the President . . . ," commented a Boston acquaintance of Charles Sumner, "*nearly* every good republican felt terribly indignant —and if you could hear the 'cussing' which your friend Fessenden received you would have thought that virtuous public sentiment was by no means extinct." [1] From all sections of the North mountains of mail descended upon the Senator from Maine, denouncing him for his vote. "Fessenden: *You villainous Traitor!*" wrote a disappointed Radical from Philadelphia. "Betrayer of your country! Double-eyed Judas! Of course, you don't intend to return to Maine. Mind, Traitor, if you dare the attempt, the *bullet* is cast, the *pistol* ready, to confront you . . . , and send your rotten carcass to the vile dust from whence it sprung, and your debased soul to 'its own place.'" [2] And from a citizen of Maine, then traveling through Ohio:

I have heard many traitors, who fought against their country, say here and on the way that you are a *God damned* good fellow. Why is this?

You have not truly represented the loyal men of your own Maine, and the country in the vote you gave, and may God forgive you, for the Republicans of Maine never can, and never, *no never* will.[3]

Attacks by the Radical press were especially severe and appeared aimed at fanning public indignation. Even a few days before the May 16

results were known, the *New York Times,* in referring to the abusive
treatment meted out by the press to the "recreant" Republican Senators, had declared:

> The leading organs of the Republican Party have exhausted their
> ingenuity in heaping upon them . . . every possible form of oppro-
> brium and obloquy. Their motives have been aspersed, their char-
> acters blackened, and every possible effort has been made to render
> them odious and infamous in the public judgment.[4]

To the Washington *Chronicle,* mouthpiece for Congressional Radicals,
Fessenden seemed a base betrayer of his party and his country. "Do you
suppose history will justify you in such a conclusion?" asked the *Chronicle* shortly after the vote. "Do you suppose that posterity will? Do you
imagine that you are now so cool, so collected, and self-poised beyond
all your contemporaries and associates, as to see clearly to the end of
this business?"[5] The *Chronicle* could find but one explanation for
Fessenden's behavior. He had obviously recognized the fact that his
power in the Senate was slipping, that he was losing his leadership and
influence to younger and more progressive men, and his vote against
conviction had represented a final desperate effort to rule or ruin. The
New York Tribune agreed, but felt that a more specific motive for Fessenden's vote could be found in his hatred and jealousy of Ben Wade,
a feeling of long-smoldering antagonism which had not many months
before been fanned by the Radical Wade's victory over Fessenden for
the office of president pro-tempore of the Senate. As Schuyler Colfax
had written to Young of the *Tribune* mid-way through the trial: "It
would seem that he [Fessenden] must know that if he votes to acquit, the
whole country will understand that it is based on unfriendliness to
Wade, who beat him for the Prest. of the Senate, and by conviction of
the Prest. would go to the White House instead of himself."[6] Even less
kind was the Bangor *Jeffersonian,* leading Republican journal for
Penobscot County, Maine, where young Pitt Fessenden had tried his
hand at law thirty-five years before. Was it cash in hand, "less direct
pecuniary interest," or frustrated ambition, wondered the *Jeffersonian,*
that had caused Fessenden to commit "the most villainous act that ever
disgraced a Republican or any other kind of government?"[7]

Among this great harvest of thorns there were for Senator Fessenden scattered roses. Democratic praise of his vote naturally ran high. Writing to him in early August after Fessenden had returned to Maine, Senator James Dixon of Connecticut, former Republican recently driven to Democratic ranks by Radical excesses, declared:

It will not be until all the actors in that scene are in their graves, that the full extent of the good which you then had the opportunity and the courage to do, will be fully seen. Whether Andrew Johnson should be removed from office, justly or unjustly, was comparatively of little consequence, but whether our government should be Mexicanized, and an example set which would surely, in the end, utterly overthrow our institutions, was a matter of great consequence. To you and Mr. Grimes it is mainly due, that impeachment has not become an ordinary means of changing the policy of government by a violent removal of the Executive, whenever either party shall have the power.[8]

Even Portland's *Eastern Argus,* so long and so outspokenly Fessenden's political antagonist, could find nothing but kind words for the Senator and his recusant followers. "In the record which impartial history shall write of this momentous and eventful period," commented the *Argus* soon after the May 16 vote, "the names of FESSENDEN, FOWLER, GRIMES, HENDERSON, ROSS, TRUMBULL, VAN WINKLE will be surrounded with a halo of glory, as men who in the discharge of a great public duty could not be deceived, betrayed, cajoled nor driven into a violation of their consciences and oaths. . . ."[9]

More gratifying to the Senator, however, were those messages of approbation from members of his own party. From his former law-partner, William Willis of Portland, and from his industrialist friend, J. M. Forbes of Boston, Fessenden received high tribute for his courageous stand. And from the venerable jurist Benjamin Curtis, who had so ably assisted in the defense of Andrew Johnson, came a warm letter commending the Senator for his outstanding service to the nation. "I say with entire sincerity," Curtis wrote, "that no man in my time has been in the position to render so great a service to the constitution of our country . . . , and that you have completely performed the work. Looking at all the aspects of the affair, I am as sure of this as I can be of anything."[10] High praise indeed, but amid the staggering mass of criticism and denunciation from his Republican colleagues, the reassuring words of the woefully few Curtises of the nation were for Mr. Fessenden only whispers in the wind.

To a man of Fessenden's sensitivities the abuse to which he was subjected by members of his own party proved most trying. Writing to his friend Forbes in late June, the Senator confessed himself sorely disturbed by the attacks still being made upon him by many of the Republican journals. Outwardly, however, he refused to be affected by party hostility, and he certainly gave no indication of anything approaching repentance. After all, as he explained to Forbes: "A man who has knowingly and deliberately put at hazard all that most public men value, in obedience to his sense of right, will not be likely to throw away all the consolation that remains to him—his own approval." [11]

After the impeachment trial had ended, Congress returned to its legislative affairs, and for the remainder of the session, which lasted until late July, Fessenden went about his duties in much the same way as before, maintaining his same lukewarm views on Radical reconstruction, behaving in his same somewhat imperious manner, and becoming involved in his customary quarrels with Charles Sumner. During this period he voted on most occasions with his Republican colleagues, although both in the original Senate vote and in the later override of President Johnson's veto, he refused to support his party's successful attempt to admit six Southern states which had been reconstructed under the Radical program. At first, after the trial, he was conscious of a great feeling of antagonism towards him on the part of many of his colleagues, but as the weeks passed he sensed that time was rapidly healing the wounds. In this respect time was unquestionably given a substantial boost by the fact that party managers had no desire to alienate prospective support during a presidential election year. This much was made clear to Fessenden not long after the trial when the Republican party's newly-chosen presidential nominee, General Grant, sent his personal assurances of esteem and high regard to the Senator from Maine. Thus, by late June, Fessenden could write to his ailing friend Grimes: "We are getting along stupidly as usual here. The impeachers are not particularly happy, though most of them have become very civil. Wade is said to be very cross and refuses to be comforted. . . . Stanton I never hear spoken of." [12]

It has usually been stated that Fessenden, like his six recusant colleagues, caused his own political ruin by voting against the conviction of Andrew Johnson. Whether or not this was actually true in Fessenden's case is a question that will never be resolved, since death intervened before the Senator could stand for reelection in 1871. Certainly his popularity rating was low enough in his home state during the months immediately following the trial. In the state elections held in September of that year (1868), Senator Fessenden's supporters fared badly against the Blaine-directed opposition of the Maine Republican machine, with the result that a strongly anti-Fessenden Legislature was sent to Augusta. In the following January the Augusta Legislature proceeded to elect the Senator's long-time rival Hannibal Hamlin to the United States Senate over the Fessenden-preferred incumbent, Lot Morrill. Poor Fessenden, lamented old Gideon Welles when he learned of Morrill's defeat, "Fessenden, who for years has been all-powerful in Maine . . . is said not to have a friend in the legislature." [13]

And yet all indications suggest that within a surprisingly few months after the conclusion of the impeachment trial Senator Fessenden's stock among his party colleagues was slowly but perceptibly on the rise. This fact can be accounted for in part by his active and exceedingly effective role in campaigning for General Grant in the late summer and early autumn of 1868. For some time Fessenden had been convinced that Grant was the man to win with, and although the Senator had initially felt some reluctance to beat the electioneering drum for Radical reconstruction, which he had so consistently refused to support on the floor of the Senate, he ultimately had little difficulty in persuading himself to do so, lest the Democrats succeed in carrying through their plan to topple the entire program for restoring the South.

For Fessenden, however, the greatest issue of the campaign centered about the popular "Ohio Idea," supported by the Democracy and brought personally into Maine during late August by its leading exponent, "Gentleman George" Pendleton of Cincinnati. Briefly described, the "Ohio Idea" called for redemption of the war-time five-twenty Government bonds in legal-tender notes rather than coin, a scheme which to Fessenden's way of thinking was little more than outright repudiation. As the leading financial figure in the Senate and a person who had helped father the five-twenty bonds, Senator Fessenden was naturally reckoned as a powerful weapon with which to thwart the "soft-money" plans of the Democracy. Consequently, during the early autumn of 1868 many of his Republican colleagues in other states, who had but a few months before been so ready to berate him, now saw fit to call upon him to aid them in combating "repudiation." Because of the poor condition of his health, however, the Senator was compelled to restrict his activities to Maine, where he did yeoman work in behalf of Grant and hard-money payments. There was no honesty in the Democratic paper-money doctrine, Fessenden assured his Maine audiences. There was but one honorable way to deal with the problem, and that was for the Government to "pay its debts and redeem its obligations in good faith, in common honesty, in the face of the world, and in the spirit as well as the letter of the contract." [14] Convinced that a triumph of the Democratically supported "Ohio Idea" would lead to national disgrace and most probably to financial disaster, Senator Fessenden was especially gratified by the victory of General Grant in early November. "The nation is saved a terrible calamity," he wrote to his friend George Harrington, "and we are afforded one more opportunity to save what we fought for." [15]

Upon his return to Washington for the reconvening of Congress in early December, Fessenden found that indignation against him had waned noticeably during the recess. He was in fact somewhat amused by the great friendliness now shown him by several members who had hardly spoken to him during the weeks immediately following his impeachment vote. As he had explained to Harrington a month before:

> I am convinced that the general feeling now is that had impeachment prevailed, the party would have been beaten. Even those who are most anxious to destroy my influence and standing . . . do not dispute the fact that we probably saved the election. Impeachment was a great blunder—on the part of some a crime—and of others pure cowardice. At the time I believed that my vote would destroy me politically. It looks now as if I should survive it.[16]

Even from Charles Sumner kind words were now audible on occasion, particularly after Fessenden let it be known not long after the session had begun that he considered Sumner the most logical and deserving choice for Secretary of State in General Grant's Cabinet. To a relative the Senator explained that he was convinced that Sumner would perform well in the position. Furthermore, it would be a relief to get him out of the Senate. From that time on, relations between the two New England Senators became more cordial, and in early March of 1869 their colleagues were treated to the unbelievable spectacle of Charles Sumner and Pitt Fessenden defending one another on the Senate floor. "I am glad to know how kindly he felt to me before his death," Sumner remarked a few months later.[17]

For General Grant's incoming administration Fessenden had high hopes. "I have great confidence in his capacity," the Senator declared soon after Grant's election, "and perfect reliance on his patriotic devotion to the best interests of the country." [18] But in Grant, Senator Fessenden was soon disillusioned, and within a few months after the General's inauguration Fessenden was forced to admit that President Grant was apparently more interested in the honors associated with his high office than in carrying out its duties and responsibilities.

Especially disturbing to Senator Fessenden was Grant's deference to the Radicals, particularly in matters of patronage. "Never was so disgraceful a scramble for office seen," Fessenden noted in mid-April. "The sweep has been almost universal, good and tried Republicans, soldiers, who have been but a short time in office, being unceremoniously turned out in many instances. I am very much disappointed and disgusted." [19] To Grant's old crony Elihu Washburne of Illinois was tendered the post of Secretary of State, as a gesture of friendship on the part of the new President. Fessenden was amazed. "Whoever heard before of a man nominated Secretary of State merely as a compliment?" he growled.[20] But for Washburne the position proved something more than a compliment, for before being succeeded by Hamilton Fish after a scant five days in office, the ephemeral Secretary proceeded to "shake up" the foreign missions for the sake of making room for his deserving Radical friends. Among those removed by Washburne was George Harrington of the Swiss mission, friend and appointee of Senator Fessenden. "I made every effort to continue your mission," the Senator later explained to Harrington, "but with no encouragement. Washburn[e] said you would have to come home and Fish could not stay the tide. . . . The whole line of foreign appointments is very weak, many of them, as I am told, having been procured beforehand, and arranged by Washburn[e] before he went out." [21]

Fessenden had no intention of being bullied out of his patronage, however, foreign or otherwise, and his success in retaining Freeman

Morse in the much-coveted London consulate indicates that his influence in the party was still a factor to be reckoned with—particularly so
after Grant's appointment of Fessenden's long-time friend Hamilton
Fish as Washburne's replacement in the State Department. When word
reached the Senator in mid-March that Morse, who had been left un-
disturbed by President Johnson, was now to be removed by Grant,
presumably in favor of a Blaine appointee, Fessenden was quick and
loud in his protestations. "I feel an unusual degree of interest in this
matter . . . on Morse's account," he declared to Fish, "because he is
poor, eminently capable, has rendered great services, and is my friend."
But there were also reasons of a more personal nature for his wanting
Morse retained. "I consider myself entitled to some considerations from
the President, from my age and standing in the party—and I do not like
to be overridden." [22] As a result of Fessenden's remonstrances Morse
was not only continued in office, but within two weeks' time was advanced by Grant to the grade of consul-general, despite the opposition
of Blaine and his Lower House colleagues from Maine.

The third and final session of the 40th Congress ended in early March
of 1869 with the advent of the Grant administration, and, in accordance
with the Meeting of Congress resolution of January 1867, was followed
immediately by the first session of the 41st, which in turn lasted until
late April. During this entire period Senator Fessenden was noticeably
less active in debate than in previous sessions. He did, however, in
mid-December take long and successful issue with Democratic Senator
T. A. Hendricks of Indiana on the matter of restoring Southern militias,
a proposal which Fessenden favored since he felt it would conduce to
greater tranquility within the Southern states. On the fifteenth amendment the Senator also spoke at some length, voicing his support for the
resolution shortly before it passed the Senate on February 9. But for
Senator Oliver Morton's subsequent plan to include this "impartial
suffrage" amendment as a prerequisite for admitting those Southern
states still unreconstructed, Senator Fessenden had little sympathy. To
impose new conditions for reconstruction at this late date would, he
felt, be both unfair and unwise, and he consequently voted with the
minority against Morton's proposal.

On March 6 the Senator had occasion to argue, but without avail, for
repeal of the Tenure of Office Act, a standing grievance with him since
its inception two years before. But unquestionably Fessenden's most

outstanding performance during this long sitting was that given in late February in support of a bill which would pledge the Government to repay its five-twenty loans in coin. In a speech delivered at a late hour in the evening Senator Fessenden again declared, as he had during the campaign of the previous autumn in Maine, his uncompromising belief in the obligations of the Government to honor its debts in full rather than with depreciated greenbacks. "It was one of the most telling speeches Mr. Fessenden . . . ever uttered upon the Senate floor," noted a correspondent covering the scene:

> The Maine statesman roused like a blooded racing charger to his last full bent, poured out on the Senate, under the glow of the midnight lamps, his most eloquent, fervid speech for years. The old members of the Senate gathered around him at its close, assuring him that he had equaled his best thing.[23]

In late April of 1869 Senator Fessenden took final leave of his colleagues and of the city where he had spent so great a part of his time since his first election to the United States Senate in 1854. It was doubtless with a feeling of some satisfaction that he sensed himself now, less than a year after his impeachment vote, largely redeemed in the eyes of his Washington associates. He was well aware, however, that he stood less high in the estimation of the Republican machine in his own home state, and upon his return to Portland he discovered a strong movement afoot to trade him in for young Blaine in the Senatorial election scheduled for January of 1871. In a letter written to his friend Grimes in early August, Senator Fessenden did, in fact, confess fears that in his coming attempts for reelection he would be forced to "contend at some disadvantage." [24] But for Fessenden there was no longer any need to worry about the political future.

During the night of September 7–8, 1869, a savage storm swept through New England. Streams were flooded; bridges were washed away, and trees uprooted. Against the Fessenden home on State Street the wind and rain lashed mercilessly. On the front lawn the Senator's favorite tree, which he himself had planted many years before, snapped and fell before the tempest, and inside the great brick house shortly before four o'clock in the morning, Senator William Pitt Fessenden of Maine answered his final roll. He had been taken ill scarcely more than a week before, after an evening of whist with friends. He had retired in apparently good health, but about midnight his son William had heard the Senator call out and had gone up to find his father pacing the floor in great pain. "His physician was at once summoned," Francis Fessenden recorded in the biography of his father. "He administered morphine, which allayed the pain and permitted the senator to go back to bed. He never left it. The attack was a rupture of the lower intestine, resulting from an irritation of many years' standing." [25]

On the Saturday morning following his death, funeral services were held for the Senator at the First Parish Church in Portland. Large crowds formed outside the church long before it was opened, and remained to join in a great procession through the streets of Mr. Fessenden's beloved city by the sea. All flags in the city and on ships in the harbor flew at half-mast. Church bells were tolled and cannons fired from the fort and arsenal in a final tribute to the great statesman. And then early in the afternoon of September 11, 1869, while Jay Gould and Jim Fisk were busily engaged in their attempts to corner the nation's gold supply, the remains of Senator Fessenden were committed to the Maine earth in the family lot at Evergreen Cemetery.

For the man who had recently been so roundly condemned and vilified by a great majority of his countrymen, there could now be found few words too laudatory. "When the Senate meets next winter, the tall form of the grave and dignified Senator from Maine will not be there," declared the *New York Times*, "and no face or form will leave a deeper impress upon that body." [26] Commented the Portland *Eastern Argus*, powerful Democratic journal which had dogged the Senator's political footsteps for nearly thirty years:

> Such men in public life are now unhappily too rare and we fear that we shall long have occasion to mourn over the void his death will create in the public service. His conduct was ever without fear and without reproach; no one doubted his integrity, and those who most confided in him found him most faithful and true.[27]

Meeting for the special purpose of paying homage to the memory of Senator Fessenden, the members of the Cumberland County Bar Association outdid one another in eulogizing their late colleague. Said one:

His public life was singularly free from stain or blemish. He was never seduced by corrupting influences to the desertion of high principles. He was never deterred from the declaration and vindication of these principles by either popular clamor or the frowns of power. His great end and aim was to do right. He never sought the popularity that floats merely upon the passing breeze, and dies away long before it can reach posterity.[28]

A few months later at the State Capitol in Augusta, the Maine Senate unanimously adopted a memorial resolution introduced by the Senator's young friend and political protégé, Thomas B. Reed:

As a stateman [the resolution read] he was a friend of liberty when her friends were few. He was tried on many critical occasions and was equal to all, and at last crowned a life of long service by steadfastly enduring for what he thought right the reproaches of friends and the praise of foes. The example of his stainless character and of the steady courage with which he met obloquy for the sake of convictions, in its effect upon the lives of those who come after him, will carry his influence and power to centuries which his name may never reach.[29]

Nor was there any lack of tribute to Senator Fessenden from among his Washington associates. "He among us today will be fortunate indeed," declared Lyman Trumbull on the floor of the Senate in mid-December, "if, when his work on earth is done, he shall leave behind him a life so pure and useful, a reputation so unsullied, a patriotism so ardent, and statesmanship so conspicuous as William Pitt Fessenden." [30] A great and good man, agreed Senators Williams and Anthony. "The purity of his life challenges and commands our admiration," commented the Senator's long-time political foe Hannibal Hamlin.[31] And from Charles Sumner came laments that without his esteemed colleague Fessenden, the Senate would hardly seem the same. "If sparkles fell where they should not have fallen," remarked Sumner in final tribute, "they cannot be remembered now." [32]

Three thousand miles away in Switzerland, Fessenden's devoted companion Grimes inhaled the mountain air in a last futile effort to regain his health. Upon learning that his great friend had fallen, he had felt an overpowering sense of grief and emptiness. Pondering the past and the future, himself not far removed from death, James Grimes perhaps of all men could understand most clearly the immensity of the loss. "He was the highest-toned, truest, noblest man I ever knew," Grimes wrote to a friend in Iowa. "I never knew or expect to know a man who can approach him in the qualities that go to make a grand man and a noble statesman. The man does not live who can take his place in the Senate." [33]

Notes

CHAPTER I

1. Unpublished diary of the Reverend William Fessenden, in possession of Miss Mary Barrows, Fryeburg, Maine.

2. Daniel Webster to Carlton Hurd, August 25, 1842, in Daniel Webster, *Writings and Speeches* (National Edition: Boston, 1903), XVIII, 147.

3. Claude M. Fuess, *Daniel Webster* (Boston, 1930), I, 67–76. See also: Charles Lanman, *The Private Life of Daniel Webster* (New York, 1857).

4. Webster to James Bingham, January 19, 1806, in Webster, *Writings*, National Edition, XVII, 220.

5. Samuel Fessenden to Ruth Greene, March 12, 1806, in possession of Miss Mary Barrows, Fryeburg, Maine.

6. L. C. Hatch (ed.), *Maine, a History* (New York, 1919), II, 368–69.

7. Francis Fessenden, *Life and Public Services of William Pitt Fessenden* (Boston, 1907), I, 32.

8. Helen Coffin Beedy, *Mothers of Maine* (Portland, 1895), pp. 203–204.

9. William Willis, *A History of the Law, the Courts, and the Lawyers of Maine* (Portland, 1863), pp. 544–45. See also: William A. Robinson, "Samuel Fessenden," in *Dictionary of American Biography* (edited by Allen Johnson and Dumas Malone), VI, 346.

10. Samuel Fessenden, *An Oration Delivered Before the Federal Republicans of New Gloucester and the Adjacent Towns, July 4, A.D., 1811* (Portland, 1811), p. 2.

11. Willis, *Lawyers*, pp. 548–49.

12. *Maine Register and United States Calendar, 1820* (Portland, 1820), pp. 126–27.

13. Horatio Bridge, *Personal Recollections of Nathaniel Hawthorne* (New York, 1893), p. 16.

14. William Pitt Fessenden, "Prospects of the South American States," 1823, in unpublished Public Exercises Records of Bowdoin College (Bowdoin College Library, Brunswick, Maine).

15. Bridge, *Hawthorne*, p. 25.

16. Unpublished Faculty Records of Bowdoin College, July 16, 1823 (Massachusetts Hall, Bowdoin College).

CHAPTER II

1. William Pitt Fessenden to Samuel Fessenden, July 4, 1826, in Fessenden Family Collection (Bowdoin College Library).

2. W. P. Fessenden, *An Oration Delivered Before the Young Men of Portland, July 4, 1827* (Portland, 1827). Copies of this pamphlet may be found at the Maine State Library in Augusta, and at the Maine Historical Society in Portland.

3. Fessenden to Samuel Fessenden, December 13, 1827, in Fessenden Family Collection.

4. Fessenden, *Life*, I, 6.

5. Fessenden to Charles Daveis, January 13, 1832, in Daveis Collection (Maine Historical Society).

6. See *Kennebec Journal* (Augusta, Maine), January 27, 1832.

7. Fessenden to Charles Daveis, January 13, 1832, in Daveis Collection (Maine Historical Society).

8. Fessenden to Maine Legislature, February 15, 1832, in Fessenden Papers (Library of Congress).

9. Fessenden to Maine Legislature, February 16, 1832, in Fessenden Papers (Library of Congress).

10. Samuel Fessenden to William Lloyd Garrison, December 14, 1832, in Anti-Slavery Papers (Boston Public Library).

11. Samuel Fessenden to Garrison, July 13, 1847, in Anti-Slavery Papers (Boston Public Library).

12. As reprinted in the *Eastern Argus* (Portland), September 10, 1840.

13. Henry A. Ford (ed.), *History of Penobscot County* (Cleveland, 1882), p. 677.

14. Penobscot County Supreme Judicial Court Records, 1833–35 (unpublished), County Courthouse, Bangor.

15. Cumberland County Supreme Judicial Court Records, 1837 (unpublished), County Courthouse, Portland.

CHAPTER III

1. Webster to Fessenden, April 8, 1837, in Fessenden Family Collection.

2. Fessenden to William Willis, May 11, 1837, in Willis Collection (Maine Historical Society).

3. Fessenden, *Life*, I, 13.

4. *Ibid.*, pp. 15–16.

5. *Ibid.*, p. 12.

6. September 26, 1837.

7. *Kennebec Journal*, March 17, 1840.

8. John Hodsdon to F. O. J. Smith, March 23, 1840, in Smith Collection (Maine Historical Society).

9. Freeman Morse to Fessenden, May 16, 1840, in Fessenden Papers (Library of Congress).

10. September 7, 1840.

11. September 12, 1840.

12. Thomas Fessenden to William Pitt Fessenden, November 20, 1840, in Fessenden Papers (Library of Congress).

CHAPTER IV

1. Charles Dickens, *American Notes* (London, 1842), pp. 135–36.

2. Thomas Hart Benton, *Thirty Years View* (New York, 1854–56), II, 360.

3. Glydon G. Van Deusen, *The Jacksonian Era* (New York, 1959), p. 143.

4. Fessenden to William Willis, June 6, 1841, in Willis Collection (Maine Historical Society).

5. Fessenden to Samuel Fessenden, July 29, 1841, in Fessenden Family Collection.

6. *Congressional Globe,* 27th Congress, 1 session, p. 167.

7. C. F. Adams (ed.), *Memoirs of John Quincy Adams* (Philadelphia, 1874–77), X, 499.

8. *Congressional Globe,* 27th Cong., 1 sess., p. 205.

9. August 16, 1841.

10. Fessenden to William Willis, June 6, 1841, in Willis Collection (Maine Historical Society).

11. *Congressional Globe,* 27th Cong., 1 sess., p. 134.

12. *Ibid.,* p. 323.

13. Adams (ed.), *Memoirs,* X, 529–30.

14. Henry Clay to Francis Brooke, July 4, 1841, in Calvin Colton (ed.), *Private Correspondence of Henry Clay* (New York, 1855), p. 454.

15. Daniel Webster to Edward Everett, July 28, 1841, in Fletcher Webster (ed.), *Private Correspondence of Daniel Webster* (Boston, 1857), II, 106.

16. Fessenden, *Life,* I, 21.

17. *Ibid.*

18. Daniel Webster to Hiram Ketchum, September 10, 1841, in Fletcher Webster (ed.), *Private Correspondence,* II, 110.

19. Fessenden to Charles Daveis, April 22, 1842, in Daveis Collection (Maine Historical Society).

20. *Cong. Globe,* 27th Cong., 2 sess., p. 118.

21. *Appendix to the Congressional Globe,* 27th Cong., 2 sess., p. 734.

22. Adams (ed.), *Memoirs,* XI, 166.

23. Fessenden to Charles Daveis, June 7, 1842, in Miscellaneous Manuscript Collection (Maine Historical Society).

24. Dickens, *American Notes,* p. 140.

25. Fessenden, *Life,* I, 22–23.

26. Henry W. Longfellow to Fessenden, February 15, 1842, in Longfellow Papers (Craigie House, Cambridge, Massachusetts).

27. Fessenden to William Willis, June 6, 1841, in Willis Collection (Maine Historical Society).

CHAPTER V

1. Fessenden to James S. Pike, April 9, 1859, in Pike Papers (Calais).

2. City of Portland Taxbook, 1853 (unpublished), City Hall, Portland. The Cumberland County Registry of Deeds (unpublished) at the Portland County Courthouse reveals that during the period 1841–1870, Fessenden was involved in seventy-four real estate transactions, many of which were undoubtedly handled for clients. His wife's name, however, appears on the books a total of one hundred and eighty-eight times from 1851 to 1870. In most of these dealings Fessenden exercised his power of attorney over an extensive property which had come to his wife on the death of her wealthy father in 1851. See vols. 173–373.

3. Registry of Deeds for Cumberland County, 1841 (unpublished), vol. 173, p. 133, in County Courthouse, Portland.

4. "Veazie vs. Williams," in *Federal Cases . . . in the Circuit and District Courts of the United States,* Book 28, pp. 1124–35.

5. "Veazie vs. Williams, Me., 1850," in *United States Supreme Court Digest,* III, 160.

6. Printed circular letter, January 5, 1852, in F. O. J. Smith Collection (Maine Historical Society).

7. *Eastern Argus*, April 10, 1844.

8. Fessenden to James Fessenden, October 5, 1848, in Norcross Collection (Massachusetts Historical Society).

9. John Marsh, *The Napoleon of Temperance: Sketches on the Life and Character of Neal Dow* (New York, 1852), p. 7.

10. Neal Dow, *A History of Prohibition in Maine*, p. 111. Undated pamphlet at the Maine State Library, Augusta.

11. Marsh, *Napoleon of Temperance*, p. 9.

12. *Ibid.*, p. 14.

13. Fessenden to William Fessenden (uncle), July 17, 1848, in Miscellaneous Collection (Maine Historical Society).

14. *Ibid.*

15. *Ibid.*

16. August 15, 1850.

17. Charles Hamlin, *Life and Times of Hannibal Hamlin* (Cambridge, 1899), p. 231.

18. Samuel Fessenden to Ellen Fessenden, June 6, 1852, in possession of John Baxter, Brunswick, Maine.

19. *New York Tribune*, June 21, 1852

20. *Ibid.*, June 19, 1852.

21. Fessenden to Hannibal Hamlin, November 17, 1852, in Hamlin Collection (Maine Historical Society).

CHAPTER VI

1. Neal Dow, *Reminiscences* (Portland, 1898), pp. 432–47.

2. *Ibid.*, p. 451.

3. *Kennebec Journal*, April 7, 1853.

4. Willis, *Lawyers*, p. 453.

5. Hamlin, *Life and Times*, p. 217.

6. Fessenden to Hannibal Hamlin, December 27, 1853, in Hamlin Collection (Maine Historical Society).

7. As cited in Dow, *Reminiscences*, p. 478.

8. Fessenden to Judge Tenney, December 17, 1864, in Fessenden Letterbook (Library of Congress).

9. Fessenden, *Life*, I, 33.

10. W. W. Nisston to Francis Fessenden, August 15, 1878, in Fessenden Papers (Library of Congress).

11. Dow, *Reminiscences*, pp. 487–94.

12. February 6, 1854.

13. Fessenden to William Crosby, February 11, 1854, in Fessenden Papers (Library of Congress).

14. Samuel C. Fessenden to William Pitt Fessenden, February 11, 1854, in Fessenden Papers (Library of Congress).

15. James S. Pike to Fessenden, February 10, 1854, in Pike Papers (Library of Congress).

16. Fessenden, *Life*, I, 40–41.

CHAPTER VII

1. Charles Sumner, *Works* (Boston, 1875–83), XIII, 190.
2. James S. Pike, *First Blows of the Civil War* (New York, 1879), p. 219.
3. *Appendix to the Congressional Globe*, 33rd Cong., 1 sess., pp. 319–324.
4. Benjamin Wade to "Cal," March 4, 1854, in Wade Papers (Library of Congress).
5. Samuel Longfellow, *Life of Henry Wadsworth Longfellow* (Boston, 1886–87), II, 267.
6. David Pratt to Fessenden, March 20, 1854, in Fessenden Papers (Library of Congress).
7. Fessenden, *Life*, I, 47.
8. Pike, *Civil War*, p. 220.
9. *Ibid.*, p. 221.
10. Pike to Fessenden, May 15, 1854, in Pike Papers (Library of Congress).
11. *Kennebec Journal*, March 10, 1854.
12. As reprinted in the *Kennebec Journal*, March 10, 1854.
13. Dow to Hannibal Hamlin, April 7, 1854, in Hamlin Collection (Maine Historical Society).
14. Freeman H. Morse to Fessenden, June 9, 1854, in Fessenden Papers (Library of Congress).
15. Fessenden, *Life*, I, 48.
16. *Ibid.*
17. As reprinted in the *New York Tribune*, June 22, 1854.
18. Fessenden to Pike, August 14, 1854, in Pike Papers (Calais).
19. *Appendix to the Congressional Globe*, 33rd Cong., 1 sess., p. 219.
20. Fessenden, *Life*, I, 51–61.
21. August 16, 1855.
22. August 15, 1855.
23. Fessenden, *Life*, I, 63.

CHAPTER VIII

1. Dana to Pike, undated, in Pike Papers (Calais).
2. Fessenden, *Life*, I, 78.
3. *Appendix to the Congressional Globe*, 34th Cong., 1 sess., pp. 301–306.
4. Allan Nevins, *Hamilton Fish* (New York, 1936), pp. 59–60.
5. Wade to Fessenden, April 15, 1856, in Fessenden Papers (Library of Congress).
6. Dana to Pike, June 11, 1856, in Pike Papers (Calais).
7. Fessenden to William Willis, June 15, 1856, in Willis Collection (Maine Historical Society).
8. James W. Stone to Fessenden, May 6, 1856, in Fessenden Papers (Library of Congress).
9. Fessenden to Elizabeth Warriner, July 10, 1856, in Fessenden Papers (Library of Congress).
10. Sumner to Raymond, March 2, 1856, in Raymond Papers (New York Public Library).
11. Fessenden to Fish, December 17, 1859, in Fish Papers (Library of Congress).
12. Fessenden to Francis Fessenden, June 15, 1856, in Fessenden Family Collection.
13. William Salter, "William Pitt Fessenden," in *Annals of Iowa*, 3rd series, VIII (April, 1908), 323.

14. Fessenden to Trumbull, November 16, 1856, in Trumbull Papers (Library of Congress).

15. R. P. Cutler to Fessenden, December 5, 1856, in Fessenden Papers (Library of Congress).

16. Fessenden to Trumbull, November 16, 1856, in Trumbull Papers (Library of Congress).

CHAPTER IX

1. Fessenden to Sumner, February 12, 1857, in Sumner Papers (Houghton Library, Harvard University).

2. *Cong. Globe*, 34th Cong., 3 sess., pp. 29–36.

3. Sumner to Fessenden, December 11, 1856, in Fessenden Family Collection.

4. Fessenden to Sumner, December 18, 1856, in Sumner Papers (Houghton Library, Harvard University).

5. Fessenden to Elizabeth Warriner, December 7, 1856, in Fessenden Papers (Library of Congress).

6. Samuel Fessenden to Ellen L. Fessenden, March 31, 1857, in possession of John Baxter, Brunswick, Maine.

7. March 7, 1857.

8. Fessenden, *Life*, I, 88.

9. *Ibid.*

10. Ware to Fessenden, March 12, 1857, in Fessenden Papers (Library of Congress).

11. *New York Tribune*, March 7, 1857.

12. Joseph Fessenden to W. P. Fessenden, August 2, 1857, in Fessenden Papers (Library of Congress).

13. Fessenden, *Life*, I, 92.

14. *Cong. Globe*, 35th Cong., 1 sess., p. 8.

15. *Ibid.*, p. 5.

16. *Ibid.*, p. 411.

17. Fessenden to Pike, February 2, 1858, in Pike Papers (Calais).

18. Pike to Fessenden, April 9, 1858, in Pike Papers (Library of Congress).

19. Buchanan to Colonel Baker, January 11, 1858, in John Bassett Moore (ed.), *Works of James Buchanan* (Philadelphia, 1908–10), X, 177.

20. Horace White, *Life of Lyman Trumbull* (Boston, 1913), p. 83.

21. James G. Blaine, *Twenty Years of Congress* (Norwich, Connecticut), I, 142.

22. Fessenden, *Life*, I, 96.

23. Fessenden to Samuel Fessenden, May 9, 1858, in Fessenden Family Collection.

24. *Ibid.*

25. Fessenden to Pike, August 24, 1858, in Pike Papers (Calais).

26. Fessenden to Pike, August 30, 1858, in Pike Papers (Calais).

27. *Eastern Argus*, September 4, 1858.

28. September 7, 1858.

29. Fessenden to Pike, September 26, 1858, in Pike Papers (Calais).

30. *Eastern Argus*, September 6, 1858.

CHAPTER X

1. Fessenden to Fish, December 18, 1858, in Fish Papers (Library of Congress).

2. Fessenden, *Life*, I, 104.

3. Fessenden to Elizabeth Warriner, December 11, 1860, in Fessenden Papers (Library of Congress).

4. Fessenden to Fish, December 18, 1858, in Fish Papers (Library of Congress).

5. Fessenden to William Fessenden, January 22, 1859, in Fessenden Family Collection.

6. Fessenden to William Fessenden, March 1, 1859, in Fessenden Family Collection.

7. Fessenden to Elizabeth Warriner, June 26, 1859, in Fessenden Family Collection.

8. Pike to Fessenden, September 6, 1859, in Pike Papers (Library of Congress).

9. Fessenden to Pike, July 23, 1859, in Pike Papers (Calais).

10. Pike to Fessenden, July 25, 1859, in Pike Papers (Library of Congress).

11. Fessenden to Elizabeth Warriner, June 26, 1859, in Fessenden Family Collection.

12. Fessenden to Pike, September 4, 1859, in Pike Papers (Calais).

13. C. H. Webb, "Old John Brown at Harper's Ferry," printed poem in the Executive Papers of Governor Henry A. Wise (Virginia State Library, Richmond).

14. Fessenden to William Fessenden, December 15, 1859, in Fessenden Family Collection.

15. February 13, 1860.

16. Emory Washburn to Fessenden, April 27, 1860, in Fessenden Papers (Library of Congress).

17. Dana to Pike, March 10, 1860, in Pike Papers (Calais).

18. Blaine to Fessenden, March 6, 1860, in Fessenden Family Collection.

19. Blaine to Fessenden, February 17, 1860, in Fessenden Family Collection.

20. Fessenden, *Life*, I, 112–13.

21. Fessenden to Elizabeth Warriner, May 27, 1860, in Fessenden Family Collection.

22. Pike to Fessenden, September 7, 1860, in Pike Papers (Library of Congress).

23. Fessenden to Pike, September 12, 1860, in Pike Papers (Calais).

24. *Ibid.*

CHAPTER XI

1. Fish to Fessenden, December 11, 1860, in Fessenden Papers (Library of Congress).

2. Fessenden to Fish, December 15, 1860, in Fish Papers (Library of Congress).

3. Joseph Fessenden to Fessenden, January 10, 1861, in Fessenden Papers (Library of Congress).

4. Fessenden to William Fessenden, February 17, 1861, in Fessenden Family Collection.

5. Fessenden to Abraham Lincoln, January 20, 1861, in Lincoln Papers (Library of Congress).

6. Simon Cameron to Fessenden, June 1, 1861, in Fessenden Family Collection.

7. Fessenden to Elizabeth Warriner, March 17, 1861, in Fessenden Family Collection.

8. *Ibid.*

9. Roy P. Basler, et al. (eds.), *Collected Works of Abraham Lincoln* (New Brunswick, New Jersey, 1953), IV, 284.

10. Carl Sandburg, *Abraham Lincoln, the War Years* (New York, 1936–39), III, 369.

11. Salter, "Fessenden," 325.

12. Sandburg, *War Years*, I, 313–14.

13. *Ibid.*, I, 434.

14. *Cong. Globe,* 37th Cong., 1 sess., p. 317.

15. Davis R. Dewey, *Financial History of the United States* (London, 1903), pp. 263, 303.

16. *Cong. Globe,* 37th Cong., 1 sess., p. 259.

17. Fessenden to William Fessenden, July 22, 1861, in Fessenden Family Collection.

18. Fessenden to Pike, September 8, 1861, in Roger Taney Papers (Library of Congress).

19. Fessenden to William Fessenden, July 14, 1861, in Fessenden Family Collection.

20. Fessenden, *Life,* I, 189.

21. Fessenden to Grimes, September 26, 1861, in Salter, "Fessenden," p. 327.

22. *Ibid.*

23. Fessenden to Pike, September 8, 1861, in Taney Papers (Library of Congress).

24. September 3, 1861.

25. Cassius Clay to James Doolittle, October 17, 1861, in Doolittle Papers (Library of Congress).

26. Fessenden to James Grimes, September 26, 1861, in Salter, "Fessenden," p. 326.

27. Fessenden to Pike, September 8, 1861, in Taney Papers (Library of Congress).

28. Adam Gurowski, *Diary* (Boston, 1862), I, 98.

CHAPTER XII

1. Fessenden to J. M. Forbes, November 10, 1861, in Fessenden Family Collection.

2. Fish to Fessenden, January 25, 1862, in Fish Letterbook (Library of Congress).

3. G. S. Ward to Fessenden, January 23, 1862, in Fessenden Papers (Library of Congress).

4. Fessenden to William Fessenden, December 15, 1861, in Fessenden Family Collection.

5. *Cong. Globe,* 37th Cong., 2 sess., pp. 16–17.

6. *Ibid.,* p. 31.

7. Chase to Fessenden, January 15, 1862, in Fessenden Family Collection.

8. Fessenden to William Fessenden, January 17, 1862, in Fessenden Family Collection.

9. Samuel Fessenden to Fessenden, January 18, 1862, in Bixby Collection (Huntington Library).

10. Washburn to Hannibal Hamlin, May 23, 1862, in I. Washburn Papers (Library of Congress).

11. George Julian, *Political Recollections* (Chicago, 1884), pp. 212–13.

12. Fessenden to John Andrew, March 9, 1862, in Andrew Collection (Massachusetts Historical Society).

13. Stevens to Simon Stevens, November 18, 1862, in Richard N. Current, *Old Thad Stevens* (Madison, 1942), p. 171.

14. James G. Randall (ed.), *Diary of Orville Hickman Browning* (Springfield, Illinois, 1925), I, 534.

15. *Cong. Globe,* 37th Cong., 2 sess., p. 1963.

16. Browning, *Diary,* I, 560.

17. Fessenden to Fish, July 15, 1862, in Fish Papers (Library of Congress).

18. Fessenden to William Fessenden, February 15, 1862, in Fessenden Family Collection.

19. March 1, 1862.

20. *Cong. Globe,* 37th Cong., 2 sess., p. 765.

21. Fessenden to Pike, August 2, 1862, in Pike Papers (Calais).

22. *Ibid.*

23. Dewey, *Financial History,* p. 301.

24. *Cong. Globe,* 37th Cong., 2 sess., p. 1038.

25. Dewey, p. 302.

26. Fessenden to William Fessenden, March 15, 1862, in Fessenden Family Collection.

27. Fessenden to Pike, August 2, 1862, in Pike Papers (Calais).

28. Fessenden to Francis (Frank) Fessenden, March 8, 1862, in Fessenden Family Collection.

29. *Ibid.*

30. Salter, "Fessenden," p. 328.

CHAPTER XIII

1. This information was taken primarily from an undated clipping from the Portland *Eastern Argus,* which was kindly called to my attention by Mr. F. M. O'Brien, collector of manuscripts and rare books, Portland.

2. Fessenden to George F. Shepley, December 24, 1862, in Shepley Collection (Maine Historical Society).

3. December 12, 1862.

4. Browning, *Diary,* I, 587-88.

5. Fessenden to William Fessenden, December 6, 1862, in Fessenden Family Collection.

6. Fessenden to Elizabeth Warriner, December 20, 1862, in Fessenden Family Collection.

7. John G. Nicolay and John Hay, *Abraham Lincoln* (New York, 1890), VI, 265.

8. Browning, *Diary,* I, 603.

9. Fessenden to Pike, April 5, 1863, in Taney Papers (Library of Congress).

10. Fessenden to Elizabeth Warriner, January 10, 1863, in Fessenden Family Collection.

11. Fessenden to Elizabeth Warriner, February 21, 1863, in Fessenden Family Collection.

12. Fessenden to Pike, April 5, 1863, in Taney Papers (Library of Congress).

13. Gideon Welles, *Diary* (Boston, 1911), I, 367.

14. *Ibid.,* I, 163.

15. *Cong. Globe,* 37th Cong., 3 sess., p. 592.

16. *Ibid.,* pp. 505-13.

17. Fessenden to Pike, April 5, 1863, in Taney Papers (Library of Congress).

18. *Cong. Globe,* 37th Cong., 3 sess., p. 897.

19. February 6, 1863.

20. Fessenden to Pike, March 9, 1864, in Taney Papers (Library of Congress).

21. Fessenden to Pike, April 5, 1863, in Taney Papers (Library of Congress).

CHAPTER XIV

1. Salter, "Fessenden," p. 329.

2. Fessenden to William Fessenden, January 15, 1864, in Fessenden Family Collection.

3. Fessenden to William Fessenden, February 7, 1864, in Fessenden Family Collection.

4. Fessenden to William Fessenden, March 12, 1864, in Fessenden Family Collection.

5. Fessenden to Thomas Deblois, March 9, 1864, in Fessenden Family Collection.

6. *Cong. Globe,* 38th Cong., 1 sess., pp. 60–61.

7. Fessenden to Elizabeth Warriner, December 27, 1863, in Fessenden Family Collection.

8. Fessenden to William Fessenden, March 12, 1864, in Fessenden Family Collection.

9. Fessenden to Pike, March 9, 1864, in Taney Papers (Library of Congress).

10. *Cong. Globe,* 38th Cong., 1 sess., p. 481.

11. William Lloyd Garrison to Henry Wilson, February 20, 1864, in Norcross Collection (Massachusetts Historical Society).

12. *Cong. Globe,* 38th Cong., 1 sess., p. 139.

13. *Ibid.,* pp. 370–71.

14. Fessenden to Elizabeth Warriner, December 18, 1863, in Fessenden Family Collection.

15. *Cong. Globe,* 38th Cong., 1 sess., p. 336.

16. Sandburg, *War Years,* III, 132–33.

17. Fessenden to William Fessenden, April 2, 1864, in Fessenden Family Collection.

18. Fessenden to Pike, March 9, 1864, in Taney Papers (Library of Congress).

19. Fessenden to Elizabeth Warriner, June 1, 1862, in Fessenden Family Collection.

20. Fessenden to William Fessenden, May 7, 1864, in Fessenden Family Collection.

21. Hamlin, *Life,* p. 480.

22. *Ibid.,* p. 481.

23. Simon Cameron to Fessenden, June 15, 1864, in Fessenden Family Collection.

CHAPTER XV

1. Fessenden to William Fessenden, July 1, 1864, in Fessenden Family Collection.

2. David Donald (ed.), *Inside Lincoln's Cabinet: The Civil War Diaries of Salmon P. Chase* (New York, 1954), p. 223.

3. James Ford Rhodes, *History of the United States, 1850–1877* (New York, 1896–1900), IV, 480.

4. Nicolay and Hay, *Lincoln,* IX, 99.

5. Fessenden, *Life,* I, 317.

6. Fessenden to Lincoln, July 2, 1864, in Fessenden Family Collection.

7. Fessenden, *Life,* I, 317.

8. Salter, "Fessenden," p. 330.

9. Fish to Fessenden, July 5, 1864, in Fessenden Family Collection.

10. July 4, 1864.

11. As reprinted in the *Kennebec Journal,* July 8, 1864.

12. July 8, 1864.

13. Fessenden to John Cisco, July 6, 1864, in Fessenden Letterbook (Library of Congress).

14. Ellis P. Oberholtzer, *Jay Cooke, Financier of the Civil War* (Philadelphia, 1907), I, 435.

15. July 27, 1864.

16. Harrington to Fessenden, August 6, 1864, in Harrington Papers (Library of Congress).

17. Fessenden to Harrington, August 12, 1864, in Bixby Collection (Huntington Library).

18. Fessenden to William Fessenden, August 27, 1864, in Fessenden Family Collection.

19. August 2, 1864.

20. "Report of the Secretary of the Treasury, 1864," in *Appendix to the Congressional Globe*, 38th Cong., 2 sess., p. 28.

21. Oberholtzer, *Cooke*, I, 448–49.

22. Treasury Department Circular, December 13, 1864, in Treasury Department Records (National Archives).

23. Fessenden to Hugh McCulloch, March 24, 1865, in McCulloch Papers (Library of Congress).

24. Oberholtzer, *Cooke*, I, 484–85.

25. *Ibid.*, I, 487.

26. February 20, 1865.

27. *New York Tribune*, March 4, 1865.

28. March 4, 1865.

29. Fessenden to Harrington, May 12, 1866, in Bixby Collection (Huntington Library).

CHAPTER XVI

1. Dana to Pike, December 12, 1864, in Pike Papers (Calais).

2. Blaine to Hamlin, October 17, 1864, in Hamlin Collection (Maine Historical Society).

3. Browning, *Diary*, I, 186–87.

4. Fessenden to Israel Washburn, December 29, 1864, in Fessenden Papers (Library of Congress).

5. Fessenden to C. L. Gilman, December 30, 1864, in Fessenden Letterbook (Library of Congress).

6. Fessenden to Washburn, November 18, 1864, in Fessenden Papers (Library of Congress).

7. Fessenden to N. Wilson, December 3, 1864, in Fessenden Letterbook (Library of Congress).

8. Elisha Allen to Fessenden, January 5, 1865, in Fessenden Papers (Library of Congress).

9. Fessenden to Maine Legislature, February 10, 1865, in Fessenden Letterbook (Library of Congress).

10. Salter, "Fessenden," p. 335.

11. Rhodes, *History*, V, 532n.

12. Sumner to Wade, August 3, 1865, in Wade Papers (Library of Congress).

13. R. Webb, "William Pitt Fessenden," in *Collections and Proceedings of the Maine Historical Society*, 2nd Series, X (1899), 249–50.

14. Theodore Tilton to Thaddeus Stevens, December 6, 1865, in Tilton Papers (Library of Congress).

15. Salter, "Fessenden," 332. See also Welles, *Diary*, II, 448.

16. Fessenden to George Harrington, February 3, 1866, in Bixby Collection (Huntington Library).

17. Fessenden to Elizabeth Warriner, February 3, 1866, in Fessenden Family Collection.

18. Fessenden to Elizabeth Warriner, February 17, 1866, in Fessenden Family Collection.

19. February 26, 1866.

20. *Cong. Globe*, 39th Cong., 1 sess., p. 982.

21. Fessenden to Pike, April 6, 1866, in Taney Papers (Library of Congress).

22. Fessenden to William Fessenden, March 31, 1866, in Fessenden Family Collection.

23. Fessenden to Elizabeth Warriner, June 9, 1866, in Fessenden Family Collection.

24. Fessenden to William Fessenden, July 8, 1866, in Fessenden Family Collection.

25. Fessenden to Elizabeth Warriner, December 24, 1865, in Fessenden Family Collection.

26. J. R. Doolittle to T. A. Hendricks, June 19, 1884, in Doolittle Papers (Library of Congress).

27. Fessenden to Pike, April 6, 1866, in Taney Papers (Library of Congress).

28. Fessenden to William Fessenden, March 31, 1866, in Fessenden Family Collection.

29. Benjamin B. Kendrick, *Journal of the Joint Committee of Fifteen on Reconstruction* (New York, 1914), pp. 50–51.

30. Fessenden, *Life*, II, 23.

31. *Cong. Globe*, 39th Cong., 1 sess., p. 705.

32. Fessenden to Elizabeth Warriner, March 3, 1866, in Fessenden Family Collection.

33. Robert Dale Owen, "Political Results from the Varioloid," in *Atlantic Monthly*, XXXV (June, 1875), 662–64.

34. Fessenden to William Fessenden, April 21, 1866, in Fessenden Family Collection.

35. Owen, "Varioloid," p. 666.

36. Fessenden to Francis Fessenden, May 18, 1866, in Fessenden Family Collection.

37. Fessenden to George Harrington, May 24, 1866, in Bixby Collection (Huntington Library).

38. Salter, "Fessenden," p. 332.

39. June 8, 1866.

40. Fessenden to Elizabeth Warriner, June 9, 1866, in Fessenden Family Collection.

41. Broadside entitled, "Appeal from Portland," July 7, 1866, in Fessenden Papers (Library of Congress).

42. Fessenden to Elizabeth Warriner, February 17, 1866, in Fessenden Family Collection.

CHAPTER XVII

1. September 21, 1866.

2. Fessenden to McCulloch, September 15, 1866, in McCulloch Papers (Library of Congress).

3. S. W. McCall, "Washington during Reconstruction," in *Atlantic Monthly*, LXXXVII (June, 1901), 824–25.

4. Campbell to Doolittle, April 25, 1866, in Doolittle Papers (Library of Congress).

5. Fessenden to McCulloch, August 29, 1866, in McCulloch Papers (Library of Congress).

6. Fessenden to McCulloch, September 15, 1866, in McCulloch Papers (Library of Congress).

7. Fessenden to McCulloch, November 11, 1866, in McCulloch Papers (Library of Congress).

8. *Cong. Globe*, 39th Cong., 2 sess., p. 1518.

9. *Ibid.*, p. 1556.

10. Pierce, *Sumner*, II, 314.

11. Fessenden, *Life*, II, 306.

12. Fessenden to James Norman, March 30, 1867, in Fessenden Papers (Library of Congress).

13. Fessenden to Thomas Bayard, May 9, 1867, in Garrett Papers (Library of Congress).

14. March 5, 1867.

15. Rhodes, *History*, VI, 62.

16. Fessenden to Grimes, June 18, 1867, in Fessenden Family Collection.

17. *Cong. Globe,* 40th Cong., Special Session of the Senate, p. 829.

18. Salter, "Fessenden," p. 333.

19. Fessenden to William Fessenden, July 7, 1867, in Fessenden Family Collection.

20. *Cong. Globe,* 40th Cong., 1 sess., pp. 750–53.

21. Boston *Daily Advertiser,* August 29, 1867.

22. *Springfield Republican,* September 5, 1867.

23. Fessenden to Grimes, September 20, 1867, in Fessenden Family Collection.

24. Fessenden to Pike, July 31, 1867, in Taney Papers (Library of Congress).

25. Fessenden to Grimes, September 20, 1867, in Fessenden Family Collection.

CHAPTER XVIII

1. October 1, 1866.

2. Horace White to Zachariah Chandler, August 20, 1867, in Chandler Papers (Library of Congress).

3. Fessenden to McCulloch, September 2, 1867, in McCulloch Papers (Library of Congress).

4. Fessenden to William Fessenden, November 23, 1867, in Fessenden Family Collection.

5. Fessenden to Elizabeth Warriner, December 8, 1867, in Fessenden Family Collection.

6. Fessenden to William Fessenden, May 3, 1868, in Fessenden Family Collection.

7. Fessenden to Elizabeth Warriner, April 19, 1868, in Fessenden Family Collection.

8. Fessenden to William Fessenden, April 27, 1868, in Fessenden Family Collection.

9. Edmund Quincy to Sumner, April 16, 1868, in Sumner Papers (Houghton Library, Harvard).

10. Fessenden to Elizabeth Warriner, March 21, 1868, in Fessenden Family Collection.

11. Fessenden, *Life,* II, 222.

12. May 13, 1868.

13. G. H. Baker to Simon Cameron, May 14, 1868, in Cameron Papers (Library of Congress).

14. Benjamin Butler to J. Russell Young, May 12, 1868, in Butler Papers (Library of Congress).

15. Richmond *Dispatch,* May 15, 1868.

16. New York *Nation,* May 14, 1868, p. 385.

17. A. W. Howard to Sumner, May 13, 1868, in Sumner Papers (Houghton Library, Harvard).

18. Edward Kingley to Sumner, May 13, 1868, in Sumner Papers (Houghton Library, Harvard).

19. G. W. Renna to Simon Cameron, May 14, 1868, in Cameron Papers (Library of Congress).

20. Fessenden to Elizabeth Warriner, March 31, 1868, in Fessenden Family Collection.

21. Fessenden to Rufus Dwinell, May 15, 1868, in Fessenden Family Collection.

22. March 31, 1868.

23. *Cong. Globe*, 40th Cong., 2 sess., p. 3790.

24. George F. Dawson, *The Life and Services of General John A. Logan* (Chicago, 1887), p. 133.

25. May 18, 1868.

26. George S. Boutwell, "Impeachment of Andrew Johnson," in *McClure's Magazine*, XIV (December, 1899), 182.

27. Blaine, *Twenty Years*, II, 365.

28. *Springfield Republican*, May 5, 1868.

29. Moorfield Storey, *Charles Sumner* (Boston, 1900), p. 349.

30. J. W. Schuckers, *The Life and Public Services of Salmon P. Chase* (New York, 1874), p. 577.

31. Charles Sumner, *Works* (Boston, 1875–83), XII, 317.

32. Welles, *Diary*, III, 336.

33. Edwin M. Stanton to J. Russell Young, May 13, 1868, in Young Papers (Library of Congress).

34. T. A. Hendricks to Samuel J. Tilden, May 13, 1868, in Manton Marble Papers (Library of Congress).

35. As cited in E. Merton Coulter, *William G. Brownlow: Fighting Parson of the Southern Highlands* (Chapel Hill, 1937), p. 350.

36. Browning, *Diary*, II, 196.

37. Fessenden to William Fessenden, May 3, 1868, in Fessenden Family Collection.

38. David Dewitt, *The Impeachment and Trial of Andrew Johnson* (New York, 1903), p. 530.

39. Sumner, *Works*, XII, 280.

40. Anon., "The Next President," in *Atlantic Monthly*, XXI (May, 1868), 630.

41. William T. Sherman to John Sherman, February 28, 1868, in W. T. Sherman Papers (Library of Congress).

42. Cincinnati *Gazette*, March 8, 1868.

43. Willard H. Smith, *Schuyler Colfax* (Indianapolis, 1952), pp. 255–56.

44. "Trial of the President," in *Cong. Globe Supplement*, 40th Cong., 2 sess., p. 411.

45. Fessenden, *Life*, II, 217.

46. "Trial of the President," p. 457.

47. J. Russell Young to Stanton, May 6, 1868, in Stanton Papers (Library of Congress).

48. John Lynch to Israel Washburn, May 13, 1868, in Gaillard Hunt, *Israel, Elihu, and Cadwallader Washburn* (New York, 1925), p. 123.

49. *Cong. Globe*, 40th Cong., 2 sess., p. 2584.

CHAPTER XIX

1. W. E. Webster to Sumner, May 22, 1868, in Sumner Papers (Houghton Library, Harvard).

2. Anon. to Fessenden, May 17, 1868, in Fessenden Family Collection.

3. John Nye to Fessenden, May 20, 1868, in Fessenden Collection (Duke University).

4. May 13, 1868.

5. May 18, 1868.

6. Colfax to Young, April 16, 1868, in Young Papers (Library of Congress).

7. June 9, 1868.

8. James Dixon to Fessenden, August 9, 1868, in Fessenden Family Collection.

9. May 18, 1868.

10. Benjamin R. Curtis to Fessenden, May 18, 1868, in Fessenden Family Collection.

11. Salter, "Fessenden," pp. 337–38.

12. Fessenden to Grimes, June 24, 1868, in Fessenden Family Collection.

13. Welles, *Diary*, III, 505.

14. Fessenden, *Life*, II, 302

15. Fessenden to Harrington, November 7, 1868, in Bixby Collection (Huntington Library).

16. *Ibid.*

17. Sumner to Hamilton Fish, October 7, 1869, in Fish Papers (Library of Congress).

18. Fessenden to Harrington, November 7, 1868, in Bixby Collection (Huntington Library).

19. Fessenden to Harrington, April 18, 1869, in Bixby Collection (Huntington Library).

20. White, *Trumbull*, p. 335.

21. Fessenden to Harrington, April 18, 1869, in Bixby Collection (Huntington Library).

22. Fessenden to Fish, March 29, 1869, in Fish Papers (Library of Congress).

23. Fessenden, *Life*, II, 321–22.

24. Salter, "Fessenden," p. 341.

25. Fessenden, *Life*, II, 330. The date of the Senator's death is given erroneously here as September 9.

26. September 9, 1869.

27. September 9, 1869.

28. *Proceedings of the Bar of Cumberland County, on the Occasion of the Death of William Pitt Fessenden* (Portland, 1869), p. 9.

29. *Journal of the Senate of Maine, 1870,* 49th Legislature, pp. 77–78.

30. *Cong. Globe,* 41st Cong., 2 sess., p. 113.

31. *Ibid.*, p. 115.

32. *Ibid.*, p. 112.

33. Salter, "Fessenden," pp. 341–42.

Bibliography

MANUSCRIPTS

Personal and Family Collections

Andrew, John, Collection; Massachusetts Historical Society
Bancroft, George, Collection; Massachusetts Historical Society
Bixby Family Collection; Huntington Library
Butler, Benjamin F., Papers; Library of Congress
Cameron, Simon, Papers; Library of Congress
Chandler, Zachariah, Papers; Library of Congress
Chase, Salmon P., Papers; Library of Congress
Colfax, Schuyler, Papers; Library of Congress
Dana, Richard Henry, Collection; Massachusetts Historical Society
Daveis, Charles, Collection; Maine Historical Society
Doolittle, James, Papers; Library of Congress
Evarts, William M., Papers; Library of Congress
Fessenden Family Collection; Bowdoin College
Fessenden, Samuel, Collection; Maine Historical Society
Fessenden, William Pitt, Collection; Duke University
Fessenden, William Pitt, Papers; Library of Congress
Fish, Hamilton, Papers; Library of Congress
Fowler, Joseph, Papers; Library of Congress
Garrett Family Papers; Library of Congress
Giddings, Joshua, and Julian, George, Papers; Library of Congress
Greeley, Horace, Papers; Library of Congress
Greeley, Horace, Collection; New York Public Library
Hamlin, Hannibal, Collection; Maine Historical Society
Harrington, George, Papers; Library of Congress
Holt, Joseph, Papers; Library of Congress

Jenckes, Thomas, Papers; Library of Congress
Johnson, Andrew, Papers; Library of Congress
King, Horatio, Papers; Library of Congress
Lincoln, Abraham, Papers; Library of Congress
Marble, Manton, Papers; Library of Congress
McCulloch, Hugh, Papers; Library of Congress
Miscellaneous Collections:
    Anti-Slavery Papers; Boston Public Library
    Fessenden Family Papers; in possession of John Baxter, Brunswick, Maine
    Fessenden, Thomas A. A., Papers; in possession of Mrs. Jane Adams, Washington, D. C.
    Longfellow, Henry W., Collection; Craigie House, Cambridge, Massachusetts (photostatic copies of original papers)
    Miscellaneous Manuscript Collection (bound); Maine Historical Society
    Miscellaneous Papers on early Fryeburg, Maine; in possession of Miss Mary Barrows, Fryeburg
Morrill, Justin, Papers; Library of Congress
Morrill, Lot, Papers; Library of Congress
Norcross Family Collection; Massachusetts Historical Society
Pike, James S., Papers; Calais, Maine, Free Library
Pike, James S., Papers; Library of Congress
Raymond, H. J., Collection; New York Public Library
Schofield, John M., Papers; Library of Congress
Shepley Family Collection; Maine Historical Society
Sherman, John, Papers; Library of Congress
Sherman, William T., Papers; Library of Congress
Smith, F. O. J., Collection; Maine Historical Society
Stanton, Edwin M., Papers; Library of Congress
Stevens, Thaddeus, Papers; Library of Congress
Sumner, Charles, Papers; Houghton Library, Harvard
Sumner, Charles, Papers; Library of Congress
Taney, Roger, Papers; Library of Congress
Tilden, Samuel J., Collection; New York Public Library
Tilton, Theodore, Papers; Library of Congress
Trumbull, Lyman, Papers; Library of Congress
Wade, Benjamin, Papers; Library of Congress

Washburn C., Collection; Massachusetts Historical Society
Washburn, Israel, Papers; Library of Congress
Washburne, Elihu, Papers; Library of Congress
Welles, Gideon, Collection; New York Public Library
Welles, Gideon, Papers; Library of Congress
Willis, William, Collection; Maine Historical Society
Wise, Henry, A., Executive Papers; Virginia State Library
Young, J. Russell, Papers; Library of Congress

Unpublished Public and Institutional Records

Bowdoin College Alumni Records, Brunswick, Maine.
Bowdoin College Faculty Records, 1823.
Bowdoin College Public Exercises Records, 1821–23.
City of Portland Taxbook, 1852–70, City Hall, Portland, Maine.
Cumberland County Registry of Deeds, 1836–70, County Courthouse, Portland, Maine.
Cumberland County Supreme Judicial Court Records, 1837–41, County Courthouse, Portland, Maine.
Inventory and Tax Records of the City of Bangor, 1833–35, City Hall, Bangor, Maine.
Journal of the House of Representatives of the State of Maine, 1846, State Capitol, Augusta, Maine.
Penobscot County Register of Deeds and Land Titles, 1833–35, County Courthouse, Bangor, Maine.
Penobscot County Supreme Judicial Court Records, 1833–35, County Courthouse, Bangor, Maine.
Records of the Treasury Department of the United States, 1864–65, National Archives, Washington, D. C.

PUBLIC DOCUMENTS

Congressional Globe, 27th Congress, 33rd–41st Congresses.
Federal Cases . . . in the Circuit and District Courts of the United States, Book 28, Vol. III, 1844.
Journals of the Executive Proceedings of the Senate of the United States, Vols. XII–XVI, 1861–69.
Journals of the Senate of Maine, 33rd, 49th Legislatures, 1854, 1870.
Report of the Adjutant General of the State of Maine, 1864–65.

Reports of the Committees of the House of Representatives of the United States . . . , Serial #1273, Vol. 1, 1865–66.
United States Statutes at Large, Vols. XI–XV, 1855–69.
United States Supreme Court Digest, Vol. III, 1850.
United States Supreme Court Reports, Book 12, Vol. VIII, 1850.

NEWSPAPERS AND PERIODICALS

Baltimore American, 1852.
Bangor (Maine), *Jeffersonian,* 1868.
Bangor *Whig and Courier,* 1833–41.
Boston *Daily Advertiser,* 1865–68.
Boston Post, 1865.
Chicago *Daily Tribune,* 1860–68.
Cincinnati *Daily Gazette,* 1865–68.
Harper's New Monthly Magazine, 1868.
Kennebec Journal (Augusta, Maine), 1832–60.
New York *Journal of Commerce,* 1864–65.
New York *Nation,* 1868.
New York Times, 1854–69.
New York Tribune, 1848–69.
New York *World,* 1864–67.
Portland (Maine) *Advertiser,* 1850–63.
Portland *Eastern Argus,* 1840–69.
Richmond *Dispatch,* 1865.
Richmond *Enquirer,* 1841–43.
Richmond *Examiner,* 1868.
Springfield Republican (Massachusetts), 1854–69.
Washington *Chronicle,* 1862–68.
Washington *National Intelligencer,* 1860–68.
Wheeling (West Virginia), *Intelligencer,* 1868.
Yankee and Boston Literary Gazette (Portland, Maine), 1828.

BOOKS

Adams, John Quincy. *Memoirs of John Quincy Adams.* Edited by C. F. Adams. 12 volumes. Philadelphia: J. B. Lippincott, 1874–77.
Ambler, Charles H. *Waitman Thomas Willey, Orator, Churchman, Humanitarian.* Huntington, West Virginia: Standard Print and Publishing Company, 1954.

Barrows, Chester L. *William M. Evarts, Lawyer, Diplomat, Statesman.* Chapel Hill: University of North Carolina Press, 1941.

Barrows, John S. *Fryeburg, Maine: An Historical Sketch.* Fryeburg: The Pequawket Press, 1938.

Bates, Edward. *Diary of Edward Bates, 1859–1866 (Annual Report* of the American Historical Association for 1930, Vol. IV). Edited by Howard K. Beale. Washington: United States Government Printing Office, 1933.

Bayley, R. A. *National Loans of the United States, July 4, 1776–June 30, 1880.* Washington: United States Government Printing Office, 1882.

Beale, Howard K. *Critical Year: a Study of Andrew Johnson and Reconstruction.* New York: Harcourt, Brace and Company, 1930.

Beedy, Helen Coffin. *Mothers of Maine.* Portland: The Thurston Print, 1895.

Benton, Thomas Hart. *Thirty Years' View.* 2 volumes. New York: D. Appleton and Company, 1854–56.

Blaine, James G. *Twenty Years of Congress.* 2 volumes. Norwich, Connecticut: Henry Bill Publishing Company, 1884–86.

Boutwell, George. *Reminiscences of Sixty Years in Public Affairs.* 2 volumes. New York: McClure, Phillips and Company, 1902.

Bowers, Claude. *Tragic Era.* Boston: Houghton Mifflin Company, 1929.

Bridge, Horatio. *Personal Recollections of Nathaniel Hawthorne.* New York: Harper and Brothers, 1893.

Brooks, Noah. *Washington in Lincoln's Time.* New York: Rinehart, 1958.

Browning, Orville Hickman. *Diary of Orville Hickman Browning.* Edited by James G. Randall. 2 volumes. Springfield, Illinois: The Trustees of the Illinois State Historical Library, 1925.

Buchanan, James. *Works of James Buchanan.* Edited by John Bassett Moore. 11 volumes. Philadelphia: J. B. Lippincott, 1908–10.

Bumgardner, Edward. *Life of Edmund G. Ross.* Kansas City, Missouri: Fielding-Turner Press, 1949.

Butler, Benjamin F. *Butler's Book, Autobiography and Personal Reminiscences of General Benjamin F. Butler.* Boston: A. M. Thayer and Company, 1892.

Chase, Salmon P. *Civil War Diaries of Salmon P. Chase.* Edited by

David Donald. New York: Longmans, Green and Company, 1954.

Clay, Henry. *Private Correspondence of Henry Clay*. Edited by Calvin Colton. New York: A. S. Barnes and Company, 1855.

Cleaveland, Nehemiah. *History of Bowdoin College*. Boston: J. R. Osgood and Company, 1882.

Clemenceau, Georges. *American Reconstruction, 1865–1870*. New York: The Dial Press, 1928.

Coulter, E. Merton. *William G. Brownlow: Fighting Parson of the Southern Highlands*. Chapel Hill: University of North Carolina Press, 1937.

Cox, Samuel S. *Union, Disunion, Reunion. Three Decades of Federal Legislation*. Providence: J. A. and R. A. Reid, 1885.

Current, Richard N. *Old Thad Stevens*. Madison: University of Wisconsin Press, 1942.

Curtis, Benjamin R. *Life and Writings of Benjamin R. Curtis, a Memoir*. Edited by B. R. Curtis, Jr. 2 volumes. Boston: Little, Brown and Company, 1879.

Dawson, George F. *Life and Services of General John A. Logan*. Chicago: Belford, Clarke and Company, 1887.

DeKnight, W. F. and Tillman, J. F. *History of the Currency of the Country and of the Loans of the United States*. Washington: United States Government Printing Office, 1900.

Dewey, Davis R. *Financial History of the United States*. London: Longmans, Green and Company, 1903.

Dewitt, David. *The Impeachment and Trial of Andrew Johnson*. New York: The Macmillan Company, 1903.

Dickens, Charles. *American Notes*. London: Chapman and Hall, 1842.

Dow, Neal. *Reminiscences of Neal Dow*. Portland, Maine: The Evening Express Publishing Company, 1898.

Dunning, William A. *Reconstruction, Political and Economic, 1865–1877* (volume XXII of *The American Nation: a History*, edited by Albert Bushnell Hart, 28 volumes, New York, 1904–18). Harper and Brothers, 1907.

Durden, Robert F. *James Shepherd Pike*. Durham, North Carolina: Duke University Press, 1957.

Emerson, Ralph Waldo. *Journals of Ralph Waldo Emerson, 1820–1876*. Edited by E. W. Emerson and W. E. Forbes. 10 volumes. Boston: Houghton Mifflin Company, 1909–14.

Fessenden, Francis. *Life and Public Services of William Pitt Fessenden.* 2 volumes. Boston: Houghton Mifflin Company, 1907.

Ford, Henry A. (ed.). *History of Penobscot County.* Cleveland: L. A. Williams and Company, 1882.

Fuess, Claude M. *Daniel Webster.* 2 volumes. Boston: Little, Brown and Company, 1930.

General Catalogue of Bowdoin College, 1794–1912. Brunswick, Maine: The College, 1912.

Gorham, G. C. *Life and Public Services of Edwin M. Stanton.* 2 volumes. Boston: Houghton Mifflin Company, 1899.

Gurowski, Adam. *Diary of Adam Gurowski.* 3 volumes. Boston: Lee and Shepard, 1862–66.

Hamlin, Charles. *Life and Times of Hannibal Hamlin.* Cambridge, Massachusetts: Printed by the Riverside Press, 1899.

Hammond, Bray. *Banks and Politics in America from the Revolution to the Civil War.* Princeton, New Jersey: Princeton University Press, 1957.

Hatch, Louis C. *History of Bowdoin College.* Portland, Maine: Loring, Short and Harmon, 1927.

Hatch, Louis C. (ed.). *Maine, a History.* 3 volumes. New York: American Historical Society, 1919.

Hill, F. T. *Decisive Battles of the Law.* New York: Harper and Brothers, 1907.

Hoar, George F. *Autobiography of Seventy Years.* 2 volumes. New York: C. Scribner's Sons, 1903.

Hughes, Sarah Forbes. *Letters and Recollections of John Murray Forbes.* 2 volumes. Boston: Houghton Mifflin Company, 1899.

Hunt, Gaillard. *Israel, Elihu, and Cadwallader Washburn.* New York: The Macmillan Company, 1925.

James, Joseph B. *The Framing of the Fourteenth Amendment.* Urbana: University of Illinois Press, 1956.

Julian, George. *Political Recollections.* Chicago: Jansen, McClurg and Company, 1884.

Kendrick, Benjamin B. *Journal of the Joint Committee of Fifteen on Reconstruction.* New York: Columbia University Press, 1914.

Lanman, Charles. *Private Life of Daniel Webster.* New York: Harper and Brothers, 1857.

Lincoln, Abraham. *Collected Works of Abraham Lincoln*. Edited by Roy P. Basler and others. 8 volumes. New Brunswick, New Jersey: Rutgers University Press, 1953.

Longfellow, Samuel. *Life of Henry Wadsworth Longfellow*. 3 volumes. Boston: Houghton Mifflin Company, 1886–87.

Maine Register and United States Calendar, 1820. Portland: Rawlins Press, 1820.

McCall, Samuel M. *Life of Thomas Brackett Reed*. Boston: Houghton Mifflin Company, 1914.

McCulloch, Hugh. *Men and Measures of Half a Century*. New York: C. Scribner's Sons, 1888.

Milton, George Fort. *Age of Hate: Andrew Johnson and the Radicals*. New York: Coward-McCann, 1930.

Nevins, Allan. *Hamilton Fish*. New York: Dodd, Mead and Company, 1936.

Nichols, Roy. *Disruption of the American Democracy*. New York: The Macmillan Company, 1948.

Nichols, Roy. *Franklin Pierce, Young Hickory of the Granite Hills*. Philadelphia: University of Pennsylvania Press, 1931.

Nicolay, John G. and Hay, John. *Abraham Lincoln*. 10 volumes. New York: The Century Company, 1890.

Oberholtzer, Ellis P. *Jay Cooke, Financier of the Civil War*. 2 volumes. Philadelphia: G. W. Jacobs and Company, 1907.

Pierce, Edward. *Memoirs and Letters of Charles Sumner*. 4 volumes. Boston: Roberts Brothers, 1877–93.

Pike, James S. *First Blows of the Civil War*. New York: The American News Company, 1879.

Poore, Ben Perley. *Reminiscences of Sixty Years in the National Metropolis*. 2 volumes. Philadelphia: Hubbard Brothers, 1886.

Proceedings of the Bar of Cumberland County on the Occasion of the Death of William Pitt Fessenden. Portland, Maine: Cumberland County Bar, 1869.

Randall, James G. *Civil War and Reconstruction*. Boston: D. C. Heath and Company, 1937.

Rhodes, James Ford. *History of the United States . . . , 1850–1877*. 7 volumes. New York: Harper and Brothers, 1896–1900.

Ross, Edmund G. *History of the Impeachment of Andrew Johnson*. Santa Fe: New Mexican Printing Company, 1896.

Sandburg, Carl. *Abraham Lincoln: the War Years.* 4 volumes. New York: Harcourt, Brace and Company, 1936–39.

Schuckers, J. W. *Life and Public Services of Salmon P. Chase.* New York: D. Appleton and Company, 1874.

Schurz, Carl. *Reminiscences of Carl Schurz.* Edited by Frederic Bancroft and William A. Dunning. 3 volumes. New York: The McClure Company, 1907–08.

Seward, Frederick. *Seward at Washington.* 3 volumes. New York: Derby and Miller, 1891.

Sharkey, Robert P. *Money, Class, and Party; an Economic Study of the Civil War and Reconstruction.* Baltimore: Johns Hopkins Press, 1960.

Sherman, John. *Recollections of Forty Years.* 2 volumes. Chicago: The Werner Company, 1895.

Smith, Willard H. *Schuyler Colfax.* Indianapolis: Indiana Historical Bureau, 1952.

Storey, Moorfield. *Charles Sumner* (volume XXX of *American Statesmen* Series, edited by J. T. Morse, Jr., 31 volumes, Boston, 1889–1900). Houghton Mifflin Company, 1900.

Sumner, Charles. *Works of Charles Sumner.* Ed. anon. 15 volumes. Boston: Lee and Shepard, 1875–83.

Taussig, F. W. *Tariff History of the United States.* New York: G. P. Putnam's Sons, 1892.

Thompson, Lawrence. *Young Longfellow, 1807–1843.* New York: The Macmillan Company, 1948.

Tryon, Warren S. (ed.). *Mirror for Americans.* 3 volumes. Chicago: University of Chicago Press, 1952.

Webster, Daniel. *Private Correspondence of Daniel Webster.* Edited by Fletcher Webster. 2 volumes. Boston: Little, Brown and Company, 1857.

Webster, Daniel. *Writings and Speeches of Daniel Webster.* National Edition. 18 volumes. Boston: Little, Brown and Company, 1903.

Welles, Gideon. *Diary of Gideon Welles.* Edited by J. T. Morse. 3 volumes. Boston: Houghton Mifflin Company, 1911.

White, Horace. *Life of Lyman Trumbull.* Boston: Houghton Mifflin Company, 1913.

Williams, T. Harry. *Lincoln and the Radicals.* Madison: University of Wisconsin Press, 1941.

Willis, William. *A History of the Law, the Courts, and the Lawyers of Maine.* Portland: Bailey and Noyes, 1863.

Woodburn, J. A. *Life of Thaddeus Stevens.* Indianapolis: Bobbs Merrill Company, 1913.

Worth, Jonathan. *Correspondence of Jonathan Worth.* Edited by J. G. Hamilton. 2 volumes. Raleigh, North Carolina: Edwards and Broughton Printing Company, 1909.

Zornow, W. F. *Lincoln and the Party Divided.* Norman: University of Oklahoma Press, 1954.

ARTICLES AND PAMPHLETS

Anon. "The Next President," in *Atlantic Monthly,* XXXIX (May, 1868), 628–32.

Boutwell, George. "The Impeachment of Andrew Johnson," in *McClure's Magazine,* XIV (December, 1899), 171–82.

Dow, Neal. *History of Prohibition in Maine.* Portland, undated.

Dow, Neal and Fred. "General Neal Dow," in *Maine Historical and Genealogical Records,* IX (August, 1898), 225–29.

Fessenden, Samuel. *Oration Delivered Before the Federal Republicans of New Gloucester and the Adjacent Towns, July 4, A. D. 1811.* Portland, 1811.

Fessenden, William Pitt. *Oration Delivered Before the Young Men of Portland, July 4, 1827.* Portland, 1827.

Henderson, John B. "Emancipation and Impeachment," in *Century Magazine,* LXXXV (December, 1912), 196–209.

Kennedy, John F. "Ross of Kansas," in *Harper's Magazine,* CCXI (December, 1955), 40–44.

Marsh, John. *Napoleon of Temperance: Sketches on the Life and Character of Neal Dow.* New York, 1852.

McCall, S. W. "Washington During Reconstruction," in *Atlantic Monthly,* LXXXVII (June, 1901), 817–26.

Merrill, L. T. "General Benjamin F. Butler in Washington," in *Records of the Columbia Historical Society,* XXXIX (1938), 71–100.

Moody, Robert E. "Freeman Harlow Morse," in *Dictionary of American Biography* (edited by Allen Johnson, Dumas Malone, and Harris Starr, 21 volumes, New York, 1928–44), XIII, 243.

Owen, Robert Dale. "Political Results from the Varioloid," in *Atlantic Monthly,* XXXV (June, 1875), 660–70.

Robinson, William A. "John Fairfield," in *Dictionary of American Biography,* VI, 257–58.

Robinson, William A. "Samuel Fessenden," in *Dictionary of American Biography,* VI, 346–47.

Robinson, William A. "William Pitt Fessenden," in *Dictionary of American Biography,* VI, 348–50.

Robinson, William A. "Hannibal Hamlin," in *Dictionary of American Biography,* VIII, 196–98.

Roshe, Ralph J. "The Seven Martyrs?" in *American Historical Review,* LXIV (January, 1959), 323–30.

Ross, Edmund G. "Historic Moments: The Impeachment Trial," in *Scribner's Magazine,* XI (April, 1892), 519–24.

Ross, Edmund G. "Previous Era of Popular Madness and Its Lessons," in *Forum,* XIX (July, 1895), 595–605.

Salter, William. "William Pitt Fessenden," in *Annals of Iowa,* 3rd Series, VIII (April, 1908), 321–43.

Schofield, John M. "Controversies in the War Department: Unpublished Facts Relating to the Impeachment of Andrew Johnson," in *Century Magazine,* LIV (August, 1897), 577–83.

Sellers, James L. "An Interpretation of Civil War Finance," in *American Historical Review,* XXX (January, 1925), 282–97.

Van Cleve, Thomas C. "James Shepherd Pike," in *Dictionary of American Biography,* XIV, 595–96.

Webb, Richard. "William Pitt Fessenden," in *Collections and Proceedings of the Maine Historical Society,* 2nd Series, X (1899), 225–63.

West, Allan. "George Henry Preble," in *Dictionary of American Biography,* XIV, 183–84.

Index

Cameron, Simon (*continued*)
142; supports Hamlin for vice-presidency, 179; predicts Johnson's conviction, 239; mentioned, 105, 232
Campbell, Lewis: 212
Cass, Lewis: 56, 88
Central America: 116
Chandler, Anson G.: 63
Chandler, Zachariah: arrives in Senate, 105; and Committee on Conduct of the War, 141, 144; attacks Fessenden, 222–23; mentioned, 174, 239
Charleston convention: *See* Democratic party
Chase, Salmon P.: and 1860 Presidential nomination, 119, 122; and Loan Act of 1861, 134; supports Stanton's appointment to Cabinet, 142; and Loan Act of 1862, 147; Fessenden's opinion of, 149; and Internal Revenue Act of 1862, 149; and Senate caucus committee, 157–59; and Loan Act of 1863, 163; promotes National Currency Act, 164–65; presidential aspirations of, 168–69; and Loan Act of 1864, 175; helps draft Internal Revenue Act of 1864, 175; resigns Treasury post, 180; urges Fessenden to accept Treasury post, 181; and "ten-forties," 184n; relationship with Jay Cooke, 184–85; and corruption in Treasury, 190–91, 191n; considered for Chief Justiceship, 193; presides over impeachment trial, 235, 238–39, 243; mentioned, 117, 140, 156, 186
Chattanooga, Battle of: 167
Chicago Convention: *See* Republican party
Chicago *Times:* 155
Chicago *Tribune:* 140, 226
Cilley, Jonathan: 9
Cincinnati *Commercial:* 172
Cincinnati *Gazette:* 242
Civil Rights Bill: *See* Reconstruction
Clay, Cassius: 138
Clay, Henry: and Northeast boundary dispute, 18; entertains Webster party in Lexington, 26; and Whig program (1841), 35–37; supports bank bill, 40; and tariff, 42; mentioned, 20, 95, 98, 116
Clayton-Bulwer Treaty: 88
Clemenceau, Georges: 235n, 239
Clifford, Nathan: 84
Colfax, Schuyler: 242

Collamer, Jacob: 93, 113, 146, 148, 154, 156, 159, 165, 209
Colorado: 209, 214
Compromise of 1850: 55, 57–58, 76
Committee on the Conduct of the War: 141–42, 143–44
Confiscation Acts: 136, 145–57
Conkling, Roscoe: 224, 228
Conscription Act: 161
Conventions: *See under appropriate party*
Cooke, Jay: 167, 184–90
"Corporal's Guard": 36
Corwin, Thomas: 128
Covode, John: 144, 235
Creole Affair: 41
Crimean War: 88
Crittenden Compromise: 128
Crittenden Resolution (war aims): 135
Crosby, William: 63, 68, 70
Cuba: 79, 81, 115–16
Cumberland County Bar Association: 256–57
Curtis, Benjamin R.: 237, 249
Cushing, Caleb: 34, 37

Dana, Charles: 87, 90, 123, 192
Dana, John W.: 66
Daveis, Charles: 12, 16, 17, 41
Davis, Garrett: 171–73
Davis, Jefferson: 105, 107, 114, 121, 243
Democratic party: weakened by Compromise of 1850, 58; injured by Brooks affair, 94; controls 35th Congress, 105; weakened position in 36th Congress, 119; Charleston convention, 122; Baltimore convention, 122
Democratic party (Maine): dominates Maine politics, 15–16; defeat of Whigs (1838), 28; weakened by Maine Law, 62–63, 67–69; bolt by Morrill Democrats, 67–68, 68n; defeated (1856), 97
Depression: of 1837, 25–26, 27–28; of 1857, 104, 133
Dickens, Charles: 33, 43
Dingley, Nelson: 194
Dix, Dorothea: 79
Dix, John A.: 85n
Dixon, James: 105, 249
Doolittle, James: 138, 212
Douglas, Stephen A.: sponsors Kansas-Nebraska Act, 73–74; supports Kansas enabling bill, 88; opinion of Fessenden, 95; upbraided by Fessenden, 95–96; and Lecompton Constitution, 106,